My Biggest Research Mistake

My Biggest Research Mistake

Adventures and Misadventures in Psychological Research

Robert J. Sternberg

Cornell University

Editor

Los Angeles | London | New Delhi
Singapore | Washington DC | Melbourne

FOR INFORMATION:

SAGE Publications, Inc.
2455 Teller Road
Thousand Oaks, California 91320
E-mail: order@sagepub.com

SAGE Publications Ltd.
1 Oliver's Yard
55 City Road
London EC1Y 1SP
United Kingdom

SAGE Publications India Pvt. Ltd.
B 1/I 1 Mohan Cooperative Industrial Area
Mathura Road, New Delhi 110 044
India

SAGE Publications Asia-Pacific Pte. Ltd.
18 Cross Street #10-10/11/12
China Square Central
Singapore 048423

Printed in the United States of America

ISBN: 9781506398846

Library of Congress Cataloging-in-Publication Data

Names: Sternberg, Robert J., author.

Title: My biggest research mistake : adventures and misadventures in psychological research / Robert J. Sternberg, Cornell University, USA.

Description: First Edition. | Thousand Oaks : SAGE Publications, [2019] | Includes index.

Identifiers: LCCN 2018048724 | ISBN 9781506398846 (pbk.)

Subjects: LCSH: Psychology–Research.

Classification: LCC BF76.5 .S6874 2019 | DDC 150.72–dc23 LC record available at https://lccn.loc.gov/2018048724

This book is printed on acid-free paper.

Acquisitions Editor: Lara Parra
Editorial Assistant: Drew Fabricius
Marketing Manager: Katherine Hepburn
Production Editor: Jyothi Sriram
Copy Editor: Michelle Ponce
Typesetter: Hurix Digital
Proofreader: Caryne Brown
Indexer: Wendy Allex
Cover Designer: Scott Van Atta

SUSTAINABLE FORESTRY INITIATIVE
Certified Sourcing
www.sfiprogram.org
SFI-01075

19 20 21 22 23 10 9 8 7 6 5 4 3 2 1

CONTENTS

PREFACE

The goal of the book is to help students and professionals in the field of psychological science learn from diverse research mistakes of successful psychological scientists. The focus of the book is on the kinds of research mistakes scientists make and, usually, learn to correct only from experience. These are the mistakes that are usually *not* covered in standard textbooks. They are the mistakes that students can learn to avoid by reading about the experience of experts, thereby avoiding making those mistakes in their own work.

The motivation for the book is that whereas we learn much of what we know from our mistakes, not from what we do correctly, nevertheless, almost all publications on research methods are about what psychological scientists have "done right." In fact, much of the advantage more senior scholars in the field have over junior scholars is that they have made more mistakes to learn from, even though they infrequently talk about, and almost never write about, those mistakes. Journals often discourage articles that are written "autobiographically"—that is, that sketch the path the researcher took to arrive at the final product.

To a larger extent, this book is about what has sometimes been called "tacit knowledge"—the informal knowledge one picks up from experience rather than the formal knowledge one acquires in courses. The book is consistent with my own idea (Sternberg, 1997a, 1997b, 2003; Sternberg & Hedlund, 2002) that a major basis of professional success, including research success, is this tacit knowledge, or what we learn from the environment that often is not explicitly recognized or talked about. It's the "hidden curriculum" of professional life. In research, the hard stuff often is not what is in typical textbooks but what is not there.

That said, when one reads psychology publications, whether journals or books, one reads almost exclusively what people did right. Journals often even discourage people from reporting all their initial false leads and starts. And you are largely judged in the field on the basis of the positive contributions you have made, not on the basis of your account of how you learned from mistakes. Much of the current crisis in replication stems from the unwillingness of scientists following current paradigms to talk about what doesn't work in research. All their insights about what *not* to do are lost (Sternberg & Davidson, 1982). The result is that students (and young professionals) often do not realize how senior people in their field of psychological science have gotten to where they are largely from learning from the mistakes they have made and thinking critically about those mistakes (Dweck, 2007; Halpern, 2013; Stanovich, 2012; Sternberg, 1985; Sternberg, Roediger, & Halpern, 2006). Those who do not reach higher levels of success often fail to reach those levels because they made mistakes but did not learn from them.

Contributors to this book are distinguished psychological scientists as determined by their having been chosen for "fellow" status in the Association for Psychological Science (APS). Scientists are awarded fellow status in APS only if they reach very high levels of scientific achievement and eminence.

Contributors each were asked to address the following questions:

1. What is the biggest research mistake (that you are willing to share with others) that you have ever made?

2. What do you think led you to make it?

3. What did you learn from it?

4. If you were today facing the situation that led up to the mistake, what would you have done differently?

5. What might the students and young professionals of today learn from it?

Authors were chosen from among APS fellows to sample from most of the particular fields of psychological science that the association covers. Essays are grouped by the kind of mistake made. The kinds of mistakes were determined after the fact. When I solicited contributions, I had no idea what people would write about. After I received all the essays, I devised a classification scheme that would fit the kinds of essays I received.

In addition to the essays about mistakes, this book contains both an introduction and a final essay. The introduction focuses on the importance of learning from mistakes in the research-socialization process. The final essay analyzes the various kinds of research errors sampled and summarizes what students might learn from them. In order to help students reflect on each chapter, each chapter has several critical-thinking questions following the essay.

This book is oriented toward students and professionals in any area of psychological science. The book covers academic careers, so is not necessarily relevant to clinicians.

There are many ways to divide up research mistakes. In this book, I divide up research mistakes into 10 categories: I. Failure in Conceptualizing Research, II. Prematurely Jumping to Conclusions, III. Following a Garden Path, IV. Using Measures of Dubious Reliability/Validity, V. Carelessness, VI. Overrelying on Others, VII. Error in Statistical Analysis, VIII. Generalizability of Findings, IX. Failure to Understand the "System," and X. Societal Costs Outweigh Societal Benefits. There is nothing magical about this system. It simply divides mistakes up so that readers can understand some ways in which mistakes group together. In the final chapter of the book, I discuss these categories in more detail.

REFERENCES

Dweck, C. (2007). *Mindset: The new psychology of success*. New York, NY: Ballantine.

Halpern, D. F. (2013). *Thought and knowledge: An introduction to critical thinking*. New York, NY: Psychology Press.

Stanovich, K. E. (2012). *How to think straight about psychology* (10th ed.). Hoboken, NJ: Pearson.

Sternberg, R. J. (1985). Teaching critical thinking, Part 1: Are we making critical mistakes? *Phi Delta Kappan, 67*, 194–198.

Sternberg. R. J. (1997a). Managerial intelligence: Why IQ isn't enough. *Journal of Management, 23*(3), 463–475.

Sternberg, R. J. (1997b). *Successful intelligence*. New York, NY: Plume.

Sternberg, R. J. (2003). *Wisdom, intelligence, and creativity synthesized*. New York, NY: Cambridge University Press.

Sternberg, R. J., & Davidson, J. E. (1982, June). The mind of the puzzler. *Psychology Today, 16*, 37–44.

Sternberg, R. J., & Hedlund, J. (2002). Practical intelligence, g, and work psychology. *Human Performance 15*(1/2), 143–160.

Sternberg, R. J., Roediger, H. L., III, & Halpern, D. F. (Eds.). (2006). *Critical thinking in psychology*. New York, NY: Cambridge University Press.

ACKNOWLEDGMENTS

David Berg, Community College of Philadelphia

Coral M. Bruni, California State University, San Marcos

Tracie L. Burke, Christian Brothers University

Nathalie Franco, Broward College

Wendy Heath, Rider University

Ashley Hoffman, Elon University

Mahzad Hojjat, University of Massachusetts Dartmouth

Daniel N. Jones, University of Texas at El Paso

Daniel Kochli, Miami University

Stephanie Krauthamer Ewing, Drexel University

Angie MacKewn, University of Tennessee at Martin

Steven M. McCloud, The Borough of Manhattan Community College

Jill Rinzel, University of Washington, Waukesha

Jeffrey Sable, Christian Brothers University

Patricia Schoenrade, William Jewell College

Stephanie Smith, Indiana University Northwest

Carrie Veronica Smith, University of Mississippi

Jeannine Stamatakis, Lincoln University

Sharmin Tunguz, DePauw University

Okori Uneke, Winston-Salem State University

Zane Zheng, Lasell College

1 INTRODUCTION
How I Learned to Learn From Mistakes

Robert J. Sternberg
Cornell University

In graduate school, I learned many lessons. I could not even count them all. But, I was lucky. I learned the most important lesson the very first week I was in graduate school.

I made three mistakes that week.

1. I showed my advisor, Professor Gordon Bower, a paper I had written as an undergraduate. He said he would look it over and cross out the sections he did not think were very good. He handed it back. Almost the entire paper was crossed out. *Lesson: Don't show your advisor your work unless you are pretty sure it is work in which you can and will take pride.*

2. In an introductory proseminar, our instructor, Professor Richard Atkinson, announced that there would be a final examination at the end of the course. But I thought this idea was stupid—the course consisted of presentations by Stanford professors on their work. I thought that the work of Stanford professors was not a valid organization of knowledge. I impulsively told him what I thought, in front of the whole class. Atkinson reacted poorly, as one might expect. I'm not sure he ever quite forgot the incident. *Lesson: If you are going to take on authority, think carefully about why, how, when, and where you will do it; don't just do it on impulse.*

3. When Gordon Bower had his students over to his house for dinner, he asked each student what he (they all were male) wanted to study. I was maybe fourth in line. Everyone preceding me said "semantic memory." They knew this was what Gordon probably wanted to hear. I suspect they were not all really interested in semantic memory but rather were only succumbing to social pressure. What should I, with no real interest in semantic memory, do? When he got to me, I said: "Semantic memory." To this day, I am embarrassed by my cowardly response. I failed to stand up for what I believed. I have never chickened out again. *Lesson: In your research, follow your dreams, not someone else's.*

In the course of a professional career, we all make a *lot* of mistakes. I know that in the course of my career I have made countless mistakes. You might think that losers make a lot of mistakes but that successful scholars avoid those mistakes. If you think that, you are wrong. Everyone makes mistakes, including the most successful scholars. I am far from the most successful scholar, but I have done reasonably well in my career. The secret is *not*—Don't make mistakes. *The secret is—Make your mistakes and learn from them, as well as from the mistakes of others.*

This book is about the mistakes that eminent psychological scientists have made, what they have learned from them, and what you can learn, too. The mistakes they made were of many kinds, and were made at many different points of career. The goal of this book is for you to learn from the mistakes of others so that you don't make the same mistakes they did!

There is a theoretical basis for a book such as this (believe it or not!). In a career, what matters most is not the formal knowledge that you acquired in courses in undergraduate or graduate school. Nor is it conventional intelligence. Whereas psychologists once viewed intelligence as primarily about general ability (Sternberg & Grigorenko, 2002), today, many psychologists take a broader view (Sternberg, 1985a, 1986). Rather, what matters most, perhaps, in career success is the informal or tacit knowledge you acquire from experience—your practical and social intelligence (Sternberg, 1997a, 1997b; Sternberg et al., 2000; Sternberg & Hedlund, 2002; Sternberg & Smith, 1985). It's the stuff that you pick up along the way through your day-to-day work tasks, your interactions with colleagues, and your interactions with the field as a whole. Your creative insights matter, of course (Sternberg & Davidson, 1982), but without tacit knowledge about how to conduct yourself in your career, you are pretty much lost (see Sternberg, 2016, 2017). I have known any number of gifted scientists who probably did very well in school and on standardized tests (Sternberg, 1981) but who failed to "learn the ropes," so to speak, of how to manage a career (Sternberg et al., 2000). They are good critical thinkers (Sternberg, 1985b) and perhaps even good creative thinkers (Sternberg & Davidson, 1982) but not good practical thinkers. One of the most important aspects of managing a career is making and learning from mistakes—not just one's own but also others'—so that one does not repeat these mistakes.

I hope this book will help you learn from the mistakes of others and thereby enhance your work in school, in your career, or in your life more generally.

Good luck in all you do and accomplish!

REFERENCES

Sternberg, R. J. (1981). A componential theory of intellectual giftedness. *Gifted Child Quarterly, 25*, 86–93.

Sternberg, R. J. (1985a). Human intelligence: The model is the message. *Science, 230*, 1111–1118.

Sternberg, R. J. (1985b). Teaching critical thinking, Part 1: Are we making critical mistakes? *Phi Delta Kappan, 67*, 194–198.

Sternberg, R. J. (1986). Inside intelligence. *American Scientist, 74*, 137–143.

Sternberg. R. J. (1997a). Managerial intelligence: Why IQ isn't enough. *Journal of Management, 23*(3), 463–475.

Sternberg, R. J. (1997b). What does it mean to be smart? *Educational Leadership, 54*(6), 20–24.

Sternberg, R. J. (2016). *Psychology 101½: The unspoken rules for success in academia* (2nd ed.). Washington, DC: American Psychological Association.

Sternberg, R. J. (2017). *Starting your career in academic psychology.* Washington, DC: American Psychological Association.

Sternberg, R. J., & Davidson, J. E. (1982, June). The mind of the puzzler. *Psychology Today, 16*, 37–44.

Sternberg, R. J., Forsythe, G. B., Hedlund, J., Horvath, J., Snook, S., Williams, W. M., Wagner, R. K., & Grigorenko, E. L. (2000). *Practical intelligence in everyday life.* New York, NY: Cambridge University Press.

Sternberg, R. J., & Grigorenko E. L. (Eds.). (2002). *The general factor of intelligence: How general is it?* Mahwah, NJ: Lawrence Erlbaum Associates.

Sternberg, R. J., & Hedlund, J. (2002). Practical intelligence, g, and work psychology. *Human Performance 15*(1/2), 143–160.

Sternberg, R. J., & Smith, C. (1985). Social intelligence and decoding skills in nonverbal communication. *Social Cognition, 2*, 168–192.

FAILURE IN CONCEPTUALIZING RESEARCH

2 GRANDIOSITY AND OVERAMBITION

Nick Haslam
University of Melbourne

Repression is said to be an immature defense mechanism, but I strongly recommend it. I must have committed countless research mistakes, but my inner censor has scrubbed my record clean, leaving a memory bank that is rich in remembered success and poor in error. However, as Freud explained, the occasional uncomfortable truth finds its way past the forces of repression and into awareness. When it does so, as in dreams, it often appears in disguised form. The biggest research mistake that I can recall is disguised as a minor success.

The research in question was part of my doctoral dissertation. It was inspired by a theory of elementary forms of social relationships developed by my advisor, Alan Fiske. Alan argued that all relationships are constituted from four basic relational models. *Communal Sharing* relationships are based on a sense of equivalence and shared identity, *Equality Matching* relationships on strict equality and balance, *Authority Ranking* relationships on ordered hierarchies, and *Market Pricing* relationships on a rational assessment of costs and benefits. Alan demonstrated masterfully how these abstract cognitive models had been anticipated in the theories of famous anthropologists, sociologists, and political thinkers. My dissertation research hoped to bring Alan's ideas down from the lofty heights of social theory to the lowlands of social cognition by testing how well his four models captured ordinary people's thinking about relationships. In essence, I wanted to find out whether people use these four models to conceptualize their own relationships.

In one study, I tried to answer this question in a way that I thought was rather ingenious. In a first experimental session, I asked a sample of undergraduates and community members to list up to 80 acquaintances with whom they interacted in any way. I randomly selected two nonoverlapping sets of 20 acquaintances for each participant. Using the first set of 20, participants rated every pair of acquaintances on how similar their relationship was with the two acquaintances. Using the second set, they sorted the 20 acquaintances into piles of people with whom they had similar kinds of relationship. These two tasks provided alternative ways of assessing how people think about the similarities and differences among their relationships.

At a later date, all participants returned for a second experimental session. I gave them a list of the 40 acquaintances they had rated or sorted in the first session as well as simple descriptions of the four relational models. I asked them to classify each acquaintance into one of those models based on the nature of the relationship they had with that acquaintance: Was it a *Communal Sharing*, *Equality Matching*, *Authority Ranking*, or *Market Pricing* relationship? If participants' ratings and sortings of their relationships in the first experimental session corresponded closely to how they classified those relationships—if, for example, they sorted their acquaintances into four piles, and each pile primarily contained relationships based on a different relational model—then the relational models would be a good account of their relational cognition.

Unfortunately, I did not stop there. It was not enough to find out whether the relational models captured people's relational cognition. I wanted to see if they were a *better* fit than any other theory of relationships. So, in the second session, I also asked participants to classify their 40 acquaintances in four additional ways: using a two-category theory of communal versus exchange relationship types, a four-category theory of social role types, a five-category theory of social motives, and a six-category theory of social resources. These disparate theories were drawn from an assortment of disciplines and literatures. I then statistically compared how well the five different classifications corresponded to the participants' ratings and sortings of their relationships. The relational models classification performed well, but the results were complex, and no classification emerged as the clear winner. An article based on the study was eventually published (Haslam & Fiske, 1992) and has now spent a quarter century languishing in well-deserved obscurity.

So what was my mistake? It was fundamentally one of scientific overreach, ambition, and impatience. I wanted to do too much with a single study, and as a result, I undermined my research in several ways. First, its findings were unnecessarily confusing and messy because I was contrasting five different theories containing 21 different ways of classifying relationships. Second, I created an interpretive nightmare for myself because the five theories were radically different and contained different numbers of explanatory elements. I was comparing apples and oranges (and pears, peaches, and pomegranates). Third, by explicitly contrasting the predictive success of relational models theory with other theories I was potentially antagonizing other theorists with my adversarial approach. Indeed, when I submitted the article manuscript to a scientific journal a reviewer argued that research should examine a single theory rather than contrast alternative theories. I was outraged by this argument at the time, because I thought it was the duty of scientists to replace worse theories with better ones. But I now see the reviewer's point: Direct adversarial contests between theories are usually less conducive to scientific progress than research programs that explore the merits of single theories.

What led me into this mistake is easy to see in retrospect. I was passionate about my advisor's theory, and I wanted to do something big and important that established its pre-eminence over other theories. I wanted to make a contribution that went beyond social psychology and joined a conversation with big ideas in social theory and one that elevated one set of ideas above all others. In short, I was grandiose. If

I were doing the work now, with the benefit of hindsight, I would be humbler and more patient. I would carry out a series of simpler studies, rather than trying to squeeze all my questions into a single, overstuffed study design. I would downplay or avoid direct empirical comparison of different theories and emphasize how well (or poorly) my one preferred theory fared in making sense of the data. And I would be more tentative, modest, and generous toward alternative theories in my interpretation of results and study conclusions.

Methodological overambition is something I see quite often in beginning researchers. They are excited by their ideas—something no advisor would want to discourage—and want to make a major splash with their work. They often don't appreciate that a single study rarely changes a field. Psychological science advances more by the steady accumulation of findings that demonstrate the value of a new idea, rather than by a revolutionary study that overturns received wisdom or slays an established theory. The intense competition for places in graduate programs and for faculty positions exacerbates this urge to do something momentous. In addition, new researchers often don't appreciate that methodological simplicity is a virtue. Rather than cramming many alternative theories or experimental factors into a single study design, it is generally better to break them up into several simpler, bite-size studies.

My mistake was not especially shameful. It was an error of immodesty and a lack of scientific humility, not of ethical blind spots or stupidity. It did not lead me to draw a false conclusion or to fail to draw a correct one. But it did take me down a dead end and make my research less impactful than it might have been.

REFERENCE

Haslam, N., & Fiske, A. (1992). Implicit relationship prototypes: Investigating five theories of the elementary cognitive forms of social relationship. *Journal of Experimental Social Psychology, 28*, 441–474.

CRITICAL THINKING QUESTIONS

1. Do you agree that adversarial comparison of alternative theories in research studies is usually an unproductive way to advance science?

2. What might be the best way to ensure that study designs are not excessively complex?

3. What are some statistical problems that might arise in highly complex, overambitious studies?

3 SEPARATING DATA-BASED FROM NON-DATA-BASED EVALUATIONS

Harry P. Bahrick

Ohio Wesleyan University

I describe how undocumented assumptions/beliefs shaped memory research and how my ignorance of these effects influenced my career.

Before the 19th century, psychological phenomena were assumed to involve the soul, a theological construct not suitable for scientific study. In the 19th century, biologists and physicists initiated psychophysical investigations relating sensory experiences to physical stimuli. Their success encouraged other scientists to study more complex conscious processes.

Scientific study of memory began with Ebbinghaus's seminal finding that retention of lists of syllables followed a predictable course over time. Ebbinghaus used experimentation, the preferred method of 19th-century physics. His demonstration helped to gain acceptance of psychology as a scientific discipline in universities. It not only made experimentation the obligatory method for subsequent memory research, it also made it symbolic of scientific psychology. Experimental psychologists formed an elite division of the American Psychological Association (APA), founded an honor society limited to those performing experiments, and published the *Journal of Experimental Psychology*, a premier journal of psychological research. Alternative methods were used in other domains of psychology, but for nearly a century, publication and funding of memory research depended upon using the experimental method.

Philosophers had postulated much earlier that all memories consisted of associations. Psychologists took over this assumption and used experiments to study how associations among syllables or words are learned and retained. However, many other memory phenomena could not be investigated experimentally. My own interest as a graduate student focused on memory for complex knowledge, for example, foreign languages and mathematics. Learning and memory of such knowledge involves long periods that do not lend themselves to experimental controls. My teachers, whom I hold in high esteem, assumed that only experimental investigations of memory were good science, that associations were the units of all knowledge, and that the experimental study of associations would ultimately suffice to account for complex memory phenomena.

Gestalt psychologists had demonstrated holistic principles of perception, indicating that the whole is more than the sum of its parts. I thought that this principle could also apply to complex memory content, as Bartlett (1932) had suggested much earlier. However, given the beliefs of my teachers and the dominant tradition in memory research, I thought it ill advised to launch my career on nonexperimental memory research. Instead, I worked on methodological issues within the experimental tradition.

Fast-forward 20 years. Pursuing my early interest, my associates and I completed a 50-year study of memory of names and faces of high school classmates. We bootlegged this study into an National Institutes of Health (NIH) grant for conventional memory research, and we substituted statistical for experimental controls of key variables. We submitted the study to the *Journal of Experimental Psychology* with little hope that it would become the first nonexperimental investigation published in that journal. Surprisingly, the editor never raised that issue. The study was published (Bahrick, Bahrick, & Wittlinger, 1975) and was well received by memory psychologists who had been influenced by the cognitive revolution that challenged traditional assumptions.

Neisser (1978), a pioneer of cognitive psychology, published a highly provocative paper asserting that experimental memory research had never dealt with any of the important issues regarding memory and that naturalistic methods were needed to make memory research ecologically relevant. The attack by an outstanding scholar threatened the status and careers of traditional experimentalists and motivated strong responses. The counterattack was delivered by Banaji and Crowder (1989) in a paper entitled "The Bankruptcy of Ecological Memory Research." Other memory scholars supported Banaji and Crowder, reinstating a hostile climate for alternatives to laboratory memory experiments.

My own publications had never directly challenged the merit of memory experiments; I only advocated an expanding methodology. The controversy of experimentation versus naturalistic investigations became an issue only after Neisser denied the merits of laboratory experimentation. This controversy culminated when the *American Psychologist* (1991, (46) issue 1, pp.16–48) devoted an entire issue to this topic. The consensus of contributors was in accord with common sense. Laboratory and naturalistic investigations are not mutually exclusive. Rather, they are complementary, enabling scholars to address more diverse memory phenomena. That resolution is also in accord with a more general guideline regarding the validity of scientific methods: The validity of scientific methods depends upon shedding new light on the phenomena of interest, not upon meeting a specific standard of control.

The foregoing account illustrates how prevailing assumptions and undocumented beliefs affect scientific issues. Such assumptions/beliefs may reflect views held by the larger society, for example, that psychological phenomena are not suitable for scientific study because they involve the soul. The assumptions may also be made by a majority of scholars, for example, that associations are units composing complex memory phenomena. Finally, assumptions may be supported by individuals or groups of scholars who reject ideas that challenge their status and contributions, for example, that traditional memory experiments have no merit because they fail to address the important issues regarding memory.

Many other scientific issues are strongly affected by undocumented assumptions/ beliefs. Arguments about evolutionary theory continue over 150 years following Darwin's publication. Support of research related to assisted suicide, abortion, climate change, gene modification, and racial or gender differences is affected by beliefs of the larger society, groups of scholars, or motivated individuals.

I advocate research focused on exploring effects of non-data-based assumptions/ beliefs on the evaluation of scientific proposals. Much research is subject to such assumptions/beliefs. These beliefs and their effects may well be beneficial to society for a variety of reasons. However, evaluations of research reflecting non-data-based criteria should not be confounded with data-based aspects of evaluation. Separating these criteria of evaluation would clarify and improve the validity of evaluations and help individual scholars plan their research

REFERENCES

Bahrick, H. P., Bahrick, P. O., & Wittlinger, R. P. (1975). Fifty years of memory for names and faces: A cross-sectional approach. *Journal of Experimental Psychology: General, 104,* 54–75.

Banaji, M. R., & Crowder, R. G. (1989). The bankruptcy of everyday memory. *American Psychologist, 44,* 1185–1193.

Bartlett, F. C. (1932). *Remembering.* UK: Cambridge University Press.

Neisser, U. (1978). Memory: What are the important question? In M. M. Gruneberg, P. E. Morris, & H. N. Sykes, (Eds.), *Practical aspects of memory* (pp.3–24). London, UK: Aca.

CRITICAL THINKING QUESTIONS

1. Why is it important to consider not only data-based but also non-data-based criteria in the evaluation of research proposals?

2. How could we differentiate non-data-based criteria that should affect evaluations from those that should not affect evaluations?

3. How could graduate programs prepare scholars to consider non-data-based criteria in planning their research programs?

4 TOO CLEVER BY HALF

Judy S. DeLoache
University of Virginia

This title is based on a saying I've often heard English friends use. As can probably be inferred relatively easily, "*too clever by half*" means that one has erred by trying to be smarter than can realistically be expected in a given situation.

My "too clever" error involved a study I conducted several years ago. The focus of the experiment was to see how well very young children can recognize faces. Hence, black-and-white photographs were taken of a number of individuals—both men and women, boys and girls—that were to be presented to the participants.

As my intent was to *focus specifically on facial recognition, everything else that was in the original photographs was cut out, leaving only the faces*—no hair or clothing was visible.

Each of the 3- to 5-year-old children participating in the experiment was first familiarized with the set of photographs presented one at a time. To test whether the children could recognize the individuals they had seen in the photographs, they were then presented with pairs of photos of either two boys or two girls or two men or two women. One of the photos in each pair was one that had been presented to the children before; the other was one that they had not seen. The children were then asked to indicate which photo was the one they had seen.

To my great surprise, the children were very poor at indicating which person they had seen before. They were, in fact, not above chance.

In trying to figure out why the children's performance had been so poor, I closely scrutinized the photos that had been used in the study. The faces in the photos were perfectly clear, but I realized—belatedly—that the limiting of the depictions to just the faces per se, with no hair visible, resulted in very peculiar facial representations. Apparently, the strange faces simply did not register with our young participants.

This experience was a good lesson in how any research, and especially research conducted with young children, needs to be designed and executed with a keen sense of what can reasonably be expected of the participants.

By being "*too clever by half*," I had wasted the time of everyone involved—the students running the study, the children who participated, their parents who brought them to the lab, and myself.

CRITICAL THINKING QUESTIONS

1. What difference in the design of this study would have made it more likely that the young participants would perform better than they did?

2. What can be learned from the fact that a seemingly minor aspect of the experimental protocol had such a substantial effect on the children's performance in the study?

3. How different might the results of this research have been if the participants had been a few years older?

5 DEATH IS NOT THE ANSWER

Barbara Finlay
Cornell University

When I was in graduate school, in the soon-to-be-renamed psychology department at MIT, a graduate student senior to me, Doug Frost, was trying to visualize the first outreach of axons in the developing visual system, and he was suffering. At that time, the only high-definition way to trace axons used a technique developed by MIT's Walle Nauta, exploiting an unusual affinity of dying axons for silver molecules. If an axon tract was cut, Nauta's method could show where those degenerating axons connected. Doug, who could be found draped over his microscope any hour of day or night, was trying to modify this technique for the developing brain. He complained bitterly that the developing brain was so full of death and degeneration that he couldn't distinguish the degeneration of the axons he cut from the charnel-house of development itself. This peculiar observation struck me, and I tucked it away for the future. I proceeded with my own thesis on the development of maps of visual space in the brain and got a job at Cornell.

The psychology department at Cornell was an idiosyncratic and singular place. Its "psychobiologists" pioneered an early version of "evo-devo" (the study of how evolution interacts with the developmental, neural, and physiological mechanisms available to selection), while, Gibsonians (Jimmy and Jackie Gibson themselves, their students, and Dick Neisser) literally denied the idea that the brain could tell us the slightest thing about perception and cognition. They insisted on studying perception and cognition in its actual, functional, real-world complexity, against the reductionist trend. In this peculiar context, I cast around for the project I would actually do and thought back to Doug's developing, degenerating brains. Cognitive neuroscience has oscillated between periods where belief in innate brain mechanisms for perception and cognition dominates (such as built-in face recognizers or grammar modules) versus periods emphasizing plasticity and learnability of such constructs. Pushing the pendulum toward plasticity just then were the observations of two major contributors to plasticity, early axonal "exuberance," the propensity of growing axons to reach past their typical adult projection zones (Innocenti, 1995) and "cell death," the generic name for the developmental process including the extreme early overproduction and death of neurons (sometimes 80% or more of the original population [Oppenheim, 1981]). I wanted to know how perception works, particularly vision, and how vision, both its mechanisms and content, is constructed in the brain.

Neuron death, in combination with overproduction and pruning back of axon connections offered a way the brain might produce adaptations without much innate specification. The brain might connect itself up in a very general manner and allow the world, in combination with whatever behavior worked best, to direct its wiring, discarding the mismatches. The first looks into neuron death in the 1930s had shown that, in some cases, neuron death regulated the numbers of neurons in interconnecting populations or could sculpt a particular form, such as fingers out of a paddle-shaped appendage (Hamburger & Levi-Montalcini, 1949). Even more, perhaps cell death removed errors and defined connectivity. Best of all, an easy pathway to selection and evolution suggested itself, as complicated adaptive behavioral mechanisms would not need to be slowly formed by natural selection but could be constructed in a generic brain with generic learning mechanisms. For a particular experiment, it was known that when one eye was occluded or removed in very early development, the remaining eye filled in the vacated spots with new projections.

Pay dirt! The remaining eye had much less neuron death, potentially producing the neurons commandeering new neural space for the remaining eye. The paper was published in *Science*, useful for the coauthors, a graduate student seeking a job and an assistant professor seeking tenure (Sengelaub & Finlay, 1981); at the Society for Neuroscience meeting, our poster (posters were an innovation that year) was thrillingly mobbed. We went on to describe the normal incidence of cell death in the visual system and perhaps implicated cell death in the sculpting of high neuron density in the center of the retina. Neuron loss looked as if it might be a central mechanism of sexual differentiation of the nervous system, starting from the different musculature and organs that need to be connected up to the spinal cord for each sex.

But then . . . more research showed that the spared retinal neurons truly existed, but they proved to be mostly an artifact of a detail of optic chiasm formation. Neuron death helped produce a retinal specialization (the extra density, high-acuity patch of neurons in the central retina that most mammals have) but only in animals with very minor central increased acuity, not in carnivores or primates like ourselves. In most regions of the brain, and in the cortex particularly, neuron loss had nothing to do with correction of errors of projection or assembly of circuits. It didn't match up the numbers of neurons in connecting populations with any sensitivity, for example, between retina and midbrain, or midbrain and cortex. Only in the case of massive losses, such as loss of the whole eye, did we see effects. The insensitivity of neuron death to anything but catastrophic variations in development dealt a deathblow to evolutionary speculations that it might be an "easy" way toward evolutionary adaptations (all reviewed in Finlay, 1992). Neuron loss did, in fact, contribute to the sexual differentiation of the spinal cord (Sengelaub, 1989). Even now, I cannot identify any overall function that best describes the purpose of the massive early neuron loss in the brain, other than perhaps a minor contribution to multiple developmental construction processes? I look at ensuing work with helpless knowledge. Neuroscience repeats earlier work over and over as better and fancier labeling techniques have been developed, performing the same experiments with new techniques. When immunological methods could recognize the particular proteins involved in apoptosis (the technical word for the cell suicide), new scientists went down the same road I had gone.

Where's the mistake? I could use cell-biology techniques, but I am not a cell biologist. I was interested in how perception and cognition developed in the brain, not apoptosis. In choosing to study this peculiar developmental phenomenon, I hoped that it and my real questions would somehow link up, but after 15 years there was no linkage. Systematically asking what neural mechanisms were central to the development of perception and cognition should have been my starting point. Here is an explicit version! Never take a sexy-looking phenomenon, some unexpected "effect" in an experiment, and try to figure it out as a research goal. Do not study "models" where the sexy effect was observed. First, describe the subject you want to understand, then study it directly.

Perhaps 15 years of work weren't entirely wasted, as students and I finally began see how the developing nervous system behaved across our multiple experimental interventions (Finlay & Pallas, 1989; Xiong & Finlay, 1996). Some broad evo-devo principles eventually emerged from the brains subjected to our unwittingly random perturbations (Finlay, Darlington, & Nicastro, 2001). It's an unacknowledged truth that many experiments will produce apparently random, nonsensical or zero results. A cause of these "failures" is that much formal hypothesis testing is hopelessly premature, testing theories with little relationship to reality, instead of the carefully planned events textbooks will claim it is. Even so, the results can be useful. To see why, consider the following analogy to two other cases where exquisitely organized structures get hit with the equivalent of hammers or lightning bolts. Both our dreams and the scattering of subatomic particles after collisions in particle accelerators in physics experiments can be described as the outcomes of random disruption of highly nonrandom, organized structures. Dreams may arise from automatic mechanisms in the cortex imposing order on the random activations produced by the subcortical stimulation that initiates REM sleep and have been useful in identifying which brain components and what kinds of experiences get incorporated into dream narratives (Hobson & Pace-Schott, 2002). Nuclei and atomic particles exploded by high energy bursts don't just vaporize but reveal new particles and specific energy output. Psychology and neuroscience experiments are usually not intended to be blunt instruments but often return results as surreal as dreams and obscure as diagrams of particles escaping exploding nuclei. If you can decouple your expectations from the actual response of the system you study, the underlying logic of complex structures may reveal itself over time.

REFERENCES

Finlay, B. L. (1992). Cell death and the creation of regional differences in cell numbers. *Journal of Neurobiology, 23*, 1159–1171.

Finlay, B. L., Darlington, R. B., & Nicastro, N. (2001). Developmental structure in brain evolution. *Behavioral and Brain Sciences, 24*, 263–307.

Finlay, B. L., & Pallas, S. L. (1989). Control of cell number in the developing visual system. *Progress in Neurobiology, 32*, 207–234.

Hamburger, V., & Levi-Montalcini, R. (1949). Proliferation, differentiation and degeneration in the spinal ganglia of the chick embryo under normal and experimental conditions. *Journal of Experimental Zoology, 111*, 457–502.

Hobson, J. A., & Pace-Schott, E. F. (2002). The cognitive neuroscience of sleep: Neuronal systems, consciousness and learning. *Nature Reviews Neuroscience, 3*(9), 679–693.

Innocenti, G. M. (1995). Exuberant development of connections, and its possible permissive role in cortical evolution. *Trends in Neurosciences, 18*, 397–402.

Oppenheim, R. W. (1981). Neuronal death and some related regressive phenomena during neurogenesis: a selective historical review and progress report. In W. M. Cowan (Ed.), *Studies in Developmental Neurobiology* (pp. 74–133). New York, NY: Oxford University Press.

Sengelaub, D. R. (1989). Cell generation, migration, death and growth in neural systems mediating social behavior. In J. Balthazart (Ed.), *Advances in Comparative and Environmental Physiology* (Vol. 3, pp. 239–267). Berlin: Springer-Verlag.

Sengelaub, D. R., & Finlay, B. L. (1981). Early removal of one eye reduces normally occurring cell death in the remaining eye. *Science, 213*, 573–574.

Xiong, M., & Finlay, B. L. (1996). What do developmental mapping rules optimize? *Progress in Brain Research, 112*, 350–361.

CRITICAL THINKING QUESTIONS

1. What prevents you from examining your question in the real world, instead of in reduced laboratory preparations or via Mechanical Turk questionnaires?

2. Are you proceeding to hypothesis testing before you actually have observed or described what you would like to understand? If not, your tests of your hypotheses will be meaningless, or at minimum, won't have the meaning you desired.

3. Why so humble, and why so cowardly? If your papers start with "Important person X showed Y, and Y is not well understood" you are neither underlining your own substantive choice nor willing to take credit or blame for the eventual outcome.

6

THINKING MORE IS MORE WHEN LESS IS MORE

E. Tory Higgins
Columbia University

Right from the start, I made my biggest research mistake. I was a psychology graduate student at Columbia University planning my doctoral research. My "burning issue" was interpersonal communication. A major communication issue in those days (early 1970s) was the extent to which communicators took the characteristics of their audience into account when formulating and transmitting their message. According to Grice's cooperative principle (Grice 1975), they should do so. But does everyone do so?

According to Piaget (1926), young children (preschoolers) can fail to take into account that what they know about something is different from what their audience knows, thereby producing "egocentric," noncooperative messages (see also Flavell, Botkin, Fry, Wright, & Jarvis, 1968; Glucksberg & Krauss, 1967). An example of this is giving directions. When you live in a neighborhood, you know the names of locations, such as the names of parks or streets or buildings. When giving directions to a neighbor, you can use these names, such as "To get to the parade, go to St. Joseph's church. It starts there." A neighbor also knows the names. But such directions would not help a stranger in the town. It would be egocentric to use the names.

I wanted to study the development of this kind of communicative perspective-taking in elementary school children (Grades 4, 5, 6, and 8). In the experimental room was a small miniature town with different buildings, streets, and vehicles. Three children were run at a time. Two of the children, the future communicator and the future "neighbor" audience, were taught the names of all of the buildings in the town, as if they lived in the town. The third child, who was the future "stranger" audience, was not given this information. The communicator child was then shown a story of an accident between two cars that happened on a street of the town. The communicator's task was to tell the accident story to the "neighbor" audience and to the "stranger" audience, in separate interactions, so that each audience would be able to choose the correct scene from a set of pictures for each part of the story. Notably, having a "neighbor" versus a "stranger" audience was an independent variable, and it could interact with developmental grade: Might there be stronger developmental differences for the "stranger" audience than for the "neighbor" audience because younger children's egocentric communication would be revealed with the "stranger" audience?

By having actual children in the role of the audience making choices about what happened in the car accident based on the communicator's message, it was possible to study the communication performance of both the communicator (encoder) and the audience (decoder). Thus, communication role (encoder *vs.* decoder) was another variable in the study, which could interact with the developmental variable: Might developmental differences be stronger for encoders than for decoders?

Wait, there's more. For both encoders and decoders, there was a manipulation of motivation. There was a monetary reward for accuracy, which was 25 times greater in the high- than the low-motivation condition. Might developmental differences be reduced when the motivation for accuracy is higher? Interesting question, I thought. But even more interesting, I thought, was the question: Might social class differences be reduced when the motivation for accuracy is higher? Oh . . . did I forget to tell you that a major aim of the study was to examine whether there are social-class differences in communication effectiveness? Half of the participants in each developmental grade were middle class, and half were lower class. Social class differences in communication effectiveness had received relatively little attention up to then. That was interesting in itself, but there was also the possibility that developmental grade and social class could interact: Might social class differences be greater in the higher grades? Another interesting question.

Wait, there's still more. [I know. You are saying: Are you kidding me?] At the time of the study, all developmental and social-class studies on communication were oral-communication studies. Might developmental or social-class differences be stronger for written communication than for oral communication? Or might they be weaker? Each of these possible interactions was reasonable. I thought: This also needs to be investigated.

Now you can see what having a "burning issue" can do to a researcher. I did not want my study to overlook any interesting question. I wasn't just eager . . . I was *over*eager. I had developmental grade differences, a "neighbor" versus "stranger" audience difference, a high- versus low-motivation difference, a social-class difference, and an oral versus written difference, plus encoder versus decoder. Did I mention all of the possible interactions among them? Not to worry. I had a whopping sample of 192 participants.

Of course, this meant that I needed some of my manipulations, and certainly most of the interactions, to have no effect on what happened. I didn't really realize that. I just wanted to study as much as I could. It was the biggest mistake I have made in designing a study. I look back at it now and it makes me laugh. How could I have done that?

I was lucky that the social-class variable and the motivation variable had no effects on communication accuracy. There was some evidence that the younger-grade communicators did better in the written than the oral channel. But mostly what I found were effects from the developmental grade differences, with the Grade 4 children clearly performing the worst and the Grade 8 children clearly performing the best for both the "neighbor" audience and the "stranger" audience (Higgins, 1977).

Looking back, I realize that I did not treat my questions seriously enough. They needed separate studies. I know now that those questions that I found so interesting, and especially the interactions that I wanted to investigate, were not actually tested in my study. The study was way too complicated and would have needed many more participants to address those questions. By being overeager in the number of issues I wanted to address, I was unable to test them all adequately. More is not more. Less is more.

Without doubt, I needed many more participants in my study. But my big mistake was not just having too few participants. It was trying to do too much in a single study. Each of my questions deserved its own separate study. As I mentioned earlier, my study did find that the younger grade communicators did better in the written than in the oral channel. Interesting. But why did this happen? I don't know. If I had only investigated development and communication channel, I might have thought more about what interactions might be found and what might explain each interaction if it was found. Then I would have included measures in the study that related to each of these possible explanations, such as a memory measure that could show that when younger children communicate in the written (*vs.* oral) channel they remember better what happened in the car accident. And then this could be followed by another study to find out why their memory is better in the written (*vs.* oral) channel. Less is more because you can think about your questions more deeply and prepare better to account for what you find.

I would like to end by saying that my dissertation research taught me a lesson that changed forever how I designed my research. In fact, it took a few more years of designing overly complicated studies before I really learned that less is more. I did a study on cognitive dissonance, for example, where three different independent variables were manipulated, and attitude change was measured three times, including twice in a second session that occurred two weeks after the first session (Higgins, Rhodewalt, & Zanna, 1979). That study did not need the second session to answer the central question. But I was overeager again to examine two additional questions. Stick to the central question in one study. Less is more.

REFERENCES

Flavell, J. H., Botkin, P. T., Fry, C. L., Wright, J. W., & Jarvis, P. E. (1968). *The development of role-taking and communication skills in children*. New York, NY: John Wiley & Sons.

Glucksberg, S., & Krauss, R. M. (1967). What do people say after they have learned how to talk? Studies of the development of referential communication. *Merrill-Palmer Quarterly, 13*, 309–316.

Grice, H. P. (1975). Logic and conversation. In P. Cole and J. L. Morgan (Eds.). *Syntax and semantics, (Vol. 3): Speech acts* (pp. 365–372). New York, NY: Seminar Press.

Higgins, E. T. (1977). Communication development as related to channel, incentive, and social class. *Genetic Psychology Monographs, 96*, 75–141.

Higgins, E. T., Rhodewalt, F., & Zanna, M. P. (1979). Dissonance motivation: Its nature, persistence, and reinstatement. *Journal of Experimental Social Psychology, 15*, 16–34.

Piaget, J. (1926). *The language and thought of the child*. New York, NY: Harcourt Brace.

CRITICAL THINKING QUESTIONS

1. Is it a good idea or a bad idea to plan a study to answer many interesting questions?

2. What are the downsides of conducting a study with several independent variables that could interact with one another?

3. What is the main lesson of this essay?

7 MANIPULATION CHECKS CAN RUIN YOUR STUDY

Ying-yi Hong
The Chinese University of Hong Kong

This essay is about a research mistake that I will never forget. Despite its happy ending, I still remember the experience vividly, probably because it was an emotional event that caused a lot of self-doubt and frustration. I learned such a powerful lesson from this mistake that I will never take common research practices for granted again. My mistake stemmed from a research practice called *manipulation check*, which is in general a good practice for most studies. Manipulation check refers to the assessment of whether the manipulation is effective. It often makes sense to assess whether a manipulation implemented does work; however, it did not work for my research, and it actually ruined the findings. Let me tell you the story.

I returned to teach in Hong Kong right after receiving my PhD in 1994 from Columbia University. By then, Hong Kong was approaching the future transfer of her sovereignty in 1997 from Britain to China. As a social psychologist, I was determined to study something with high social relevance for Hong Kong. Therefore, I decided to examine the social identity of Hong Kong people and intergroup relations between Hong Kong people and Chinese Mainlanders. In a study, I sought to examine how Hong Kong people perceive Chinese Mainlanders and whether prejudice was involved. Because this is a sensitive matter and most Hong Kong respondents probably would not be forthcoming in expressing blatant prejudice against Chinese Mainlanders, we invented an indirect method to assess respondents' attitudes. The respondents were told that researchers in the university had observed a group of Hong Kong persons and Chinese Mainlanders over the past six months and had collected some behaviors that were displayed by the two groups of people. The respondents were shown one behavior at a time and were asked to guess if the behavior was more likely to be performed by a Hong Kong person or a Chinese Mainlander. In fact, we made up the behaviors; there were seven positive, seven negative, and seven neutral behaviors. These behaviors were pilot tested and showed clear valence as predicted. We told participants at the beginning that they would be shown 42 behaviors but actually we showed them only 21 behaviors. In this way, the participants weren't able to balance their choices of behaviors between the two groups. At the end, we would examine all the behaviors assigned to Chinese Mainlanders and count how many were positive, negative, and neutral. A higher than chance level (one third) of negative behaviors and lower than chance level (one third) of positive behaviors would indicate prejudice. We defined prejudice as preconceived, usually unfavorable, feelings toward people because of their group membership (such as Chinese Mainlanders). Regardless of whether these preconceived unfavorable feelings were based on actual experience with the group, the feelings were overgeneralized to all members and contexts. Indeed, we found some Hong Kong people more prejudiced and some less prejudiced against Chinese Mainlanders. We could predict the individual differences.

How? We hypothesized that participants' self-claimed identity and their beliefs (implicit theory) in the malleability of moral character *matter*. If the Hong Kong participants identified themselves as "Chinese," they would include the Chinese Mainlanders as their in-group because they are both Chinese. Moreover, people who believe that moral character is malleable (we call this incremental theory) would be less judgmental than those who believe that moral character is fixed (called entity theory). Indeed, we found that incremental theorists who held an inclusive "Chinese" identity assigned about equal number of positive, negative, and neutral behaviors to Chinese Mainlanders, suggesting that they were not prejudiced against Chinese Mainlanders. By contrast, participants who held a "Hongkonger" identity, which excluded Chinese Mainlanders, or those who believed in an entity theory, assigned significantly more negative behaviors and fewer positive behaviors to Chinese Mainlanders, indicating that they were more prejudiced.

Despite the findings being interesting, they were correlational in nature because I had only measured the participants' self-claimed identity and their chronic endorsement of the implicit theory of moral character. Because I did not manipulate participants' identity or theory, I cannot discern whether those two factors indeed caused different levels of prejudice. To fill in this gap, I needed to conduct another study to manipulate identity and implicit theory and thereby see if I could replicate the findings.

I had a good opportunity to conduct a second study when I moved to the University of Illinois at Urbana-Champaign in 2002. I was quite shocked by the incident of the Rodney King riots that happened in Los Angeles in 1992, when some Korean-American store owners got into intense conflicts with African Americans. Therefore, I wondered if Asian Americans would show prejudice against African Americans. Employing a logic similar to that in the Hong Kong case, the Asian Americans could identify themselves as American (an inclusive identity) or Asian American (an exclusive identity). Therefore, extrapolating from the Hong Kong findings, participants who held an American identity and incremental theory should show significantly less prejudice against African Americans than participants who held an Asian-American identity or those who believed in the entity theory of moral character. Unlike the first study in Hong Kong, we sought to manipulate participants' identity and implicit theory.

I and my graduate student at that time, Jill Coleman, came up with a new way to manipulate Asian Americans' identity. We asked participants to write a short essay (about 250 words) first, allegedly for a study on writing style; but, in fact, we asked half of the participants to write an essay from the perspective of "American" and the other half from the perspective of an "Asian American" in order to activate their "American" and "Asian American" identities, respectively. To ensure that writing the essay would induce the different identity as predicted, we inserted a manipulation check item right after participants finished writing the essay: They were asked, "How do you identify yourself?" The options ranged from "American" to "Asian American." Then, we manipulated participants' implicit theory of moral character by asking them to read a "scientific" essay advocating either an incremental or an entity theory of moral character (this method has been commonly used in manipulating implicit theories; see Chiu, Hong, & Dweck, 1997). Subsequently, we assessed participants' prejudice toward African Americans using the symbolic racism scale. Our prediction was that participants who wrote the "American" essay and read the incremental theory essay would show lower prejudice toward African Americans than would those who wrote the "Asian American" essay or read the entity theory essay. To our surprise, we did not find any significant results! If anything, only the implicit-theory manipulation worked. We were so disappointed!

What had gone wrong? Was it because what I found in Hong Kong cannot be generalized to the United States? Was it because the measures and procedures we used in Hong Kong and the United States were very different? Jill and I thought hard and were puzzled.

Interestingly, we also found that participants' self-reported identity in the manipulation check actually showed our predicted effect. That is, participants who self-identified as "American" and read the incremental theory essay showed the lowest prejudice toward African Americans. All of a sudden, we got it—in the manipulation check, we asked our participants to report on their identification as American or Asian American, which could have flipped participants back to their chronic identity and thus wiped out the effect of the identity manipulation!

With this insight, we reran the study in an identical way but removed the manipulation check item. Finally, we found what we had predicted and replicated the same pattern of findings as in Hong Kong. We published this research in Hong et al., 2004.

From then on, I would not take common research practices for granted. It is important to think through each measure or procedure in the context of your study. Some good practices may turn out to be "bad" practices if they are used in the wrong context.

REFERENCES

Chiu, C., Hong, Y., & Dweck, C. S. (1997). Lay dispositionism and implicit theories of personality. *Journal of Personality and Social Psychology, 73*, 19–30.

Hong, Y., Coleman, J., Chan, G., Wong, R. Y. M., Chiu, C., Hansen, I. G., … & Fu, H. (2004). Predicting intergroup bias: The interactive effects of implicit theory and social identity. *Personality and Social Psychology Bulletin, 30*, 1035–1047.

CRITICAL THINKING QUESTIONS

1. When should you use a manipulation check? Why?

2. When should you not use a manipulation check? Why?

3. If you decide not to use a manipulation check, how can you assess the effectiveness of the manipulation method?

8

BEWARE OF POPULAR PREMISES

Jerome Kagan
Harvard University

Readers must first appreciate the ideological commitments held by many psychologists during the 1950s in order to understand the mistake I made in selecting a test of personality to administer to young adults. My assignment was to create a battery of measures designed to evaluate select personality traits in young adults on whom extensive longitudinal data were available. The details of the study can be found in the book *Birth to Maturity* (Kagan & Moss, 1962). The concepts of motive and conflict were important to both behaviorism and Freud's psychoanalytic ideas, both of which were popular at the time. Many psychologists assumed that measurement of personality traits required indirect methods because people were reluctant to admit to undesirable traits. This belief explains the widespread use of a person's interpretations of 10 ink blots, called the Rorschach test, and the stories told to a series of black-white pictures illustrating one or more individuals in settings allowing multiple interpretations of the thoughts of the persons illustrated. This procedure was called the Thematic Apperception Test. These methods were called projective because investigators assumed the person projected his or her conflicts and desires on to the test materials. These methods proved to be insensitive and are rarely used in research today

A projective test called The Make-A-Picture-Story test required adults to sort arrays of cardboard figures into a number of groups that shared a common property (Shneidman, 1949). The figures, which varied in age, gender, and social role, were designed to suggest the motives of hostility, nurture, dependence, and sex, and the emotions of anger, fear, and sadness. I assumed that the content of the six groups each adult produced to each of two different arrays of figures would be related to the extensive evidence gathered on them during a contemporary interview, as well as by others who had gathered observations on each individual from infancy to adolescence.

I was disappointed by the lack of any relation between the content of the groups the adults generated and the evidence on their motives or conflicts in the past or present. Rather, most of their groupings were based either on a shared physical feature (for example, a boy, policeman, and woman who were standing or a woman, beggar, and doctor with a raised arm), or a relationship between two figures in a group (for example, a boy and his mother or a married couple).

Fortunately, I had recorded the latency to each grouping because my experience as a graduate student had taught me the value of recording as many measures as possible. After spending many hours poring over the evidence, I realized one night that the adults who produced many groupings based on similar physical features took a few seconds longer to respond than those who generated groups based on a relationship. Equally important, the longitudinal data revealed that those with longer latencies were behaviorally less impulsive than those who produced many relationship sorts quickly. That surprising discovery led to several years of fruitful research on the concepts of a reflective or impulsive conceptual style measured with the Matching Familiar Figures Test (Kagan, 1966).

LESSONS LEARNED

This episode contains four lessons with implications that have been affirmed during the remainder of my career. Here they are!

First, measure as many variables as you can that might be relevant to the question being asked. Because every psychological outcome can be the product of more than one cascade of processes, it is wise to base inferences on patterns of measures rather than single variables.

Second, be skeptical of all popular premises, especially those you favor. Major advances often follow experiments designed to disprove, rather than affirm, a popular idea. Harry Harlow and his colleagues placed infant monkeys in a room with either a wire surrogate that was a source of food or a cloth-covered surrogate with no food to disprove the behaviorist's seminal hypothesis that satisfaction of a biological drive was the most powerful reward (Harlow & Harlow, 1966). Garcia and Koelling (1966) are celebrated because their experiments disproved the popular assumption that any combination of a conditioned and unconditioned stimulus produced conditioning.

The third lesson is recognition of the limitations on conclusions based on one study in one setting with an unrepresentative group of subjects generating one kind of evidence. Conclusions about processes, such as anxiety, memory, or shame, require sentences that specify the agent—a rat, infant, or college student—the response measured—a behavior, verbal report, or biological reaction—and always the context in which the evidence was gathered—an unfamiliar laboratory, a home, or a social gathering.

The final lesson is to be suspicious of the words people use and to trust direct observations because words omit important details in every event. Watching a football game is more informative than listening to a narrator on the radio. If psychologists could observe me several hours a day for 20 days they would have a far more accurate understanding of my personality than if they inferred my traits from any current questionnaire. This suggestion runs counter to the recent suggestion that investigators declare the results they expect to find before they perform a study. If past scientists had followed this regime many of the most significant discoveries would have been delayed. These include the nucleus of the atom, the structure of DNA, and the functions of the primary visual cortex. Most scientific progress has been the result of unexpected observations by minds examining carefully gathered observations with patience and an obsessive attention to detail.

REFERENCES

Garcia, J., & Koelling, R. (1966). Relation of cue to consequence in avoidance learning. *Psychonomic Science, 4*, 123–124.

Harlow, H. F., & Harlow, M. K. (1966), Learning to love. *American Scientist, 54*, 244–272.

Kagan, J. (1966). Reflection-impulsivity. *Journal of Abnormal Psychology, 71*, 21–26.

Kagan, J., & Moss, H. A. (1962). *Birth to Maturity.* New York, NY: John Wiley.

Shneidman, E. S. (1949). *The Make-a-Picture-Story Test.* New York, NY: The Psychological Corporation.

CRITICAL THINKING QUESTIONS

1. Why should we be suspicious of conclusions about the localization of a psychological property in a brain site from one measure of brain activity in a sample of 20 college students observed in a magnetic scanner?

2. Even though English has one only word for *consciousness*, is it possible that there are multiple states of consciousness?

3. Psychologists do not understand why the gap in income and education between Americans who grew up with parents who did not graduate from high school and those with parents who had a college degree is growing. If a philanthropy gave you a million dollars a year for five years to gather evidence that would help us understand why heathy, family-raised children from these two groups differ in language skills and behavior as early as age three, what kind of study would you propose?

9 THE NEED FOR BLIND TESTING

Saul M. Kassin

John Jay College of Criminal Justice

I had been studying false confessions for years. It's inconceivable, I once thought, that anyone would confess to a serious crime he or she did not commit. Unless you held a gun to my head, I would never do that.

Then I read the manuals on how police interrogate people to get them to confess. Using subtle but persuasive forms of trickery and deceit, the techniques they use could have been scripted in Stanley Milgram's obedience experiments. Prodding a beleaguered suspect with phrases such as "We know everything," "We have your fingerprints," and "If I were in your situation I would have done the same thing," police can persuade an innocent person to confess. My colleagues and I have tested these tactics in the laboratory. The effects can be devastating. Indeed, nearly 30% of all wrongful convictions uncovered by the Innocence Project involved false confessions (for a review, see Kassin et al., 2010).

That false confessions happen is only the first part of a bigger problem. The second part is that judges and juries unflinchingly trust the confessions they hear in court—regardless of who the confessor is and how it came about. Time and again, I've seen this in jury research: When there is a confession in evidence, even when the defendant recanted it, claimed it was coerced, and insisted he or she was innocent; and even if there was no other evidence, juries vote for conviction. How, then, does the legal system protect us? Where is the safety net?

While presenting my research, sometimes to law enforcement groups, I heard so many detectives say it that I lost count: "Don't worry. *I'd know a false confession if I saw one.*" Well, that's an easy claim to make, I thought. "But how do you know?"

This seemed like a hypothesis worth testing. So along with a former Williams College student, who was by then in the social psychology PhD program at Harvard, I packed my video equipment into the car and headed to Boston. Through a friend of a friend, I had gained access to the Suffolk County Correctional Facility. Once there, and with Institutional Review Board (IRB) approval in hand, we recruited a number of inmates, all male, at a rate of $20 each. We set up shop in a room, where I would sit on one side of a table, and the inmates would sit opposite me. Behind me, my student operated a video camera, which was set up on a tripod facing the inmate. An audio recorder was also placed on the table.

30

One by one, the inmates would come in, and I would instruct them to confess to the crime for which they were being incarcerated—statements I verified by their records. In each case, they would give their confession, after which I was prepared with a standard set of follow-up questions to ensure a minimum level of detail. Then I would ask those same inmates to fabricate a confession to a crime they did not commit (specifically, the confession I asked for was to a crime that the previous participant had actually committed). Being good experimentalists, we counterbalanced the order in which we took the two confessions. Half the inmates gave their true confession first; half gave their false confession first.

After leaving the facility, we created a stimulus videotape and corresponding audiotape that depicted 10 different individuals, once each, confessing to one of five crimes. Half the confessions were true; the other half were their false counterparts. We then showed the tapes to college students and to experienced detectives, telling them that some of the statements they will see are true, others false. In contrast to the claim that "I'd know a false confession if I saw one," the results showed that the detectives, while confident, could not tell the difference any better than the average person. At 48%, their accuracy rate was so low they may as well have guessed or flipped a coin.

This study was published and is highly cited (Kassin, Meissner, & Norwick, 2005). Sometime afterward, however, I was reviewing a manuscript for a journal involving a study in which interviewers questioned people who were instructed either to lie or tell the truth. I was critical of the fact that the interviewers knew ahead of time which people were in which condition. The experimenter should have been "blind" to the truth vs. lie condition while conducting the interviews, I noted, to avoid unwittingly altering their questions, intonation, or demeanor.

The need for "blind" testing is basic—and has been ever since Robert Rosenthal published his work on experimenter expectancy effects. In a classic experiment, Rosenthal and Fode (1963) asked two groups of students to train rats to run a maze. Some students were told their rat was bred to be "bright;" others were told that their rat was bred to be "dull" (in fact, all rats were drawn from the same population). The results showed that the so-called bright rats learned the mazes more quickly. Somehow, the students had influenced the performance of their rats, depending on what they were led to expect. Later, Rosenthal and Jacobson (1966) found that when elementary school teachers were led to believe that certain students were on the verge of an intellectual growth spurt, those selected students exhibited greater improvement in academic tests. Whether training rats or teaching students, it appears that people unwittingly act upon their beliefs in ways that produce the expected outcomes.

Back to our prison study. I took two confessions from each inmate—one true, the other false, in counterbalanced order. I personally instructed them, so I knew whether each statement was true or false when asking my standardized follow-up questions (on a couple of occasions, the prisoner's false statement was so convincing that I had to confirm the condition with my student!). Is it possible that I had inadvertently shaded the way I asked my follow-up questions based on what I knew to be the condition? I can't totally exclude that possibility. In light of experimenter-expectancy effects, it was a mistake not to blind myself—which would have been easy by having my student instruct each inmate in my absence before I interviewed him.

From a practical standpoint, I don't really worry that our main results were tainted. Had I somehow shaded my interviews, treating the inmates differently during their true vs. false confessions, I would expect the two sets of statements to be distinguishable to observers. In fact, neither police nor college students could tell the difference. I also don't worry because this main result was replicated in a later study involving juvenile offenders (Honts, Kassin, & Craig, 2014) and is highly consistent with research showing that people in general are not accurate at distinguishing other people's truths and lies (Vrij, 2008).

This study demonstrated what often happens in the real world whenever judges and juries convict innocent defendants because they erroneously believed their false confessions. That said, the failure to blind myself, the interviewer, was a mistake too often seen, unfortunately, in behavioral research—and in the real world. If we were to conduct this study again, I would rewrite the protocol, allowing for my students to instruct participants in my absence.

REFERENCES

Honts, C. R., Kassin, S. M., & Craig, R. (2014). "I'd know a false confession if I saw one": A constructive replication with juveniles. *Psychology, Crime and Law, 20,* 695–704.

Kassin, S. M., Drizin, S. A., Grisso, T., Gudjonsson, G. H., Leo, R. A., & Redlich, A. D. (2010). Police-induced confessions: Risk factors and recommendations. *Law and Human Behavior, 34,* 3–38. [Official White Paper of the American Psychology-Law Society]

Kassin, S. M., Meissner, C. A., & Norwick, R. J. (2005). "I'd know a false confession if I saw one": A comparative study of college students and police investigators. *Law and Human Behavior, 29,* 211–227.

Rosenthal, R., & Fode, K. (1963). The effect of experimenter bias on performance of the albino rat. *Behavioral Science, 8,* 183–189.

Rosenthal, R., & Jacobson, L. (1966). Teachers' expectancies: Determinants of pupils' IQ gains. *Psychological Reports, 19,* 115–118.

Vrij, A. (2008). *Detecting lies and deceit: Pitfalls and opportunities.* Chichester, England: Wiley.

CRITICAL THINKING QUESTIONS

1. What are experimenter-expectancy effects?

2. Why are experimenter-expectancy effects important for researchers to understand?

3. How might such effects have influenced the study described in this chapter?

4. What should the investigators have done differently to avoid experimenter-expectancy effects?

10 FINDING IMPLICIT MEMORY IN POSTHYPNOTIC AMNESIA

John F. Kihlstrom
University of California, Berkeley

Following appropriate suggestions and the termination of hypnosis, some subjects are unable to remember the things they did or experienced while they were hypnotized—a phenomenon called posthypnotic amnesia (PHA). After the administration of a prearranged reversibility cue, the memories come back into awareness, marking this amnesia as a disruption of memory retrieval, rather than encoding or storage.

I wanted to see how PHA affected different aspects of memory (Kihlstrom, 1980). Cognitive psychologists distinguish between declarative and procedural memory, and between two forms of declarative memory, episodic and semantic. Because PHA affects memory for experiences, it should impair episodic memory but leave semantic memory intact. An earlier experiment by John Williamsen had found that PHA affected free recall and recognition of a word list memorized during hypnosis but did not prevent amnesic subjects from using the forgotten words as responses on a free-association test (Williamsen, Johnson, & Eriksen, 1965). I decided to perform a conceptual replication of his study: If you're beginning a new program of research, it's best to start where previous investigators left off, to make sure that you can see what they saw.

In my first experiment, subjects were hypnotized, memorized a list of words, like *girl*, that were strong associates of other words, like *boy*, and then received a suggestion for PHA. Highly hypnotizable subjects performed very poorly on a free-recall test administered while the amnesia suggestion was in effect but continued to use the list items as responses on a word-association test. In a second experiment, in which subjects memorized lists consisting of highly salient category instances, such as *foot*, highly hypnotizable subjects were densely amnesic on the test of free recall but still used the list items when asked to generate instances of categories such as *part of the human body*. Endel Tulving (1983) later cited this study as one of four convincing demonstrations of his distinction between episodic and semantic memory.

I had succeeded in replicating Williamsen's study, but I also had another motive for doing the experiment. Meyer and Schvaneveldt (1971) had reported semantic priming effects in a lexical decision task. Subjects responded faster to associated pairs of words, such as *bread-butter* and *doctor-nurse*, compared to unrelated pairs such as *bread-nurse* and *doctor-butter*. Apparently, processing the first word of a related pair facilitated processing the second word. Similar priming effects had been observed in the amnesic syndrome, and I wanted to see if there were similar priming effects in PHA. Williamsen hadn't been looking for priming effects: Cognitive psychologists didn't seriously think about priming until Meyer and Schvaneveldt published their experiment more than five years later.

Would having just memorized words like *girl* make them come more readily to mind as free associates to words like *boy*? Would having just memorized words like *foot* make them come more readily to mind as instances of *part of the human body*—despite the fact that my subjects could not remember having memorized them? Yes: Priming effects occurred in PHA, just as they occurred in the amnesic syndrome.

Nobody would have been surprised to learn that priming accompanied *conscious* recollection, but at the time, nobody had a name for preserved priming during amnesia. All I could do was refer, somewhat clumsily, to "a residual effect of the original learning episode on a subsequent task involving retrieval from 'semantic' memory" (p. 246). Only later were these unconscious priming effects, occurring in the absence of conscious recollection, labeled as instances of *implicit memory* (Schacter, 1987). It's not a mistake exactly, but I wish I had thought of that term first.

Although my paper appeared to demonstrate a dissociation between explicit (conscious) and implicit (unconscious) memory, it wasn't completely definitive. I had compared free recall with priming and found a difference between them. But that comparison entails a confound: Free recall tests involve very minimal retrieval cues—really, they just specify the time and place the target event occurred, but the free-association and category-generation tests provided additional cues, in the form of the free-association stimuli or category labels. The most convincing demonstration of explicit-implicit dissociations come from studies where the two tests are matched for the informational value of the cues provided to the subjects. For example, *boy* should be presented as a retrieval cue in the explicit memory task as well as a free-association stimulus in the implicit memory task. But nobody realized that until much later (Graf, Squire, & Mandler, 1984). Fortunately, Amanda Barnier and her colleagues performed a conceptual replication of my experiment with matched cues and confirmed my finding (Barnier, Bryant, & Briscoe, 2001). Moreover, Dan David and his colleagues employed Jacoby's (1991) process-dissociation procedure to confirm that priming in PHA was a product of automatic (unconscious), rather than controlled (conscious), processing (David, Brown, Pojoga, & David, 2000).

At the time I did my experiment, nobody had given the name *implicit memory* to priming in the absence of conscious recollection. Nobody understood that we should match the cues provided on tests of explicit and implicit memory. And the process-dissociation procedure hadn't been invented yet. They weren't mistakes, really, but there were certainly things I would have done differently. But the nice thing about science is that it's cumulative: each study builds on what went before. Just as I built on an earlier experiment, the later experiments built on mine, to yield a much better understanding of posthypnotic amnesia. That's the way science is supposed to work.

REFERENCES

Barnier, A. J., Bryant, R. A., & Briscoe, S. (2001). Posthypnotic amnesia for material learned before or during hypnosis: Explicit and implicit memory effects. *International Journal of Clinical & Experimental Hypnosis, 49*(4), 286–304. doi: http://dx.doi.org/10.1080/00207140108410079

David, D., Brown, R., Pojoga, C., & David, A. (2000). The impact of posthypnotic amnesia and directed forgetting on implicit and explicit memory: New insights from a modified process dissociation procedure. *International Journal of Clinical & Experimental Hypnosis, 48*(3), 267–289. doi: http://dx.doi.org/10.1080/00207140008415246

Graf, P., Squire, L. R., & Mandler, G. (1984). The information that amnesic patients do not forget. *Journal of Experimental Psychology: Learning, Memory, and Cognition, 10*, 164–178. doi: http://dx.doi.org/10.1037/0278-7393.10.1.164

Jacoby, L. L. (1991). A process dissociation framework: Separating automatic from intentional uses of memory. *Journal of Memory & Language, 13*, 513–541. doi: http://dx.doi.org/10.1016/0749-596X(91)90025-F

Kihlstrom, J. F. (1980). Posthypnotic amnesia for recently learned material: Interactions with "episodic" and "semantic" memory. *Cognitive Psychology, 12*, 227–251. doi: http://dx.doi.org/10.1016/0010-0285(80)90010-9

Meyer, D. E., & Schvaneveldt, R. W. (1971). Facilitation in recognizing pairs of words: Evidence of a dependence between retrieval operations. *Journal of Experimental Psychology, 90*, 227–234. doi: http://dx.doi.org/10.1037/h0031564

Schacter, D. L. (1987). Implicit memory: History and current status. *Journal of Experimental Psychology: Learning, Memory, and Cognition, 13*, 501–518. doi: http://dx.doi.org/10.1037/0278-7393.13.3.501

Tulving, E. (1983). *Elements of episodic memory.* Oxford, UK: Oxford University Press.

Williamsen, J. A., Johnson, H. J., & Eriksen, C. W. (1965). Some characteristics of posthypnotic amnesia. *Journal of Abnormal Psychology, 70*, 123–131. doi: http://dx.doi.org/10.1037/h0021934

CRITICAL THINKING QUESTIONS

1. What is priming, and how does it reflect implicit memory?

2. Why is it important to replicate previous research?

3. Is it important for scientists to have names for the phenomena they discover?

11 SOCIAL COORDINATION IN THE WILD

Joachim I. Krueger

Brown University

Johannes Ullrich

University of Zurich, Switzerland

This is not the story of a catastrophic breakdown of scientific thinking but rather of a minor case of forecasting myopia, which, we think, is diagnostic of a larger point. Our forecasting failure occurred when we were studying the decision to make a prosocial sacrifice in the so-called Volunteer's Dilemma (VoD). The VoD is a rather challenging situation of interpersonal interdependence where the best outcome for the group is when exactly one person agrees to make a sacrifice. To give a stark example, who will run into the burning house to save the baby when mom and dad are respectively standing on the front and on the back lawn? The savior will get badly burned but live; if both run in, both get burned; if neither runs in, the baby dies, and each parent's grief is worse than the burn. In a series of web-based studies, we found that the probability of volunteering increases as the social distance between the "players" decreases (Krueger, Ullrich, & Chen, 2016).

The social distance effect is compelling, assuming that people care more about the well-being of close others than distant others. They are more willing to engage in a costly prosocial act. This generally useful social-distance heuristic is potentially problematic in the VoD because it can lead to "overvolunteering." We found that when people consider a VoD involving someone near and dear, they are all too willing to make that sacrifice. There are too many cases where both volunteer, which is not what they want. They want to volunteer for someone who does not volunteer. That is what would give the sacrifice meaning in the form of added value to the other person. If both parties want to be nice, both lose.

The overvolunteering effect, though small in size, was an intriguing finding because it showed that ill can come out of good intentions, and it is most likely so when people care the most about others. That is what makes the effect ironic and intriguing. Given that we had demonstrated the effect under conditions of information dearth, we sought to replicate it with live pairs in the field. We sought a strong replication to show the robustness and social relevance of overvolunteering.

We therefore sent a student assistant to various public places (e.g., coffeehouses and parks) in the city of Berlin, Germany. Our field researcher approached 100 pairs, invited them to participate in a brief behavioral study, and gathered data from those who agreed. Our main distinction was whether the participants were partners in a close relationship (n = 46) or not, with the latter category including mostly "close friends" and "friends" but also some "acquaintances" and "strangers."

We then asked the members of each pair to sit with their backs to one another. Doing so, we sought to eliminate nonverbal communication that might help them coordinate their volunteering decisions. Setting up a modified VoD, we then gave each participant a €2 coin, told them they could keep it afterward, and instructed them to place it heads ("*Adler*") or tails ("*Zahl*") up in their palm. If one person placed the coin heads up and the other placed it tails up, the one choosing tails would win an additional €5. If both chose tails, or both chose heads, however, they would only get to keep their two "endowment" Euros. In short, choosing heads was to volunteer because it ensured that the person could not win additional money.

We predicted that the close pairs would overvolunteer, thereby retaining only their total of €4, when they could have gained a total of €9. This did not happen. In fact, three quarters of the close pairs successfully coordinated their choices such that one of them volunteered, and the other did not (74% success, $p < .01$, when tested against the chance baseline of 50%). Less close pairs coordinated with a 59% success rate, which was statistically different from 74% ($p = .02$) but not from 50% ($p = .22$).

What had happened? We had predicted a rate of volunteering so high that fewer than 50% of the close pairs would end up with exactly one volunteer. Classic (i.e., nonsocial) game theory predicted a rate of 50% volunteering and hence 50% of coordination success. Both predictions turned out to be false, and we had had no *a priori* prediction pointing to the high rate of successful coordination that we ended up finding. We were thrown back to seeking *post hoc* explanations. We discovered that Diekmann (1993) had shown that people often coordinate successfully if they have a shared perception of who is the stronger player, that is, who can more easily absorb the sacrifice. In hindsight, it makes sense that people use myriad cues about one another (age, health, wealth, reproductive fitness) to assess who may want to (or even should) make the sacrifice. People who are psychologically very close are typically very similar to one another, but they also have considerable amounts of shared information about how they differ in their capacity to tolerate a sacrifice.

Equally troubling was our neglect of participants' strategic farsightedness. In postexperimental interviews, many noted that they intended to share the proceeds. Such intentions do not directly solve or eliminate the dilemma but may encourage the weaker player to defect without contrition.

Our failure to predict this outcome may not have been a colossal misfiring of scientific reasoning, but it highlights the wisdom of laying out a panel of hypotheses to anticipate all possible outcomes, including those that may seem unlikely or even weird at the time. Such outcomes, as our example shows, often do not look as weird once they have occurred. In our case, the failure of forecasting was not a failure to anticipate a null result (in fact, we had performed an *a priori* power analysis) but a result in the opposite direction. Foresighted thinking sets the stage for theory modification and follow-up study design before the data are in.

REFERENCES

Diekmann, A. (1993). Cooperation in an asymmetric volunteer's dilemma game. Theory and experimental evidence. *International Journal of Game Theory, 22,* 75–85.

Krueger, J. I., Ullrich, J., & Chen, L. J. (2016). Expectations and decisions in the volunteer's dilemma: Effects of social distance and social projection. *Frontiers in Psychology: Cognition, 7,* article 1909. doi: 10.3389/fpsyg.2016.01909

CRITICAL THINKING QUESTIONS

1. As the example shows, post hoc reasoning often reveals a number of auxiliary assumptions that were tested together with the main hypothesis. Can you verbalize the auxiliary assumptions that we implicitly made but failed to see by focusing on our overvolunteering hypothesis?

2. Try the "imagine the opposite result" technique on another published study. Put yourself in the shoes of the authors. Can you come up with a good explanation for it that does not jeopardize the validity of the original hypothesis?

3. Now try the technique on the next study you are planning. Imagine the opposite results from what you predict. How would you explain them? Then change the design of your study to rule out these alternative explanations.

12 DATA DISTRESS

Barbara C. Malt
Lehigh University

I've found a research question I'm dying to answer. I've developed a hypothesis and figured out how to test it. I've operationalized the independent and dependent variables, got all the materials together, specified my procedures, and jumped through the Institutional Review Board (IRB) hoops. I'm all set!

Maybe! What is missing from this picture? The answer is: I haven't sat down and thought through how I'll analyze the data.

This isn't a mistake I've made just once. I've made it multiple times. It's so easy to do. Data analysis is far off when you embark on the project, there are many other things to attend to, and analysis is kind of boring compared to having the ideas and making them come to life. Furthermore, you have a general schema in place: You have some experimental groups, you'll end up with condition means, and you know how to deal with comparing them.

But the implementation of your schema is not always a no-brainer, and a lot can go wrong if you don't spend some time thinking things through ahead of time. Recently, I had a senior thesis student who was interested in how narratives affect people. We read about "narrative transportation," a reader's feeling of entering the world evoked by the narrative (e.g., Green & Donahue, 2012). We read about how readers become so engaged in that narrative world that they show "participatory responses" such as calling out a warning to a character who is about to encounter danger (e.g., Gerrig & Jacovina, 2009). We wondered if being transported by a narrative can actually change a person's physical state. Does watching Lawrence of Arabia trudging through the desert sands make you thirsty? Does reading about Shackleton's Imperial Trans-Antarctic Expedition make you cold? And, furthermore, if abstract thought is grounded in concrete thought (Lakoff & Johnson, 1980) and if a person's physical, bodily state can influence judgments and decisions related to social warmth (Williams & Bargh, 2008), can being transported by such narratives indirectly affect judgments and decisions linked to social relationships?

My student created three stories of about 5,000 words each, matched except for setting descriptors that placed the same plot in a hot summer environment, a cold winter environment, or a neutral environment. She invited people to a lab room made cozy with soft lighting, art on the walls, and a comfy stuffed chair. She had each person read one story version and then gave them measures tapping their comprehension, degree of transportation by the story and susceptibility to narrative transportation in general, and physical and social states.

Then we sat down to look at the data. There was a lot of it. Comprehension questions weren't hard to deal with: Tallying the number correct out of the total took care of them. Susceptibility to being transported by narratives and transportation by the narrative just read were also ok. They were adapted from published measures, and all responses were on a 1 to 7 scale that could be averaged to create a mean score for each construct. The most straightforward measures of current body state and body state during reading were also conveniently on scales of 1 to 7, representing very cold to very warm. But then there were some items meant to measure perceived bodily state indirectly: a choice among four beverages ranging in temperature from iced to hot, and a choice between two activities, one in the sun and one in the snow. They seemed like good ideas at the time; how could it be bad to have more ways of tapping into bodily state? The problem was, they couldn't be averaged with each other or with the temperature ratings to create a global measure, so we had four separate measures using three different types of responses. And then there were the measures of social state, meant to tap feelings of warmth toward others. One was a forced choice between doing something for yourself or for someone else; one was a choice of three among eight possible activities (some social and some not); and then there was a series of six statements to be judged on a 1 to 7 scale characterizing the self and feelings toward other people. Again, there was no way to create a global measure combining the information since there were three different response types. And here, it hardly made sense even to average across the six statement ratings because the different statements asked rather disparate questions. We had eight different measures here, really.

How to proceed? It's too much to report an analysis of the effect of story type on each of these measures. Too much for the stamina of a student writing a senior thesis, definitely, but too much, also, for any journal report of a conceptually fairly straightforward, single study asking two focused questions. Reviewers would say it was taking up too much space relative to its contribution. So we needed to make things more manageable, but that creates the dilemma of how. Do we do all the analyses and then pick the most interesting results to report? That's a no-no. Cherry-picking results that support certain conclusions hides the fact that other results didn't show the same outcome. Do we try to decide what the very best one or two measures of physical and social warmth are and report analyses based on those? A better option, but we'd already seen the data and were no longer in a position to make an unbiased decision. If it were obvious *a priori* what the best measures were, we would have chosen them to start with and not thrown in the kitchen sink. Plus, it still means reporting some results and not others.

In the end, we went with the second option, but it was not ideal. It was ok, sort of, for finishing off a senior thesis, but it would have presented a real dilemma if the study had looked like a candidate for publication. (In case you are wondering, the story setting manipulation resulted in significantly lower judgments of body temperature for the winter story than for the neutral one. However, body temperature judgments for the summer story were no higher than for the neutral one, for unknown reasons. Thus, the transportation outcome that could have mediated social warmth judgments didn't cleanly emerge and couldn't provide a good test of the potential impact of the narratives on social warmth.)

The lesson here is clear: Don't just plan to collect data. Think through how you will analyze the data before they are staring you in the face. It's too late then to fix your mistakes.

REFERENCES

Gerrig, R. J., & Jacovina, M. E. (2009). Reader participation in the experience of narrative. In B. H. Ross (Ed.), *The Psychology of learning and motivation, vol. 51* (pp. 224–254). Burlington, MA: Academic Press.

Green, M. C., & Donahue, J. K. (2012). Simulated worlds: Transportation into narratives. In K. D. Markman, W. M. P. Klein, and J. A. Suhr (Eds.), *Handbook of imagination and mental simulation* (pp. 241–256). New York, NY: Psychology Press.

Lakoff, G., & Johnson, M. (1980). *Metaphors we live by.* Chicago, IL: University of Chicago Press.

Williams, L. E., & Bargh, J. A. (2008). Experiencing physical warmth promotes interpersonal warmth. *Science, 322,* 606–607.

CRITICAL THINKING QUESTIONS

1. What are possible limitations for analyses of using a two-alternative forced choice response measure?

2. What difficulties for analysis are raised by a measure that is "Pick 3 out of the following 8 activities" (where four of the 8 are supposed to be more compatible with social warmth and four with social coolness)?

3. Do you think the hypotheses might actually turn out to be true?

A BIG MISTAKE IN INTERPRETING CULTURAL DIFFERENCES

David Matsumoto

San Francisco State University

Hyisung C. Hwang

Humintell

There are many mistakes we have made over our research careers, with probably many more to come despite how much we learn from our previous mistakes. There's no perfect study and no perfect researcher. But one of the biggest mistakes that stands out in our minds is one that one of us (DM) made many years ago in a cross-cultural study involving judgments of facial expressions of emotion. To explain what happened, let us give some background.

The original findings documenting the universality of facial expressions had emerged previously (Ekman & Friesen, 1971; Ekman, Sorenson, & Friesen, 1969; Izard, 1971), which set the basis for the understanding that people around the world have a universal way of expressing and perceiving emotions in their faces. The first evidence for cultural differences in judgments of facial expressions of emotion emerged almost two decades later (Ekman et al., 1987). That study showed that although people of different cultures perceived the same emotion portrayed in faces, they judged them to be expressed at different intensities. Those findings opened the door to a number of studies that we produced thereafter in order to replicate and extend that basic finding (Biehl et al., 1997; Matsumoto, 1989, 1992, 1993; Matsumoto & Ekman, 1989). Across those studies, we demonstrated that Americans perceived greater intensity in facial expressions of emotion compared with Japanese observers, a finding that became well established.

For over a decade, we had interpreted those findings to have occurred because people of East Asian cultures were "known" to have suppressed their facial expressions when in social contexts. That is, we thought that the U.S.–Japan cultural differences in perceptions of the intensity of facial expressions of emotion occurred because the Japanese must have been suppressing their intensity ratings, just as they suppressed the intensity of the expression of their emotions as well (which was a common thought among researchers concerning cultural differences in expression; e.g., see Ekman, 1972).

Years later, as we continued to extend those basic findings, we conducted a study that obtained intensity ratings not only of the external facial expressions (i.e., how intensely is the expression being displayed?) but also of the internal experience underlying those faces (i.e., how intensely is the person actually feeling the emotion? [Matsumoto, Kasri, & Kooken, 1999]). We did this because the intensity ratings obtained in the previous studies were ambiguous as to whether the observers were rating the external display of the expresser's face or the internal, subjective experience of the expresser. Also, we wanted to see if there would be cultural differences on both types of ratings.

As in all our previous studies, we found the same cultural differences in ratings of external displays—Americans rated the intensity of those higher than did the Japanese. But when we compared the intensity ratings of the external displays with those of the internal, subjective experiences, we found that there were no differences between these ratings for the Japanese observers; that is, the Japanese rated the intensity of the external display the same as the intensity of the underlying experience. The American observers, however, rated the external displays more intensely than the internal experiences of the expresser. These findings made clear that the Japanese were not suppressing their intensity ratings; instead, the Americans were the ones *exaggerating* their intensity ratings of external display relative to the inferred subjective experience of the expressers.

Thus, years of interpretations that the Japanese were suppressing their ratings were wrong. When we realized that we had been interpreting the data incorrectly for years, what immediately came to our mind was that we were automatically using the American data as the norm and interpreting any differences from the American data as "different." And when other cultures' data were different from the American data, we had interpreted the differences to mean that "they" were doing something different to alter reality (e.g., the Japanese were suppressing their ratings) because the American data must have reflected an objective reality.

Since then we have tried to be very careful when interpreting differences observed in our studies. Although being wary of making clear value judgments about differences (e.g., *good vs. bad, right vs. wrong*) is relatively easy, sometimes our unconscious cultural filters work in more subtle ways. Just as these filters alter how we perceive the world in our everyday lives, they can work to influence the way we conduct our research, design our studies, perceive our data, and interpret differences. These filters can especially influence how we perceive and interpret differences in cross-cultural research.

We constantly need to be reminded of such filters. As we continue to conduct cross-cultural research today, we always remind each other about being careful concerning how we interpret any observed differences between cultures. Sometimes the culture one believes is the most appropriate reference group in a comparative study should not be the basis by which observed differences are interpreted. This is true for any multigroup comparison study. Above all, any interpreted mediators (causal

mechanisms) of differences should be followed up by actual studies empirically testing one's claims about what produced those obtained differences. Else, one's claims
are just that—claims—that remain as speculations until evidence is marshalled to
support them. Of course, this is the ecological fallacy (inferences about the nature
of individuals are made on the basis of an inference about the group to which
those individuals belong), as pointed out decades ago (Campbell, 1958, 1961) and
brought back to us more recently in the cross-cultural realm as well (Matsumoto &
Yoo, 2006).

Researchers and all professionals in psychology—regardless of experience—can
always be reminded of these caveats. As we constantly deal with, read about, and
act upon studies that test group differences, this is a lesson that we must constantly
remind ourselves of.

REFERENCES

Biehl, M., Matsumoto, D., Ekman, P., Hearn, V., Heider, K., Kudoh, T., & Ton, V.
(1997). Matsumoto and Ekman's Japanese and Caucasian Facial Expressions of
Emotion (JACFEE): Reliability data and cross-national differences. *Journal of Nonverbal Behavior, 21*, 3–21.

Campbell, D. T. (1958). Common fate, similarity, and other indices of the status of
aggregates of person as social entities. *Behavioural Science, 3*, 14–25.

Campbell, D. T. (1961). The mutual methodological relevance of anthropology
and psychology. In F. L. Hsu (Ed.), *Psychological anthropology* (pp. 333–352).
Homewood, IL: Dorsey.

Ekman, P. (1972). Universal and cultural differences in facial expression of emotion. In
J. R. Cole (Ed.), *Nebraska symposium on motivation, 1971* (Vol. 19, pp. 207–283).
Lincoln: University of Nebraska Press.

Ekman, P., & Friesen, W. V. (1971). Constants across culture in the face and emotion.
Journal of Personality and Social Psychology, 17, 124–129. doi:10.1037/h0030377

Ekman, P., Friesen, W. V., O'Sullivan, M., Chan, A., Diacoyanni-Tarlatzis, I., Heider,
K., . . . Tzavaras, A. (1987). Universals and cultural differences in the judgments
of facial expressions of emotion. *Journal of Personality & Social Psychology, 53*(4),
712–717.

Ekman, P., Sorenson, E. R., & Friesen, W. V. (1969). Pancultural elements in facial displays of emotion. *Science, 164*(3875), 86–88. doi:10.1126/science.164.3875.86

Izard, C. E. (1971). *The face of emotion*. East Norwalk, CT: Appleton-Century-Crofts.

Matsumoto, D. (1989). Cultural influences on the perception of emotion. *Journal of
Cross-Cultural Psychology, 20*(1), 92–105. doi:10.1177/0022022189201006

Matsumoto, D. (1992). American-Japanese cultural differences in the recognition of universal facial expressions. *Journal of Cross-Cultural Psychology, 23*(1), 72–84.

Matsumoto, D. (1993). Ethnic differences in affect intensity, emotion judgments, display rule attitudes, and self-reported emotional expression in an American sample. *Motivation & Emotion, 17*(2), 107–123.

Matsumoto, D., & Ekman, P. (1989). American-Japanese cultural differences in intensity ratings of facial expressions of emotion. *Motivation & Emotion, 13*(2), 143–157.

Matsumoto, D., Kasri, F., & Kooken, K. (1999). American-Japanese cultural differences in judgments of expression intensity and subjective experience. *Cognition & Emotion, 13*, 201–218.

Matsumoto, D., & Yoo, S. H. (2006). Toward a new generation of cross-cultural research. *Perspectives on Psychological Science, 1*(3), 234–250. doi:10.1111/j.1745-6916 .2006.00014.x

CRITICAL THINKING QUESTIONS

1. In cross-cultural research, comparing cultures is inevitable and finding differences is sometimes easy. What are some of the ways that researchers can avoid making mistakes in interpreting differences such as the one we wrote about, especially concerning the meaning of observed differences (and even non-differences)?

2. How are these ways similar to, or different from, what can or should happen in any group comparison study?

3. As readers of group or cultural comparative research, what can we do to think more critically about the source of any differences observed in a study? And how can we avoid overgeneralization of observed differences to all members of a group/culture?

14 IN PRAISE OF PILOT STUDIES

Richard McCarty
Vanderbilt University

The field of stress research started in the first half of the 20th century, thanks to the efforts of two famous physician-scientists, Walter B. Cannon and Hans Selye (McCarty, 2016a, 2016b). Cannon popularized the concept of the fight-or-flight response and studied the emergency function of epinephrine (EPI), a hormone secreted into blood from the inner portion of the adrenal gland. (To appreciate the effects of EPI, think of a time when you were frightened, and your heart was pounding, your breathing increased, and the hair on the back of your neck was standing on end.) Selye connected the effects of stress with chronic diseases, such as hypertension, diabetes, and arthritis. More recently, stress has been linked to the onset of mental disorders, including depression, schizophrenia, and bipolar disorder.

Throughout my career, I have conducted experiments with various kinds of laboratory mice and rats on physiological and behavioral adaptations to stress. One hypothesis I have pursued is that a failure of physiological systems to adapt to chronic stress may be especially important in causing various diseases. Some early reports of stress effects on EPI secretion caught my attention. When laboratory rats were exposed to the same stressor each day for multiple days, the release of EPI into blood decreased with repeated exposure to that same stressor. At the same time, the capacity of the adrenal gland to synthesize and store EPI increased. That is, the activity of the critical enzyme for making EPI was elevated, as was the amount of EPI present in the adrenal gland (Kvetnansky, Nemeth, Vigas, Oprsalova, & Jurcovicova, 1984).

I wanted to understand this apparent paradox (i.e., EPI storage up but EPI secretion down) because it might have something to do with the ways in which stress can cause disease. It appeared that as laboratory rats gained experience with chronic intermittent stress, they released the minimum amount of EPI to maintain their internal physiological balance, or homeostasis. At the same time, the animals hedged their bets by increasing the capacity of the adrenal gland to respond to a completely different stressor, with increased synthesis and storage of EPI for a time when it might be needed.

An unresolved issue that seems so obvious now was what would happen if laboratory rats were exposed to the same stressor each day for several repetitions and were then surprised with a completely different stressor. I predicted that this combination of repeated exposure to one stressor followed by acute exposure to a different stressor would result in an elevated release of EPI into blood.

The stage was now set for me to clarify how the secretion of EPI was regulated in response to stress (for a review, see McCarty, 2016c). I had a wonderful opportunity, but I blew it. With the benefit of hindsight, I wish that we could go back and refine to a significant extent the way these experiments were designed. First and foremost, I am embarrassed to admit that I did not conduct pilot experiments to optimize the number of daily bouts of stressful stimulation. Reducing the number of exposures of animals in a chronic intermittent stress experiment is important from an animal-welfare perspective as well as from a researcher-welfare perspective, as these were grueling experiments to conduct. Our experiments were typically four weeks in duration, including over weekends, and I am now confident that we could have obtained similar results (reduced and enhanced plasma EPI responses) with many fewer days of chronic intermittent stress. I took the easy way out and simply set the length of the experiment based upon what other investigators had reported.

I am also dismayed at the three primary stressors I employed in these experiments—footshock, restraint, and swim stress. These stressors, which had been used by others, were easily administered, but they did not fit well with the day-to-day existence of laboratory rats. I wish I had included stressors that captured aspects of the normal behavioral patterns of laboratory rats. Two excellent examples I should have used are chronic social-defeat stress, which takes advantage of the aggressive and territorial behaviors of adult male laboratory rats, and exposure to the scent of a natural predator. For chronic social-defeat stress, adult male rats are placed into the cage of a resident aggressive male rat for a brief period (up to 10 minutes), and then the two rats remain in the same cage but are separated for the next 24 hours by a wire mesh barrier that allows for sensory but not physical contact. This same process is then repeated for multiple days, with test rats encountering different resident males each day (Wood et al., 2015). In human terms, these rats must confront a bully on the bus ride to school each day and then sit next to the bully in each class, eat lunch with the bully, and even ride home on the bus seated next to the bully. Last, but not least, the bully spends the night and sleeps in the top bunk bed. Each day thereafter, a new bully appears on the morning bus ride to school, and the stress cycle continues.

Brief exposure to the scent of a predator (e.g., domestic cat or a ferret) is also quite stressful for laboratory rats (Weinberg et al., 2009) and could be incorporated into a chronic intermittent-stress paradigm. Once again, this stressor scores very high in relevance for laboratory rats, as it is a life-or-death matter. When a laboratory rat detects the smell of a cat, all systems go to high alert, especially the adrenal gland.

In summary, I wish I had optimized my basic experimental design by conducting pilot studies and by employing stressors that made "sense" to the rats. Instead, I took the easy way out by using experimental designs employed by others and not thinking through carefully on the types of stressors to employ. My three take-home messages include the following:

- Step back and think carefully about what you want to achieve in a given experiment.

- Conduct pilot studies so that you know in general what to expect before committing yourself to a particular experimental paradigm.

- Be as creative and insightful as possible as you settle on a final experimental design. Be aware of what others have done, but don't take the easy way out and simply copy the experimental paradigms of others.

REFERENCES

Kvetnansky, R., Nemeth, S., Vigas, M., Oprsalova, Z., & Jurcovicova, J. (1984). Plasma catecholamines in rats during adaptation to intermittent exposure to different stressors. In E. Usdin, R. Kvetnansky, & J. Axelrod (Eds.), *Stress: the role of catecholamines and other neurotransmitters* (pp. 537–562). New York, NY: Gordon and Breach.

McCarty, R. (2016a). The alarm phase and the General Adaptation Syndrome: Two aspects of Selye's inconsistent legacy. In G. Fink (Ed.), *Handbook of stress. Volume 1, Stress: Concepts, cognition, emotion, and behavior* (pp. 13–19). San Diego, CA: Elsevier.

McCarty, R. (2016b). The fight-or-flight response: A cornerstone of stress research. In G. Fink (Ed.), *Handbook of stress. Volume 1, Stress: Concepts, cognition, emotion, and behavior* (pp. 33–37). San Diego, CA: Elsevier.

McCarty, R. (2016c). Learning about stress: Neural, endocrine and behavioral adaptations. *Stress, 19,* 449–475.

Weinberg, M. S., Bhatt, A. P., Girotti, M., Masini, C. V., Day, H. E. W., Campeau, S., & Spenser, R. L. (2009). Repeated ferret odor exposure induces different temporal patterns of same-stressor habituation and novel-stressor sensitization in both hypothalamic-pituitary-adrenal axis activity and forebrain c-*fos* expression in the rat. *Endocrinology, 150,* 749–761.

Wood, S. K., Wood, C. S., Lombard, C. M., Lee, C. S., Zhang, X.-Y., Finnell, J. E., & Valentino, R. J. (2015). Inflammatory factors mediate vulnerability to a social stress-induced depressive-like phenotype in passive coping rats. *Biological Psychiatry, 78,* 38–48.

CRITICAL THINKING QUESTIONS

1. Are there times when following a previously published experimental paradigm in your own research is warranted? If so, give several examples.

2. A great deal has been learned from studies in which laboratory mice and rats have been exposed to experimental protocols that require responses that do not match well with the normal behavioral repertoire of these species (e.g., exposure to footshock). Could you defend studies of this type to an expert in animal behavior?

3. Physiological responses to naturally occurring life stressors are thought to play a critical role in the etiology of several mental disorders, including major depressive disorder, schizophrenia, and bipolar disorder. What essential features would you employ in designing an experiment using laboratory mice and rats to model the relationship between stressful stimulation and onset of mental disorders in humans?

15 START STRONG, PLAN AHEAD

Nora S. Newcombe
Temple University

My biggest research mistake was my dissertation. It didn't give me a firm platform for launching a research program, and as I took up teaching and committee responsibilities and faced an initial tenure evaluation in five years, I spent a lot of time in panic and confusion. I'll tell the story in the hope that it provides some guidance for early career researchers, even though it was long ago and far away, in a world with very different norms and customs. Maybe those practices will be interesting, too, in an historical vein.

My first three years in graduate school went well. Entering the fourth year, I already had one publication, which concerned whether children could plan their looking time at pictures for memory tasks that would occur at varying times in the future. We simply called it planning, but today, we would see it as touching on prospective memory, meta-memory, and executive function (Rogoff, Newcombe, & Kagan, 1974). I had also given my first conference talk at SRCD in Denver in 1975 on research on whether grouping semantically related items in a memory-span task improved children's memory. Today we would conceptualize the work as involving interactions of semantic and verbal working memory. The research eventually came out as Huttenlocher and Newcombe (1976) in a journal many readers may not know, the *Journal of Verbal Learning and Verbal Behavior*, although it continues today as the *Journal of Memory and Language*.

Meanwhile, I was intrigued by memory for pictures, not so much planning to remember them but what children and adults took away from the pictures and what they ignored or forgot. I collected a data set in my third year on how sensitive children and adults were to various changes in the pictures, such as switches in vantage point; that project eventually became a paper by Newcombe, Rogoff, and Kagan (1977). I wanted to follow up on the ideas I had started to develop. But I took seriously advice I had heard that there is no point in staying in graduate school for years, aiming at the best dissertation possible. It's just one more piece of research, the pragmatists said. Do it, get out, get a job, and start your career. Don't get hung up.

And it worked, sort of. In the winter of 1976, I was offered a job at Penn State as an assistant professor, even before I had written the thesis. That couldn't happen nowadays, and in fact it couldn't have happened even a few years after I got that offer. One drawback to the practice of hiring faculty who hadn't completed their dissertations was that some of them never did. Not me—I was awarded a PhD soon after I started at Penn State in the fall of 1976. So, all was apparently well. But it wasn't. I had hurried the research, and the study was badly underpowered. I guess lack of statistical power is one element of my dissertation mistake, though it was sadly common in those days before power analysis became a basic step in research planning. Even so, lack of power wasn't the fundamental error. The essential problem was that the dissertation wasn't really the basis of a well-conceptualized research program. There was no overarching vision, no plan for what I wanted to do in the future.

I was lucky. There were people at Penn State who believed in me. There were interesting seminars led by colleagues from various departments, including a group of spatial cognition researchers (e.g., Lynn Liben and Roger Downs), in whose company I launched a research program in spatial development (Newcombe & Liben, 1982). There was a senior woman, social psychologist Carolyn Sherif, with whom I taught classes on gender that led to my only publication in social psychology (Newcombe & Arnkoff, 1979). There was a next-door colleague, Bill Ray, with whom I launched some work on sex-related differences in spatial ability. Eventually, I wrote an RO3 grant proposal on pubertal timing, brain lateralization, and spatial ability, funded on the first round (more common in those days), which led to another paper into which I poured my heart (Newcombe & Bandura, 1983). I remember writing the RO3 grant in the summer of 1978, thinking the whole time that this plan should have been my dissertation prospectus.

Today, careers have a different shape. I would have taken the fifth year in graduate school that I should have taken and sought a postdoctoral appointment. If I had chosen wisely, I would have developed the kinds of interests and plans that I eventually formulated as an assistant professor. After a three-year postdoc period or so, I would have started as an assistant professor. In short, the period from 1976 to 1980 might have been less well paid, but it would have firmed up my career vision without the fearful sword of a tenure decision looming ahead and without my having to master teaching at the same time.

Everything worked out, and in some ways, the course I took was easier than what faces graduate students today, especially women who must also consider child-bearing. I was able to start my family after tenure, a luxury inconceivable now. Still, hurrying my dissertation made for a rocky start, and I think the lesson is clear, and still has contemporary relevance. *Find a problem you really care about in graduate school, and work out the terrain in which it is embedded.* There will only be one bit of the problem that you can tackle for your thesis, but if you find a set of questions that will carry you forward, write it down (preferably as a grant), and focus on related career development (e.g., a postdoc in which you add skills needed for that plan), you can ride the wave.

REFERENCES

Huttenlocher, J., & Newcombe, N. (1976). Semantic effects on ordered recall. *Journal of Verbal Learning and Verbal Behavior, 15*, 387–399.

Newcombe, N., & Arnkoff, D. B. (1979). Effect of speech styles and sex of speaker on person perception. *Journal of Personality and Social Psychology, 37*, 1293–1303.

Newcombe, N., & Bandura, M. M. (1983). Effects of age at puberty on spatial ability in girls: A question of mechanism. *Developmental Psychology, 19*, 215–224.

Newcombe, N., & Liben, L. S. (1982). Barrier effects in the cognitive maps of children and adults. *Journal of Experimental Child Psychology, 34*, 46–58.

Newcombe, N., Rogoff, B., & Kagan, J. (1977). Developmental changes in recognition memory for pictures of objects and scenes. *Developmental Psychology, 13*, 337–341.

Rogoff, B., Newcombe, N., & Kagan, J. (1974). Planfulness and recognition memory. *Child Development, 45*, 972–977.

CRITICAL THINKING QUESTIONS

1. Select a senior researcher in your field whose work you admire, and trace back his or her early career. Were key themes evident from the start? If not, when did they emerge?

2. What are your current guiding questions? Can you describe them in an "elevator speech" of one minute? In a page, as often requested in research statements or grant summaries?

3. Why are you interested in these questions? What is their theoretical significance? Do they have translational implications?

16

A MISTAKE IN STUDYING THE ROLE OF SLEEP IN SPEECH

Howard C. Nusbaum
The University of Chicago

I study speech communication, and when I came to the University of Chicago in the Department of Psychology, I met another new faculty member, Dan Margoliash, who studies birdsong. We wanted to develop a research collaboration to study communication systems generally. There is a long history of research comparing human speech use with birdsong (see Doupe & Kuhl, 1999). We considered findings in speech perception (e.g., see Diehl, Lotto, & Holt, 2004) and in birdsong research (e.g., birds have a better neural representation of their own song than the songs of others [Margoliash, 1986]), but after 15 years of discussion, we could not find clear parallel questions that were scientifically informative.

That is, until a graduate student, Kimberly Fenn, now a tenured professor of psychology at Michigan State University, heard Dan talk about his research showing that sleep is important for birdsong learning. Over a day, a bird's song becomes more variable, but sleep seems to reset it the next morning (see Brawn & Margoliash, 2014). Kim wanted to know if speakers start out the morning with consistent speech production and over the course of the day become messier until sleep resets production to be consistent the next morning.

Why is this question interesting? Understanding the function of sleep has been a scientific problem with few definitive answers, and understanding its role in communication would be important. It would be interesting if speech and birdsong as motor behaviors show similar patterns of behavior. Communicative behavior depends on neural networks, so this would suggest at least one kind of similarity between human and bird brains. Bird brains and human brains are different in structure and complexity. There is no reason why such different brains should produce similar behavior—if they do, this would be informative about neural function and structure. Finally, songbirds are not humans' "nearest evolutionary ancestor." Nonhuman primates such as apes are thought of as much more similar to us. However, songbirds are a vocal learning species like humans but unlike nonhuman primates. If songbirds and humans are similar in some ways—vocal communication—this would be a potentially important way to think about how evolution functions that is different from the prevailing view. Evolution may shape biological substrates to support species-critical functions even if similar functions are mediated by different biological mechanisms (cf. Margoliash & Nusbaum, 2009).

We planned to test this idea by measuring the timing of different parts of speech sounds to test for change over a waking day and which is reset after sleep. This requires testing at least three times, once in the morning, then the evening, and again the next morning. It is difficult to get participants tested three different times, so we decided to focus on the first part—that speech might become sloppier from morning to evening. If true, then we could test whether speech is cleaned after sleep. There was no guarantee that sleep would reset speech production.

Kim recorded speakers saying syllables like BA and TEE in the morning and then again in the evening. Consonant-vowel syllables were spoken several times, and we measured timing with acoustic analysis software, reflecting the coordination of lips and tongue and vocal folds. The results seemed promising. There were changes in some measurements over a waking day.

Unfortunately, there was a problem. Changes were not consistent across consonants or speakers. Some speakers showed timing changes for some consonants but not others; speakers changed timing in different consonants. We should have seen similar patterns across consonants and speakers, but there was no consistency. We could not identify a single principle that would account for the changes we observed. While it was possible that sleep could affect this the next morning, there was no point if we could not explain why some sounds were affected and others were not. Another problem was that we did not control for fatigue or circadian effects, or differences in the sleep history of the participants. If we could not explain the findings, we could not compare these findings to songbirds.

After much discussion, we recognized two important problems. The direct comparison between birdsong learning and speech production in adults was not appropriate. Juvenile birds learning a song are not comparable to adult humans speaking fluently. We designed a study about motor performance, but it should have been about learning. Furthermore, we did not plan out the appropriate controls to understand what happens simply based on time of day—circadian factors. We decided to change the study to examine how speech learning was affected by a waking day or sleep. This was the key to understanding what we had done wrong.

We designed a different study of perceptual learning of hard-to-understand speech (Schwab, Nusbaum, & Pisoni, 1985). We tested and trained listeners on computer-generated speech and tested again 12 hours later. Some listeners were trained in the morning and tested in the evening, and the other half trained in the evening and were tested in the morning, after sleep. Participants never heard the same words twice. During training, people improved by 20 points (from around 25% to 45% correct identification), but over a waking day, lost about 10 points (down to 35%). However, there was no loss after sleeping. We tested control groups and found no circadian effect and recorded sleep history and drug use. Finally, to see effects in a single group, we tested and trained participants in the morning, tested them after being awake 12 hours, and then again after a time that included sleep. These results replicated between-group findings, showing 20 points of learning initially, a loss of 10 points over a waking day, and sleep restoring what was lost (Fenn, Nusbaum, & Margoliash, 2003). The results showed that sleep restores forgotten learning and protects against future forgetting.

These findings were replicated with tasks such as learning video games (Brawn, Fenn, Nusbaum, & Margoliash, 2008). Furthermore, these findings have led to new insights about rote and generalization learning as we have found that not all memories resulting from the same learning experience are consolidated by sleep—rote learning does not show a sleep benefit whereas generalization from the same learning experience does (Fenn, Margoliash, & Nusbaum, 2013). We have found there are multiple ways to conceive a scientific question. At the start, we thought we were investigating vocal variability, but we should have been studying vocal learning. While logical to consider parallels between songbirds and humans in vocalizing, the deeper parallel about learning was the real issue. We started to carry out a sleep study with little experience in sleep research, not understanding what comparisons would be needed or how to control for potential confounds. Only after our failed attempt did we start to think about the real research question and what controls were needed to make sure that we could address that question.

REFERENCES

Brawn, T. P., Fenn, K. M., Nusbaum, H. C., & Margoliash, D. (2008). Consolidation of sensorimotor learning during sleep. *Learning & Memory, 15*, 815–819.

Brawn T. P., & Margoliash, D. (2014). A bird's eye view of sleep-dependent memory consolidation. In P. Meerlo, R. Benca., & T. Abel. (Eds). *Sleep, neuronal plasticity and brain function. Current topics in behavioral neurosciences, 25*. Berlin, Heidelberg: Springer.

Diehl, R. L., Lotto, A. J., & Holt, L. L. (2004). Speech perception. *Annual Review of Psychology, 55*, 149–179.

Doupe, A. J., & Kuhl, P. K. (1999). Birdsong and human speech: Common themes and mechanisms. *Annual Review of Neuroscience, 22*, 567–631.

Fenn, K. M., Nusbaum, H. C., & Margoliash, D. (2003). Consolidation during sleep of perceptual learning of spoken language. *Nature, 425*, 614–616.

Fenn, K. M., Margoliash, D., & Nusbaum, H. C. (2013). Sleep restores loss of generalized but not rote learning of synthetic speech, *Cognition, 128*, 280–286. Margoliash, D., & Nusbaum, H. C. (2009). Language: The perspective from organismal biology. *Trends in Cognitive Sciences, 13*, 505–510.

Margoliash, D. (1986). Preference for autogenous song by auditory neurons in a song system nucleus of the white-crowned sparrow. *Journal of Neuroscience, 6,* 1643–1661.

Schwab, E. C., Nusbaum, H. C., & Pisoni, D. B. (1985). Effects of training on the perception of synthetic speech. *Human Factors, 27,* 395–408.

CRITICAL THINKING QUESTIONS

1. Why is understanding a topic thoroughly important before designing a study?

2. How does experience working in a particular experimental area help in designing a study?

3. How can you identify alternative explanations of possible results in order to control for them?

17 SHORT-TERM GAINS, LONG-TERM IMPASSE

Lisa S. Onken
National Institute on Aging, NIH

When I was at the National Institute on Drug Abuse (NIDA), my primary concern was the development of treatments for people with drug abuse and co-occurring mental disorders. Early in my career, two major forces loomed: One stemmed from the "real world" public health emergencies of the cocaine and AIDS epidemics and the other from the research community studying behavioral treatments for drug use and mental health disorders.

In the late 1980s, no treatments for cocaine dependence and no treatments for HIV were in sight. Needle sharing and risky sexual behaviors associated with drug abuse were known to spread HIV. The co-occurring, rapidly expanding epidemics produced a state of alarm within the country. For many researchers, a medication for cocaine abuse/dependence was of utmost priority, and by 1990, NIDA established the Medications Development Program, with a major focus on the development of a cocaine medication. Unlike with heroin, there was no prospect for a methadone-like medication for cocaine, and there was skepticism regarding finding an effective treatment. Behavioral treatment researchers were highly motivated to develop behavioral treatments. Meanwhile, without a foreseeable cure, a new field of HIV prevention research was born, intent upon developing HIV prevention interventions to quell the epidemic. Because of the link between drug abuse and HIV, drug abuse treatment was viewed as critical to HIV prevention.

The other force emerged from behavioral treatment researchers who wanted to produce treatments but argued that behavioral treatment development research was being stymied. The problem was a "Catch 22": To be funded to conduct a randomized clinical trial (RCT) of a behavioral treatment, pilot data was necessary; to collect the pilot data to propose an RCT, funding was required. Researchers lamented the lack of an FDA (Food and Drug Administration)-like entity for behavioral treatment development and no conceptual framework for behavioral treatment development analogous to the FDA medication development pipeline. Whereas medication development researchers were supported for "Phase I" clinical trials, behavioral treatment researchers had no comparable early phase of research treatment creation, refinement/modification, and pilot testing prior to an RCT. The field pushed to add an initial stage for (1) intervention creation, refinement, and pilot testing; to the existing stages for (2) efficacy testing; and (3) effectiveness testing. The field readily embraced this conceptual framework, as did I (Onken, Blaine & Battjes, 1997; Rounsaville, Carroll & Onken, 2001).

The good news: Many short-term gains were realized. Creativity was high, and approaches to treating drug-use disorders were developed and refined in early stage research. Behavioral treatments for cocaine dependence were developed and shown by the early 1990s to be efficacious (see Carroll, Power, Bryan, & Rounsaville, 1993; Higgins et al., 1993). In fact, the broader behavioral treatment development field has had great success in developing efficacious behavioral treatments for a variety of problems, such as mood disorders (Hollon & Ponniah, 2010), anxiety disorders (Butler, Chapman, Forman, & Beck, 2006), and conduct disorder (Scott, 2007).

After a while, though, an impasse was reached. Few efficacious behavioral interventions ever made their way to the people who needed them. Many efficacious treatments did not show effectiveness when tested outside of highly controlled research settings, and very few ever got implemented in the real world. It was so bad that the Institute of Medicine (Institute of Medicine, 2006) highlighted the failure to implement efficacious treatments, and Weisz et al. (Weisz, Jensen-Doss, & Hawley, 2006; Weisz, Ng, & Bearman, 2014) coined a term describing it: the *implementation cliff*.

In hindsight, this all seems predictable. Why would we expect efficacy to lead to real-word effectiveness? Behavioral treatments aren't like pills. Powerful, efficacious treatments like Carroll's CBT (cognitive-behavioral therapy) for cocaine dependence (Carroll et al., 1993) can be complicated and difficult to learn how to administer correctly. However, the early conceptual framework of "Create → Efficacy Test → Effectiveness Test" implied that once efficacy testing is done, the intervention is ready for effectiveness testing. In efficacy trials, attention is paid to training hired therapists and supervising them to ensure fidelity of delivery, but little if any attention is paid to training community therapists and developing methods to maximize fidelity. Moreover, often little is understood regarding the principles underlying intervention, and this knowledge could be critical to helping community therapists administer a treatment flexibly while still adhering to the principles.

The urgency to develop *something* that is efficacious overshadowed concerns about what might happen next. I have shifted this shorter term focus to a longer term one that values principle-driven intervention development, with attention to maintaining efficacy and usability *within the real world*. Additional stages/activities were needed, aimed at modifying efficacious interventions to be real-world friendly. One step in this direction was shown with CBT for cocaine dependence, for example. It was modified into the more scalable "CBT4CBT," (Computer-Based Training for Cognitive Behavioral Therapy) without losing its potency (Carroll et al., 2014). The earlier intervention development conceptual framework was refined (the "NIH Stage Model") with the goal of developing principle-driven interventions (Onken, Carroll, Shoham, Cuthbert, & Riddle, 2014) that fit into the real-world while maximizing fidelity in the community and the preliminary real-world testing of the newly packaged intervention before proceeding to large-scale effectiveness trials. This way, treatments shown to be effective have been designed to be ready for real-world implementation. It doesn't matter if treatments work if they can't ever be used.

Disclaimer

The participation of these individuals or the materials should not be interpreted as representing the official viewpoint of the U.S. Department of Health and Human Services, the National Institutes of Health or the National Institute on Aging, except where noted.

REFERENCES

Butler, A. C., Chapman, J. E., Forman, E., & Beck, A. T. (2006). The empirical status of cognitive-behavioral therapy: A review of meta-analyses. *Clinical Psychology Review*, 26, 17–31.

Carroll, K. M., Kiluk, B. D., Nich, C., Gordon, M. A., Portnoy, G. A., Marino, D. R., & Ball, S. A. (2014). Computer-assisted delivery of cognitive-behavioral therapy: Efficacy and durability of CBT4CBT among cocaine-dependent individuals maintained on methadone. *American Journal of Psychiatry, 171*, 436–44.

Carroll, K. M., Power, M. E, Bryan, K., & Rounsaville, B. J. (1993). One-year follow-up status of treatment-seeking cocaine abusers. Psychopathology and dependence severity as predictors of outcome. *Journal of Nervous and Mental Disorders, 181*(2), 71–79.

Hollon, S. D., & Ponniah, K. (2010). A review of empirically supported psychological therapies for mood disorders in adults. *Depression and Anxiety*, 27, 891–932.

Higgins, S. T., Budney, A. J., Bickel, W. K., Hughes, J. R., Foerg, F., & Badger G. (1993). Achieving cocaine abstinence with a behavioral approach. *American Journal of Psychiatry, 150*(5), 763–769.

Institute of Medicine. (2006). *Improving the quality of health care for mental and substance-use conditions: Quality chasm series*. Washington, DC: National Academies Press.

Onken, L. S., Carroll, K. M., Shoham, V., Cuthbert, B. N., & Riddle, M. (2014). Reenvisioning clinical science: Unifying the discipline to improve the public health. *Clinical Psychological Science, 2*, 22–34.

Onken, L. S., Blaine, J. D., & Battjes, R. J. (1997). Behavioral therapy research: A conceptualization of a process. In S. W. Henggeler & A. B. Santos (Ed.), *Innovative approaches for difficult-to-treat populations* (pp. 477–485). Washington, DC: American Psychiatric Press.

Rounsaville, B. J., Carroll, K. M., & Onken, L. S. (2001). NIDA's stage model of behavioral therapies research: Getting started and moving on from Stage 1. *Clinical Psychology: Science and Practice, 8,* 133–142.

Scott, S. (2007). An update on interventions for conduct disorder. *Advances in Psychiatric Treatment, 14* (1), 61–70. DOI: 10.1192/apt.bp.106.002626

Weisz, J. R., Jensen-Doss, A., & Hawley, K. M. (2006). Evidence-based youth psychotherapies versus usual clinical care: A meta-analysis of direct comparisons. *American Psychologist, 61,* 671–689.

Weisz, J. R., Ng, M. Y., & Bearman, S. K. (2014). Odd couple? Reenvisioning the relation between science and practice in the dissemination-implementation era. *Clinical Psychological Science, 2,* 58–74.

CRITICAL THINKING QUESTIONS

1. With regard to real-world implementation, how do behavioral treatments differ from medications?

2. Why is proof of efficacy often insufficient to ensure real-world effectiveness?

3. How can understanding the principles underlying an intervention help make an intervention easier to implement?

18 BE AS CAREFUL AFTER YOUR STUDY IS RUN AS YOU ARE BEFORE

Richard E. Petty
Ohio State University

A critical aspect of engaging in scientific work is being extremely careful. Whether you are mixing chemicals or psychological ingredients, you want to do it with the utmost diligence so you can provide the strongest test of your hypothesis. Hours and hours are spent *prior* to the implementation of most studies in an attempt to get the materials (independent and dependent variables) just right so that they represent the constructs of interest. Against this background, the research mistake I describe has to do with the importance of being just as careful *after* the data are collected. The mistake I describe is one that stands out in my mind because (1) it came very early in my research career (my second year as an assistant professor), and (2) it taught me a very valuable lesson.

As was my common practice then and now, the research was done in collaboration with a graduate student. Our goal was to test a new theoretical framework against the prevailing view regarding the role of personal relevance in persuasion. Prior research indicated that people tended to reject counter-attitudinal messages more when the message addressed a topic of high rather than low personal relevance. As you might imagine, as the topic becomes more personally important, people can become more defensive in guarding their initial views.

In contrast, our theory said that personal relevance makes people more interested in thinking about the information presented. Specifically, the extra thinking from the personal connection to the proposal can result in more message rejection when the message is easy to argue against. But, we argued, if the message presented very cogent arguments, the extra thinking could lead to greater acceptance. Thus, our theory predicted an interaction between personal relevance and argument quality. If the arguments were weak, high relevance would lead to greater rejection—the typical effect that was found previously. However, if the arguments were strong, more thinking under high relevance would lead to more message acceptance—the opposite of what was found previously.

To examine our hypothesis, we presented undergraduates with a counter-attitudinal proposal on a novel topic—that they should be required to take a comprehensive exam in their major in order to graduate. The students did not like this proposal at all. Then, we varied two things: (1) the quality of the arguments in the message and (2) the personal relevance of the proposal. To vary argument quality, we pretested many arguments and selected those that elicited mostly favorable thoughts as the strong ones. The weak arguments were selected so that they elicited mostly negative thoughts (counterarguments). To vary relevance, we told students in the high relevance condition that the exams were being proposed for next year, in which case all of them would be affected. In the low-relevance condition, they were told that the exams were being proposed for 10 years in the future so none of them would be affected.

We then made four tape recordings for participants to hear that represented each of the four conditions in our 2 (Argument quality: weak vs. strong) X 2 (Personal relevance: 1 vs. 10 years) experimental design. We chose an audio message rather than a written one to ensure that all participants would have some exposure to the arguments. After listening to the appropriate message over headphones, students wrote their thoughts about the message. Then, attitudes toward the proposal were assessed (e.g., rating of how good/bad it was on a 7-point scale).

The study seemed to run smoothly enough, and within a few weeks, all of the data were collected. Now it was time to look at our results, and I scheduled a meeting with the graduate student in charge. At the meeting, we went over the data for each cell of the design. First, we had replicated the standard personal relevance effect when weak arguments were presented—the students were less favorable when personal relevance was high than low. So far, so good. Then, I was stunned when I saw the strong arguments results. Here, high personal relevance produced more *rejection* of the advocacy than in any other condition. This was quite different from what we hypothesized, so we next eagerly read the students' thoughts from that condition.

The participants' thoughts in the strong arguments–high relevance condition were not at all what I expected. Rather than providing cogent counterarguments to the strong arguments, the thoughts were statements like, "I couldn't wait for this damn study to end;" "This experiment is torture;" and "That tape was so annoying." A look at thoughts in the other conditions revealed that they were just relevant reactions to the arguments presented. What had gone wrong? I asked the graduate student to play each of the tapes for me over headphones just as the participants had heard them. Three of the tapes were fine. The tape for the high relevance–strong argument condition, however, had a loud, high-pitched screeching sound every 15 seconds or so. Indeed, it was like torture to listen to it! To this day, I have no idea how this screeching was introduced, but it clearly explained why participants' attitudes in this condition were so negative.

So, what was my mistake? First, I had not observed each of the instantiations of the experimental conditions from the participants' point of view prior to running the study—nor had my graduate student. But, second and more important, I only scrutinized the study materials extra carefully after the study was completed because the data had not come out as hypothesized. What would have happened, I wondered, if the screeching tape happened to be in the high relevance–weak argument condition?

That would have helped our study come out as hypothesized—but due to an artifact in the experimental materials. I realized it would be unfortunate if extra checking did not take place just as diligently if the study had confirmed our hypothesis.

Prior scholars of research methods have written about how researchers can be biased in favor of their preferred outcome. True enough. But there is nothing like a personal experience to bring the lesson home. That is, if a study comes out "correctly," researchers are less likely to double-check experimental conditions, or redo data coding, or engage in additional data analysis, or look for outliers, or read participants' written responses for indications of suspicion. They are less likely to do all of the things that they might try if the data did *not* come out as predicted. The lesson, of course, is that all of these double-checking protocols should be in place regardless of how the data come out—in support or not in support of one's theorizing. This is something that we now aim to do with all of the studies we conduct. And, by the way, we reran the screeching study getting rid of the problem, and it was eventually published (Petty & Cacioppo, 1979).

REFERENCE

Petty, R. E., & Cacioppo, J. T. (1979). Issue involvement can increase or decrease persuasion by enhancing message-relevant cognitive responses. *Journal of Personality and Social Psychology, 37,* 1915–1926.

CRITICAL THINKING QUESTIONS

1. Why is it just as important to be careful after as before conducting an experiment?

2. What are some of the reasons that bias can enter into the scientific process after data are collected?

3. How can you avoid confirmatory bias when dealing with the results from your own studies?

LESSONS LEARNED FROM A FAILED EXPERIMENT

Paul Slovic

University of Oregon

I was taught to design experiments in order to test hypotheses derived from theories. Early on, I began to stray from that path. I designed experiments to answer questions I was curious about. Sometimes I did have a hypothesis about how the data would turn out. Often I was wrong. Then I would examine the data from multiple perspectives and sometimes come upon incidental, surprising findings that appeared more interesting to me than the question I had originally hoped to answer. I would abandon the original idea and set out to examine the new one.

Looking back, I see that many of the research paths I am most fond of turned out to have resulted from "failed" experiments, and persistent redirection. I'll briefly describe one of these paths below.

CHOICES AMONG EQUALLY VALUED ALTERNATIVES

This research path arose from a design malfunction. I set out to determine whether the choice between two items, X and Y, could be reversed by adding a third item, Z, to the choice set. For example, suppose you are offered a choice between chicken (X) and pasta (Y) on a menu, and you say you prefer chicken. Then the waiter says "beef (Z) is also available today." You don't like beef, but you say, "Ok, I'll choose the pasta." This reversal of preference makes no sense according to theories that assume we have stable values and preferences. However, I had a hypothesis about how I might reverse the choice between X and Y by strategically manipulating the description of Z. But to make it easier for Z to reverse the choice in an experiment, I decided first to make X and Y of equal value to the chooser.

I started with two baseball players, each described by their batting average and number of home runs during the previous season. Player Y was superior on home runs. Player X had a higher batting average. But, I omitted one attribute for one of the players: for example, player Y's home runs. This missing attribute was varied across subjects (see Table 19.1).

I asked each subject to fill in the missing value so as to make the two players equal in value to their team. For example, in Pair 2, Player X has a higher batting average. How many more home runs would Player Y have to hit (more than 20), to be equal to Player X in value to their team?

TABLE 19.1 ■ Pairs of Baseball Players. One Attribute Value is Missing, Marked by? Fill in the Missing Value so as to Make Player X and Player Y of Equal Value to Their Team.			
Pairs	**Players**	**Home runs**	**Batting average**
1	Player X	?	.287
	Player Y	26	.273
2	Player X	20	.287
	Player Y	?	.273
3	Player X	20	?
	Player Y	26	.273
4	Player X	20	.287
	Player Y	26	?

To test whether the players were made equal, three weeks later I asked each of the subjects to consider the two players that they had equated and indicate which one they thought was more valuable to their team. Then I brought everyone back one week later to repeat the task (camouflaged in other tasks to reduce recognition and memory). Because these players had been made equal, I expected to find about a 50-50 split in the judged value of X and Y, indicative of random choices, as if they had tossed a coin to make their decision. This didn't occur. A strong majority judged the player with the higher batting average as more valuable both times they made their choice.

I didn't quite trust the method of equating two items by filling in a missing dimension as in Table 19.1. I thought this method might be biased. So I replaced it in a new study by defining the two choice alternatives as equal. For example, consider evaluating two typists applying for a job (these were the old days before computers). Typist A is faster than Typist B, but B's advantage in quality of work exactly offsets A's speed advantage so that "you feel the overall typing quality of each is *equal*." Which one would you select? As before, subjects did not choose randomly; 88% of the subjects chose B, based on the intrinsically more important attribute, which was quality.

I scrapped my original experimental plan as it appeared that adding Z to the choice set of X *vs.* Y wouldn't make a difference. Subjects clearly were not choosing randomly but were consistently preferring the option that was better on the intrinsically more important dimension.

I subsequently tested and found support for the general hypothesis that people often resolve difficult choices by choosing the option that is superior on the most important dimension (Slovic, 1975).

These results led, 13 years later, to what Amos Tversky, Shmuel Sattath, and I called "the prominence effect," reflecting the fact that difficult choices are often made on the basis of what is seen to be the most defensible option, even when those choices violate one's stated values for the underlying attributes of those options (Tversky, Sattath, & Slovic, 1988).

Recently, I used the prominence effect to explain why American presidents, who place very high value both on protecting national security and protecting innocent foreign lives being victimized in a genocide, decide in favor of protecting security rather than acting to intervene in the genocide, no matter how many people might die as a result of this decision (Slovic, 2015). Protecting security is the more important and more prominent, that is, more defensible, consideration, and that determines the choice, as was the case for choosing baseball players and typists and many other choices I studied many years earlier.

OBSERVING DATA AS AN AID TO THINKING

Through these experiences and other experiments that didn't go as planned, I have come to see collecting data not only as a means of testing hypotheses but as an aid to thinking. Staring at surprising or misbehaving data has been, for me, a catalyst for new ideas.

I am certainly not alone in this view. The Nobel Prize-winning biochemist Albert Szent-Györgyi wrote,

> I make the wildest theories . . . but spend most of my time in the laboratory playing with living matter, keeping my eyes open, observing and pursuing the smallest detail . . . I must admit that most of the new observations I made were based on wrong theories. My theories collapsed, but something was left afterwards. (Szent-Györgyi, 1963, p.7).

When scientists are playful, persistent, and lucky, what is left may be a valuable new idea.

REFERENCES

Slovic, P. (1975). Choice between equally valued alternatives. *Journal of Experimental Psychology: Human Perception and Performance, 1*, 280–287.

Slovic, P. (2015). When (in)action speaks louder than words: Confronting the collapse of humanitarian values in foreign policy decisions. *Illinois Law Review Slip Opinions, 2015*, 24–31.

Szent-Györgyi, A. (1963). Lost in the twentieth century. *Annual Review of Biochemistry, 32*, 1–14.

Tversky, A., Sattath, S., & Slovic, P. (1988). Contingent weighting in judgment and choice. *Psychological Review, 95,* 371–384.

CRITICAL THINKING QUESTIONS

1. Is there a threshold of cost and effort for conducting an experiment, above which collecting data as an aid to thought may not be practical?

2. If data collection is costly and effortful, how can we still get the creative benefits of exploration?

3. Will the strategy of redesigning a study after looking at the data run afoul of the growing requirements for preregistering studies and other strict guidelines designed to prevent false-positive results?

20 | RAGING HORMONES

Laurence Steinberg
Temple University

I can still remember the excitement that was generated by a symposium at the 1986 meeting of the Society for Research on Adolescence in Madison, Wisconsin. The panel, which was chaired by Elizabeth Susman, was reporting on the first major study to connect variations in adolescent psychological functioning to variations in levels of different sex hormones.

I was especially interested in this session. This was the first meeting of the Society, and I was the host. My doctoral advisor, John Hill, was the first president of the Society, and he and I had planned the meeting. We made the decision to feature this symposium as the culminating event of the meeting, scheduled to take place right before a reception and banquet. At that time, the Society was small enough that there were no overlapping presentations, so the room was likely to be packed. A symposium that included "hard science" would confer special credibility on this fledgling organization.

The connection between puberty and adolescent psychological development and mental health has always been a central focus of research on this age period, of course. Beginning with the seminal work of G. Stanley Hall, virtually every aspect of adolescent functioning has been attributed in one way or another to puberty—not just changes in teenagers' appearance or sex drive but in their family relationships, status in the peer group, cognitive performance, and a wide range of problems, including moodiness, delinquency, depression, and rebellion.

Up until the time of this meeting, the measurement of puberty in adolescence research was limited to physical examinations conducted by physicians or nurses, questionnaires completed by teenagers or their parents, or observer ratings of adolescents with their clothes on. These approaches, which are still used today, are fine, but they don't really get at what most people have assumed is the reason that puberty matters for adolescents' psychological functioning: their "raging hormones."

Assessing hormone levels was too expensive for most psychological researchers to even contemplate, though, and it was far too cumbersome, requiring the collection of blood or 24 hours worth of urine, neither of which most psychologists were equipped to do.

Which is why one specific aspect of the symposium was so interesting to everyone: The presenters explained that hormonal assessments had become sensitive enough to be done on saliva, and that assays using saliva could be used in place of ones that necessitated blood or urine. Collecting saliva was a breeze, they explained. All that was required was some chewing gum to help kids salivate, glass containers for them to spit into, a picnic cooler and ice pack to keep the samples cold until they could be taken back to the lab, and a freezer in which to store them until they were analyzed. One sample of saliva was sufficient to measure at least a half dozen hormones, including testosterone, estrogen, progesterone, some important adrenal hormones, and cortisol. And the assays were cheap.

At the time, I was conducting a study of adolescents and their parents, in which we were following a sample of about 200 families as their first-born children transitioned through puberty. We were collecting data in people's homes, in the late afternoon, in the evening, and on weekends.

This was a follow-up from my doctoral dissertation, in which I studied how family relationships changed during puberty, but where my assessment of puberty was necessarily limited. We had measured puberty by surreptitiously assessing adolescents' pubertal maturation on a 1 to 5 scale, from prepubertal (no signs) to postpubertal (having adult appearance). Amazingly, in 1977, when I submitted my study for publication, this passed muster in the field's top journal, *Developmental Psychology*. Today, a reviewer would laugh at how much room for error this approach would carry.

My dissertation was the first study to show that the quality of an adolescent's family relations was better predicted by puberty than by age or cognitive functioning. I was determined to show that these findings could be replicated using a more rigorous measure of puberty than had been available and affordable 10 years previously.

The conference ended on a Sunday. On Monday morning, I had my graduate students go out and buy packs of gum, a bunch of glass vials, and a couple of Playmate coolers. I talked to Ned Kalin, a close friend of mine who was a biological psychiatrist on Wisconsin's med school faculty, about where best to send our samples for analysis. He explained that his lab, which was studying primate development, was equipped to do this sort of thing and offered to help. During the next round of family visits, we asked the adolescents to spit into our containers.

Two years later, for the second meeting of the Society, I organized a symposium at which I was eager to present our findings. I was hoping to wow the audience with our cutting-edge approach. I even invited a well-known pediatric endocrinologist, Donald Orr, to serve as the panel's discussant.

I organized the panel before we had had a chance to look at the data. Unfortunately, our findings were all over the place. We were running analyses up until the day before the conference, desperately looking for *something* to report. We found a few correlations between hormones and family relationships but nothing that told a coherent story. I figured I would just give a talk about how complicated things are but that people would be impressed with our lab's initiative and originality. And saying the word "spit" would surely get a laugh.

When it came time for the discussant to comment on our study, he began by asking some questions. Did we collect the saliva samples at the same time of day for every subject? No. (Hormone levels fluctuate over the course of the day.) Did we ask subjects how recently they had eaten? No. (Hormone levels are affected by food.) Did we record what day in their menstrual cycle the female participants were? No, we did not. You do know that female hormones vary over the course of the month, don't you? Yes, but we forgot to ask.

In other words, our hormonal data were pretty much worthless. In the end, I never published a single paper on the relation between hormones and family relationships. When you have bad data, there's not much you can do with it. The whole thing had been a big waste of time.

I can think of all sorts of reasons for this colossal mistake: hubris, ignorance, and impulsivity being the main ones. I had been out of graduate school for nearly 10 years. I was old enough to know better than to get so carried away but still so young that I was a little too motivated by my desire to impress others and scoop my fellow scientists rather than the need to do careful science. Had I spent an hour consulting with an endocrinologist, the whole mess could have been avoided.

I've had several doctoral students since then who were similarly champing at the bit to get going on a study that really excited them. And I've tried my best to gently encourage them to take it slow, to think through things before beginning, to anticipate as best they can what might go wrong, and to remember that the goal of what we do is to advance our understanding of human behavior—not to advance our own careers.

CRITICAL THINKING QUESTIONS

1. In this example, a psychologist's mistake is largely due to his lack of familiarity with another field (endocrinology). Psychologists are increasingly encouraged to conduct cross-disciplinary research, but working outside one's area carries some risk. Is cross-disciplinary research worth it?

2. In this case, the scientist's mistake resulted in a lack of findings, so nothing was ever published, but there are instances in which people have made mistakes but obtained significant findings, buried their errors, and published their findings without proper disclosure. What might be done to prevent this from happening?

3. A well-intentioned scientist discovers after a paper has been published that a mistake was made in how a key variable was coded for a portion of the sample. The analyses are rerun with the proper coding, and the researcher sees that a few entries in a table have changed in small ways, but that the main findings of the paper have not. Should the scientist do anything about this?

21 A FAILURE IN FIDELITY OF EXPERIMENTAL TREATMENTS

Robert J. Sternberg
Cornell University

I have long believed that many students would do better in their studies if they were taught in ways that better matched their patterns of cognitive skills. In my theory of successful intelligence (Sternberg, 1997a, 1997b), three kinds of skills are particularly important—analytical ones (Sternberg, 1985), creative ones (Niu & Sternberg, 2003; Sternberg & Davidson, 1982), and practical ones (Sternberg, 1997b; Sternberg & Smith, 1985). Most teachers emphasize teaching for memory and analytical-reasoning skills. Such traditional teaching tends to benefit students who are naturally analytical in their orientation, often the ones who do well on standardized tests. But these teaching methods may leave out students who are more creative or practical learners, or who have learning disabilities (Spear-Swerling & Sternberg, 1994). Students may learn better from mixed instruction—analytical, creative, and practical—that simultaneously allows them to capitalize on their strengths and to compensate for or correct their weaknesses.

In order to test these ideas, some time ago we did several research studies comparing teaching for successful intelligence (analytical, creative, and practical thinking) with teaching for traditional memory and analytical skills (e.g., Grigorenko, Jarvin, & Sternberg, 2002; Sternberg, Grigorenko, Ferrari, & Clinkenbeard, 1999; Sternberg, Torff, & Grigorenko, 1998). The results were very promising. It was possible to teach students analytically, creatively, and practically, in ways that were quite distinguishable from each other. For example, in teaching about nutrition, a teacher could teach in a way that encourages students to analyze the nutrients in different kinds of foods; or the teacher could teach students in a way that encourages students creatively to design an experiment testing a hypothesis about the nutritional benefits of one kind of food versus another; or the teacher could teach in a way that encourages students to create a practical poster advertisement for eating heathy food. Students learned better when taught according to the theory of successful intelligence than when they were taught in more conventional ways.

Because the results of the early studies were very encouraging, my colleagues and I decided to do a major upscaling. This meant that rather than trying out our techniques just in a few classrooms here and there, we would try them out in hundreds of fourth-grade classrooms with thousands of students. This was a daunting task because we had to arrange teaching and testing throughout the country. We needed to train teachers in all geographic regions of the United States and also show them how to accommodate their teaching to the new analytical, creative, and practical techniques (Sternberg et al., 2014). In the new study, students would be taught language arts, science, or mathematics (a) for successful intelligence, or (b) in a way that emphasized analytical thinking, or (c) conventionally, emphasizing memory.

Unfortunately, the upscaling was not very successful. Whereas teaching for successful intelligence had been superior to conventional methods of teaching in the few scattered classrooms in which we previously had tried it, the teaching for successful intelligence was not significantly and substantially superior to standard teaching in the upscaled version of our work. This disappointing result led us to ask what went wrong.

We checked our data analyses, of course, and also whether we entered our achievement-test-score data correctly. Whatever the problem was, it was in neither the analyses nor the entry of the data that had been analyzed. We also checked whether the classrooms we thought were supposed to be in a certain condition were actually in that condition. They were. So the problem was not one that was susceptible to an easy fix—reanalysis of the data.

We then made inquiries and looked into our observational data regarding what teachers had actually done in the classrooms—and we found out what had gone wrong (or at least one thing that went wrong!). In the smaller studies, we—the experimenters—did the teacher training. We ensured that the teachers were learning just what they needed to do to demonstrate *fidelity* to the experimental condition— that what was actually happening in each experimental condition was what was supposed to be happening. In the upscaling, there was no way we experimenters could do all the teacher training, and so we hired teacher trainers. But somewhere between the training of the teacher trainers and the training of the actual teachers and the teaching of the program to the students, something went wrong. But what?

In many experimental-group classrooms, teachers who were under many everyday pressures to teach in conventional ways (e.g., their perceived need to maximize standardized test scores) began to abandon the new techniques and to teach in ways with which they were more familiar and more comfortable. In other words, *fidelity* within the conditions to the intended experimental treatments was, at best, uneven. Many of the classrooms where teachers were supposed to be teaching for successful intelligence ended up being ones where teachers ended up teaching in more or less conventional ways. With the upscaling, we got in over our heads, and the results showed it.

What did we learn from the experience? We learned the importance of ensuring that conditions labeled as representing a particular experimental treatment truly represent that treatment. As one upscales and has more and more subjects, fidelity becomes more difficult but all the more important in order to achieve meaningful experimental results. We failed adequately to ensure fidelity to the intended treatment and realized that, in the future, we would have to build into our studies procedures more carefully to monitor and ultimately assess fidelity to intended experimental treatments. To the extent possible, we would have to create better safeguards to ensure such fidelity. My recommendation to any psychological scientist would be not to assume that because you label a treatment in a certain way, the treatment actually corresponds to the label. You need to do all you can to ensure fidelity so that the actual treatment matches whatever you have chosen to call it!

REFERENCES

Grigorenko, E. L., Jarvin, L., & Sternberg, R. J. (2002). School–based tests of the triarchic theory of intelligence: Three settings, three samples, three syllabi. *Contemporary Educational Psychology, 27,* 167–208.

Niu, W., & Sternberg, R. J. (2003). Societal and school influences on student creativity: The case of China. *Psychology in the Schools, (40)*1, 103–114.

Spear–Swerling, L., & Sternberg, R. J. (1994). The road not taken: An integrative theoretical model of reading disability. *Journal of Learning Disabilities, 27*(2), 91–103.

Sternberg, R. J. (1985). Teaching critical thinking, Part 1: Are we making critical mistakes? *Phi Delta Kappan, 67,* 194–198.

Sternberg. R. J. (1997a). Managerial intelligence: Why IQ isn't enough. *Journal of Management, 23*(3), 463–475.

Sternberg, R. J. (1997b). What does it mean to be smart? *Educational Leadership, 54*(6), 20–24.

Sternberg, R. J., & Davidson, J. E. (1982, June). The mind of the puzzler. *Psychology Today, 16,* 37–44.

Sternberg, R. J., Grigorenko, E. L., Ferrari, M., & Clinkenbeard, P. (1999). A triarchic analysis of an aptitude–treatment interaction. *European Journal of Psychological Assessment, 15*(1), 1–11.

Sternberg, R. J., Jarvin, L., Birney, D., Naples, A., Stemler, S., Newman, T., . . . Grigorenko, E. L. (2014). Testing the theory of successful intelligence in teaching grade 4 language arts, mathematics, and science. *Journal of Educational Psychology, 106,* 881–899.

Sternberg, R. J., & Smith, C. (1985). Social intelligence and decoding skills in nonverbal communication. *Social Cognition, 2,* 168–192.

Sternberg, R. J., Torff, B., & Grigorenko, E. L. (1998). Teaching triarchically improves school achievement. *Journal of Educational Psychology, 90,* 374–384.

CRITICAL THINKING QUESTIONS

1. Why do treatments sometimes not match the labels they are given?

2. What was the mismatch in the study described above—what were teachers supposed to do, and what did many of them actually do?

3. What can you, as a researcher, do to ensure that a treatment matches its label—in other words, that the treatment is what it is supposed to be?

22 STUMBLING IN THE DARK

Peter Suedfeld

The University of British Columbia

As a first-year graduate student at Princeton in 1960, I was invited by Jack A. Vernon to join his research team. Discussing his various interests, he asked if I wanted to take over his sensory deprivation (SD) lab. I only knew two things about SD: It was reputed to be extremely stressful, its effects akin to psychosis; and as a volunteer subject, eager to get $25 for lying on a bed in the dark, soundproof SD chamber and doing nothing for 24 hours, I nevertheless got panicky and quit after only three hours.

When I became the experimenter, I pondered why such negative effects were common: After all, most people spend a fair proportion of their life on a bed in a dark, silent room, and consider it pleasant. I concluded that the problem was in tangential aspects of the methodology. SD researchers required subjects to sign a legal release form in case of psychological damage, provided a "panic button" that would bring rescuers running to release the subject, and led them around the darkened room, disoriented and allowed only to feel where food, water, and the toilet were located.

I thought these features scared subjects before the SD session even started, and when I took over the lab (Jack having moved on to other research areas), I eliminated them all. No legal forms, no panic button, a monitor next door, and a low-key, friendly orientation to the illuminated room—including the ability to just get up from the bed and walk out by oneself if desired.

The effects were striking. Our early termination rate went down from about 20% to around 5%, and nobody reported the dramatic hallucinations and emotional storms common in the literature. The nonstressful procedures quite soon became standard (Zubek, 1969).

In those days, the *Zeitgeist* was changing from S-R drive reduction theory to a more cognitive, S-O-R approach. New theories proposed that rather than homeostasis—minimal arousal—the goal of the organism was a moderate level of arousal, which explained curiosity, novelty seeking, the enjoyment of surprises, and other behaviors that contradicted drive reduction theory.

I was particularly intrigued by the Yerkes-Dodson Law (1908), which posits that the optimal level of arousal for simple tasks is higher than for complex ones.

Basing research on it enabled me to combine SD with the thinking of my other mentor, Harry Schroder, and his work on cognitive complexity (Schroder, Driver, & Streufert, 1967). Research on the effects of SD on simple and complex cognitive task performance followed.

A literature review and several of our own subsequent experiments showed that SD improved performance on simple tasks such as memorization, arithmetic problems, and recall of word lists. But complex tasks, which were relatively unstructured, had many possible steps, and no predetermined endpoint (e.g., storytelling and the Unusual Uses Test) showed most improved performance in low-arousal groups and decrements in high-arousal, with moderate arousal such as SD in the middle. We also found that SD-related arousal was a function of time, while arousal related to financial competition was related to the amount offered. Complex task performance was best at 0 hours of SD or no financial reward, whereas simple tasks were best performed after 24 hours or in competition for a moderate reward ($5 for the best 25% of competitors and $20 for the best one). Longer SD (36 hrs.) or higher reward ($7.50/$30) both resulted in poorer performance. The effects of the standard 24 hours of SD did follow the Yerkes-Dodson curve for a moderate-arousal environment (Suedfeld, Glucksberg, & Vernon, 1967).

Textbooks and authors who didn't bother to read the up-to-date literature continued to rant about ultrahigh arousal effects such as model psychoses, hallucinations, and anxiety attacks. Trying to end this, my student, Rod Borrie, and I renamed the condition as the Restricted Environmental Stimulation Technique (REST), and I edited a book showing the current state of the field in 1980. Increasing information was coming in about positive effects of REST—powerful effects on habit modification such as smoking cessation, a calming effect on acting-out mental patients and drug users, and improvements in learning and memory (Suedfeld, 1980). Eventually, a version developed where the T stands for Therapy, and a number of outside reviewers characterized REST as promising beneficial outcomes but requiring more research.

In the late 1970s, flotation tanks—skin–temperature water, dense solution of Epsom salts, in darkness and silence, for one to one and one half hours rather than 24—came into fashion, thanks to John C. Lilly (1977). But the lauded results revolved around what we thought of as very low arousal: reduced muscle tension and blood pressure, reduced anxiety, improvement of tension headaches and insomnia, free flow of artistic and even scientific ideas, more hypnagogic states, and reports of deep relaxation. Neurological and physiological measures showed increased power in the prefrontal and right occipital regions and increases in theta waves.

This was a conundrum. I had invested a lot of time and effort (and grant money), in the moderate arousal hypothesis, and the new information seemed to support a low-arousal conclusion. My beautiful theory was being murdered by a gang of brutal facts (thank you for the quote, Ben Franklin).

Now, after considerable thought, I think I understand what was happening. Chamber REST has its best effects on events under the control of the volitional aspects of the central nervous system, whereas flotation REST primarily affects autonomic nervous system functioning. Volitional processes may be enhanced by chamber REST, which may in fact produce moderate arousal and may follow the Yerkes-Dodson Law (I haven't completely given up yet); the latter induces deeper relaxation, and its benefits come from low arousal. For example, attempts to produce smoking cessation by flotation have not been successful, whereas there have been at least 10 studies showing the powerful effectiveness of chamber REST. Motor performance, such as athletic skills and limb mobility, benefit from flotation. So does recovery from fatigue and muscle strain. The Epsom salts solution may be an important factor in the different effects; so may the simulation of microgravity that flotation, but not bed REST, provides. The one vs. 24-hour duration of flotation vs. chamber REST may be relevant as well.

The nature of my error was that my conclusions were overgeneralized: They fit the chamber REST data but not all REST data. I failed to realize that the two major methods of experimental stimulus reduction had such different effects, and my explanation was for a method that was overtaken by its competitor. But what bothered me the most was that I had forgotten one of my basic tenets as a researcher and teacher: Always remember that scientific conclusions are tentative and subject to disconfirmation at any time. In retrospect, I feel that I tried too hard and believed for too long in my theory.

The flotation enterprise is flourishing; hundreds of pay-to-float establishments around the world provide very relaxing environments before and after, as well as during, the float. Flotation research is also making a recovery, although more slowly. An annual conference attracts commercial tank operators and researchers from around the world (http://floatconference.com). Relatively few therapeutic agencies, and even fewer researchers, use chamber REST (but see Malůš, Kupka, & Kavková, 2013). I don't have a REST lab anymore and have turned my attention to other issues, methods, and theories, but I watch with interest to see whether my modified theory has new life in view of the new, less brutal, facts.

REFERENCES

Lilly, J. C. (1977). *The deep self: The tank method of physical isolation.* New York, NY: Simon and Schuster. doi: 671 22552-9

Malůš, M., Kupka, M., & Kavková, V. (2013). Technika omezené zevní stimulace (REST): Výpovědi ze tmy. [Restricted Environmental Stimulation Technique (REST): Statements from the dark]. In A. Neusar & L. Vavrysová (Eds.), Kvalitativní přístup a metody ve vědách o člověku XII: Hranice normality (pp. 322–330) [Qualitative approach and methods in the science of human beings XII: The boundaries of normality]. Olomouc, Czech Republic: Univerzita Palackého.

Schroder, H. M., Driver, M. J., & Streufert, S. (1967). *Human information processing.* New York, NY: Holt, Rinehart, & Winston.

Suedfeld, P. (1980). Restricted environmental stimulation: Research and clinical applications. New York, NY: Wiley. ISBN: 0471835366

Suedfeld, P., Glucksberg, S., & Vernon, J.A. (1967). Sensory deprivation as a drive operation: Effects upon problem-solving. *Journal of Experimental Psychology, 75*(2), 166–169. PMID: 6062955

Yerkes, R. M., & Dodson, J. D. (1908). The relation of strength of stimulus to rapidity of habit-formation. *Journal of Comparative Neurology and Psychology, 18*, 459–482. doi:10.1002/cne.920180503

Zubek, J. P. (Ed.). (1969). *Sensory deprivation: Fifteen years of research.* New York, NY: Appleton-Century-Crofts. ISBN 0390973424, 9780390973429

CRITICAL THINKING QUESTIONS

1. We know that new technology frequently results in new research methods. But how does it affect scientific theories, hypotheses, and the conclusions drawn from data?

2. How can researchers guard against becoming so convinced that their theories and/or findings are correct that they ignore, deny, or explain away research that shows flaws or limitations in their work?

3. Under what conditions might the practical application of research provide feedback that changes the original ideas and practices of the relevant research community?

23 PILOT, PILOT, PILOT

Rebecca Treiman
Washington University in St. Louis

A pilot study, students of psychology will have learned, is a preliminary study conducted before embarking on a full-scale research project. Pilot studies are useful for several reasons, one of which is that they can help researchers improve the design of a study before running a full version. One of my research mistakes was not doing a pilot before a large longitudinal study.

My colleagues and I have been in interested in how children learn to spell (e.g., Treiman, 1993; Treiman & Kessler, 2014). Particularly interesting is a phase of development that children may go through when they are around 4 or 5 years old. During this period, children will try to write words when asked to do so, often using recognizable letters of the alphabet and stringing the letters along a line. However, the children's spellings don't make sense from the perspective of *phonology*: how the words sound. For example, one 4-year-old wrote *drop* as ‹bninioo› and *volcano* as ‹bbi›. The letters this child used don't reflect the sounds in the words, and the child didn't even use more letters for *volcano*, which contains three syllables, than for *drop*, which contains one syllable. Such children are *prephonological spellers*. The spellings that they produce might appear to be random strings of letters that don't reveal any knowledge about spelling. But our research had shown that, as a group, prephonological spellers possess some knowledge about which letters and letter sequences tend to occur in words of their language and that they express this knowledge in their spelling attempts. This evidence came from studies in which preschool children were given paper and a pencil and were asked to write dictated real and made-up words (e.g., Pollo, Kessler, & Treiman, 2009). We identified the prephonological spellers and analyzed their productions, finding, for example, that the frequency with which these children used various two-letter sequences was related to the frequency with which these sequences occur in the words of their language.

Our next question was whether some prephonological spellers have more knowledge than others about what words look like. For example, one child might produce spellings that look rather like English words, such as ‹fepiri›. Another child of the same age might produce less word-like letter strings, such as ‹fpbczs› or ‹ccc›. Children like the former might be further along in learning to spell than children like the latter, already more knowledgeable about the letter sequences that occur in

81

the words of their language even if not more knowledgeable about how the letters symbolize sounds. If so, children like the former might be better spellers when tested several years later. This would be an exciting result, for it would suggest that the quality of a preschooler's spelling attempts can help predict that child's success in learning to spell conventionally at school. Given the importance of identifying problems sooner rather than later, such a finding would have real educational value.

We thus embarked on a longitudinal study. Our plan was to test a large group of U.S. children when they were in preschool. We would ask the children to spell a set of words and to perform several other tasks that are known to predict later spelling performance. We would identify the prephonological spellers and follow them into kindergarten and first grade, assessing their spelling at these times. Our goal was to test the hypothesis that the quality of a child's early prephonological spellings can help predict later conventional spelling.

One question that we had to address was how children should produce their spellings in the preschool test. In our previous studies showing that prephonological spellers' attempts reveal a degree of knowledge about the letter patterns of their language, children wrote by hand on paper (e.g., Pollo et al., 2009). Having children write this way promotes ecological validity, because this is how children usually write. However, young children's fine motor skills are not very good. Writing by hand can take them a long time, and it is sometimes difficult to be sure which letters they meant to write. Asking children to say what letters they meant, as we did in our previous work, might be seen to detract from the naturalness of the task. We decided, therefore, to use a different task in the longitudinal study. We would give children a board on which plastic versions of all 26 letters of the alphabet were laid out randomly in rows. We would ask children to pick the letters needed to spell each dictated word and to arrange the letters in the right order. We had used a similar task in a previous study (Pollo, Kessler, & Treiman, 2005), but we hadn't systematically compared the handwriting task and the preformed letter task with the same group of children and the same items.

Longitudinal studies are difficult and time consuming, and our longitudinal study was especially so. In the United States, children in a preschool classroom typically disperse to a number of different schools for kindergarten. It was sometimes difficult to locate and test the children when they were in kindergarten and first grade. We tried as hard as we could, and we ended up with data from over 100 children. However, when we began serious analyses of the preschool spellings, we noticed that they were somewhat different from the ones we had collected in the handwriting task, the ones that revealed some knowledge about the letter patterns of the language in prephonological spellers. In the preformed letter task, children sometimes seemed to pick letters because of such things as their adjacency on the board. They didn't seem to think very hard about which letters to use, and they didn't show a strong tendency to use letters and letter sequences in proportion to their frequency of occurrence in the language. Because of this, the data we had collected didn't provide as good a test of our hypothesis as we had hoped.

If we had conducted a pilot study, testing 20 or so preschoolers in both a handwriting task and a preformed letter task and balancing the order of the tasks across children, we would probably have noticed the problems with the preformed letter task and decided to use the handwriting task instead. But we didn't do such a pilot study. Because of our excitement and our desire to get moving, we jumped in to the full-scale study. The solution, in retrospect, is simple. Take the time to do a pilot study. You won't regret it.

REFERENCES

Pollo, T. C., Kessler, B., & Treiman, R. (2005). Vowels, syllables, and letter names: Differences between young children's spelling in English and Portuguese. *Journal of Experimental Child Psychology, 92*, 161–181. http://doi.org/10.1016/j.jecp.2005.01.006

Pollo, T. C., Kessler, B., & Treiman, R. (2009). Statistical patterns in children's early writing. *Journal of Experimental Child Psychology, 104*, 410–426. http://doi.org/10.1016/j.jecp.2009.07.003

Treiman, R. (1993). *Beginning to spell: A study of first-grade children.* New York, NY: Oxford University Press.

Treiman, R., & Kessler, B. (2014). *How children learn to write words.* New York, NY: Oxford University Press.

CRITICAL THINKING QUESTIONS

1. The essay focuses on one reason why pilot testing is valuable. Can you think of other reasons?

2. Why might a researcher not conduct a pilot test even when he or she knows it's a good idea to do so? Is it for the same reasons that people do other things that aren't good for them (e.g., overeat) and don't do things that are good (e.g., exercise)?

3. How might we assess a young child's knowledge about the spellings of words other than asking the child to write dictated words? What are the potential advantages and disadvantages of other methods?

24 FAILURE TO RECOGNIZE SURFACE DIFFERENCES DOESN'T NECESSARILY IMPLY UNDERLYING PROCESSING DIFFERENCES

Ovid J. L. Tzeng

National Chiao Tung University,
Academia Sinica
Taipei Medical University

Back in 1972, during my last year of PhD study at Pennsylvania State University, I took an advanced seminar course on educational Psychology taught by Professor Francis J. Di Vesta, who was a star teacher in the Department of Educational Psychology. I enjoyed and learned a great deal from his lectures and discussion among the graduate students in the class. In the middle of the spring quarter, Professor Di Vesta gave me a mid-term assignment, in which I was asked to review the literature on learning to read. He specifically wanted me to find out whether there are differences in learning to read English and learning to read Chinese. At that time, I thought this should be an easy task because there was a common belief that Chinese characters were picture-like symbols, each with a unique shape and associated with a specific meaning and sound, and hence, learning to become skilled readers of Chinese was assumed to depend on nothing more than rote memory. In contrast, learning to read English, as well as other alphabet-based scripts, depends on successful acquisition of a set of grapheme-phoneme conversion rules (GPC assemble route), in addition to establishing a visual lexicon for word recognition via the addressed route. The difference was so apparent with respect to visual perception, to memorial processes and finally to a lexical retrieval route, such that it would be easy to run a word recognition experiment with native Chinese readers to demonstrate the specific differences underlying the processing of these two different kinds of script. Thus, in addition to making a grand synthesis of reading literature of cross-language reading acquisition, I thought it would be an excellent idea to actually run a real experiment that showed the processing differences between reading English words and Chinese characters. I thought setting up a standard word recognition experiment would be a piece of cake, and all I had to do was choose a conventional experimental paradigm like the word-recognition paradigm in English but replace the English words with Chinese characters.

Still, I needed to find a unique phenomenon that was commonly known in cognitive psychology and that would allow me to demonstrate the expected processing difference between reading these two kinds of scripts. In the early 1970s, an amazing elucidation of different processing modes (roughly, language primarily in the left hemisphere vs. nonlinguistic spatial perception primarily in the right hemisphere) was shown in split-brain patients, at least after the removal of the corpus callosum, which connects the two hemispheres of the brain (Gazzaniga, 1967). The split-brain effect excited many cognitive psychologists, who began to simulate the differential processing modes in healthy subjects with a special experimental paradigm. Basically, this divided visual field paradigm was an experimental technique that involved measuring task performance when visual stimuli were presented very briefly in a tachistoscope (T-scope) to the left or right visual hemifields. If a visual stimulus appeared in the left visual field (LVF), the visual information was assumed to initially project to the right cerebral hemisphere (RH), and conversely, if a visual stimulus appeared in the right visual field (RVF), the visual information was assumed initially received by the left cerebral hemisphere (LH). In this way, if one of the cerebral hemispheres had functional advantages over the other hemisphere on some aspect of a particular task, an experimenter might observe improvements in task performance when the visual information is presented to the contralateral visual field. Based on results from the visual half-field experiments, visual word recognition in alphabetic languages such as English had been shown to have left-hemisphere lateralization and was assumed to be linked to the LH superiority in language processing. On the other hand, Chinese character recognition had been sometimes shown to be more bilateral or right-hemisphere lateralized and thus to be a counterexample to this claim (Hatta, 1977; Tzeng, Hung, Cotton, & Wang, 1979).

I set up the standard visual half-field experiments with the tachistoscope in the Department of Educational Psychology, prepared single Chinese character cards as stimuli to be presented half in the right visual field and the other half in the left visual field, with a randomization procedure to make sure all characters had equal probability to be projected onto either visual field. The Chinese readers served as subjects and were recruited from the Chinese Students Association at Pennsylvania State University. They were all right handed, and all volunteered to participate in the experiments without being paid. In the experiment, the subject was asked to identify and name the briefly presented Chinese character as fast as possible. Their naming times were recorded by a clock connected to a voice key, the activation of which stopped the clock. It took almost two weeks to complete the experiment with 30 Chinese readers. Statistical analyses on the mean naming times for each individual subject across the right and left visual hemifields were carried out upon completion of the experiment. A left visual field advantage should be expected, implying a right-hemispheric superiority in processing Chinese characters.

To my dismay, a glance at the results indicated no left visual-field superiority effect, not at all; instead, a tendency toward right visual-field advantage was observed (implying left hemispheric processing) but was not statistically significant. What was going on? I checked and rechecked the data recoding sheets, and they were all right! I checked the stimulus characters with respect to the location of their presentation, and there was no right and left visual field bias in the presentation of certain characters. Since the stimulus characters were randomized across subjects with respect to frequency of usage, there should be no frequency advantage in either field. Another confounding factor might be the handedness reports. Because the Chinese culture condemned left handers in general, children with a left-handedness predisposition were corrected throughout their life. I suspected some of the subjects might be "corrected right handers." After a brief telephoned interview with every one of the subjects and a check of their handedness history, I thus deleted data of four subjects with questionable handedness preferences. The results of the new analysis of the data, after removing data from the four subjects, made no difference: There was not a hint of the expected left visual field (right hemisphere) advantage in naming briefly presented Chinese characters in the tachistoscope experiment.

The texts written in Chinese characters and in English alphabetic letters are visually so different. Clearly, the configurative layouts of the characters are visually distinctive, and their processing must have been heavily loaded with intricate spatial analyses. The split-brain effect of two modes of processing had been followed up by dichotic listening as well as visual hemifield experiments with normal subjects. Moreover, the studies in Japan (Hatta, 1977) had shown the differentiated processing of Kanji (Chinese characters) and Kana (syllable-based symbols) in visual hemifield tachistoscope experiments, with the left visual-field advantage for the former and the right visual-field advantage for the latter, respectively. It was puzzling that no left visual-field (right hemisphere) advantage was observed in my carefully set up visual half-field experiment of naming Chinese characters.

Of course, against those experiments that showed the superiority effect for English (or other alphabetic scripts) words presented in the right visual field (LH), failure to find a left visual-field superiority effect for processing Chinese characters in my tachistoscope experiment might be interpreted as that the Chinese characters were bilaterally represented in the brain. But I thought it was a not good way to suggest a new and ad hoc interpretation based upon a non-result after the completion of a single simple experiment. I decided to report the failed experiment to Professor Di Vesta's seminar class, with a concluding remark: Surface differences do not necessarily lead you to find underlying processing differences.

FOLLOW-UP STUDIES

After giving the report in the seminar class, I went back to my rented apartment, feeling stressed and uneasy about my simple-minded experiment. All along, I thought that from the literature of visual half-field experiments on word recognition and on object configuration, and the associated results of right- and left-visual field superiority effects, respectively, a left visual field (RH) superiority effect should be a straightforward prediction for processing Chinese characters. But the prediction was not confirmed by results from my rigorously constructed and carefully conducted simple experiment. Why? The perceptual differences of the English and the Chinese scripts were so apparent, and literature on reading research had identified two modes of processing (i.e., assembled and addressed routes) in English word recognition, while the prevalent view of Chinese character recognition could be accomplished only by accessing the visual lexicon via the addressed route. Failure to obtain a left-visual-field (RH) advantage in character recognition by native Chinese readers, compared with the seemingly robust right-visual-field (LH) advantage in English word recognition, might be taken to mean that our conventional wisdom about reading Chinese characters was a big mistake.

I was fooled by the pronounced difference between these two scripts, which led me to advance a prediction based upon my gut feeling that so apparent a surface difference must have implicated a difference down below, cognitively! The gut feeling turned out to be wrong, totally wrong!

First of all, later restudies on processing Chinese characters uncovered a speech recoding process in short-term memory as well as in sentence reading (Tzeng, Hung, & Wang, 1977), similar to that observed in experiments with English letters and words (Crowder, 1976). This finding provided a strong evidence against the conventional view that reading Chinese characters was a simple mapping between the visual symbols and their meaning stored in a visual lexicon.

Second, the above speech recoding result was further supported by the evidence that scores on a phonemic awareness measure were found to be highly correlated with reading achievement in Chinese children's reading acquisition (Hung & Tzeng, 1981). How could this be when there was no need for extracting the grapheme-phoneme conversion rule (the so-called G-P conversion rule in English) embedded in the Chinese orthography? Maybe the assumption of no G-P Conversion rule in the Chinese orthography was wrong?

Third, and most important, the assumption was indeed simply wrong. Basically, more than 85% of all Chinese characters were phonograms, in which one component of the character formation was a significate radical, which gave a semantic clue to the meaning of the general category, and the other component was a phonogram radical, which gave a syllabic clue of how to sound out the characters (Tzeng, 1991). The morpho-syllabic nature of the Chinese orthography implied an exploration of the systematic G-P (grapho-phonological) conversion rule in order to establish an assembled route for faster processing, just as in the case of reading English (Hung, Tzeng, & Lee, 1995).

Finally, recent neuroimaging studies of reading Chinese characters consistently showed a left lateralized hemispheric processing and the active site of neuro-activity lay in the Broca area for speech processing (Kuo et al., 2001).

CONCLUDING REMARKS

When I ran my first Chinese reading experiment back in 1972, during the last year of my graduate study, I was totally committed to the conventional view that processing of the logographic Chinese characters must be different from the processing of the alphabetic English words, because the scriptal structure of these two writing systems were so perceptually very different. It was commonly assumed that recovering meanings of the Chinese characters could only be accomplished by the addressed route and nothing else. Failure of my simple visual half field experiment with a T-scope setup indicated that the above assumption was wrong. It took me years and through running studies after studies under various experimental paradigms to find out that reading Chinese was more than just retrieval from rote memory. The evolutionary success of a mature and efficient writing system is the establishment of speech-based orthography, and Chinese is no exception, even though the written script is perceptually very different from the alphabetic script.

The lesson I learn from the study of Chinese reading is that young investigators are vulnerable and easily taken in by strong surface differences. They tend to jump to the conclusion that underlying the differences must be the associated processing differences. In fact, it is the failure to find the expected underlying differences that leads us to uncover the processing complexity of reading Chinese characters. Many excellent studies on Chinese psycholinguistics and neurolinguistics mushroomed and tried to resolve the complexity with respect to learning to read as well as to skillful reading of Chinese as a second language. A recent study by Rueckl et al. (2015) provides an important final lesson to all of us who work on cross-language comparisons. In the study, corresponding fMRI experiments were carried out in native speakers of Spanish, English, Hebrew, and Mandarin Chinese, which vary in orthographic depth (ambiguity of spelling-to-phonology mapping). This mapping is largely unambiguous in Spanish and highly ambiguous in Chinese, with English and Hebrew falling in between. During fMRI, skilled adult readers of these four distinct, highly contrasting languages performed identical semantic categorization tasks with spoken and written words. Results from three complementary analytic approaches demonstrate limited language variation, with speech–print convergence emerging as a common brain signature of reading proficiency across the selected languages, whether their writing system is alphabetic or logographic, opaque or transparent, and regardless of the phonological and morphological structure it represents. In other words, the results give a universal signature on the neurolinguistics underpinning of reading across writing systems.

In retrospect, I am glad I had the opportunity to run that failed experiment several decades ago.

REFERENCES

Crowder, R. G. (1976). *Principles of learning and memory.* Hillsdale, NJ: Lawrence Erlbaum Associates.

Gazzaniga, M. S. (1967). The split brain in man. *Scientific American, 217*(2), 24–29.

Hatta, T. (1977). Recognition of Japanese Kanji in the right and left visual fields. *Neuropsychologia, 15*(4-5), 685–688.

Hung, D. L., & Tzeng, O. J. L. (1981). Orthographic variations and visual information processing. *Psychological Bulletin, 90*(3), 377–414.

Hung, D. L., Tzeng, O. J. L., & Lee, W. L. (1995). A conspiracy effect in the recognition of Chinese characters. In B. de Gelda & J. Morais (Eds.), *Speech and reading: A comparative approach* (pp. 303–335). Hove, England: Erlbaum (UK), Taylor & Francis.

Kuo, W.-J., Yeh, T.-C., Duann, J.-R., Wu, Y.-T., Ho, L.-T., Hung, D. L. . . . Hsieh, J.-C. (2001). A left-lateralized network for reading Chinese words: A 3T fMRI Study. *Neuroreport, 12*(18), 3997–4001.

Rueckl, J. G., Paz-Alonso, P. M., Molfese, P. J., Kuo, W.-J., Bick, A., Frost, S. J. . . . Frost, R. (2015). Universal brain signature of proficient reading: Evidence from four contrasting languages. *Proceedings of the National Academy of Sciences of the United States of America, 112*(50), 15510–15515. http://doi.org/10.1073/pnas.1509321112

Tzeng, O. J. L. (1991). Writing about writing: It is speech after all! *Contemporary Psychology, 36,* 982–983.

Tzeng, O. J., Hung, D. L., Cotton, B., & Wang, W. S.-Y. (1979). Visual lateralisation effect in reading Chinese characters. *Nature, 282*(5738), 499–501. http://dx.doi.org/10.1038/282499a0

Tzeng, O. J., Hung, D. L., & Wang, W. S-Y. (1977). Speech recoding in reading Chinese characters. *Journal of Experimental Psychology: Human Learning and Memory, 3*(6), 621–630. http://dx.doi.org/10.1037/0278-7393.3.6.621

CRITICAL THINKING QUESTIONS

1. Apparent surface differences may or may not imply underlying processing differences. Why are investigators, in particular, those who engage in cross-language studies, so easily taken in to believe that surface differences must imply underlying processing differences?

2. In the visual half-field study described above, can the investigator use the result of no visual field difference to claim that Chinese characters are stored bilaterally in both hemispheres?

3. What can you, as a researcher, do to avoid running experiments just for proving that surface differences must imply underlying cognitive processing differences?

25 FARFEL FLEES FROM HIS FEAST

Bernard Weiner

University of California, Los Angeles

As a graduate student, I had a humiliating and unforgettable experience that proved invaluable to my development as a research psychologist but closed a valuable research direction. My graduate school mentor was John Atkinson, known for his studies of achievement motivation. He identified some individuals (labeled as high in need for achievement) who prefer to undertake tasks of intermediate difficulty, whereas a contrasting group (labeled low in achievement needs) appeared to favor the selection of very easy tasks (where they would not fail) or very difficult tasks (where they would not be blamed for failure).

My friend, Paul Slovic, was a graduate student in the program of mathematical psychology and, with his insights, we recognized that these disparate behaviors could be interpreted as contrasting approaches to variance preferences: Individuals low in achievement needs desire greater disparities or dispersion in their choices than do individuals considered high in achievement needs.

We thought about investigating the belief that there are stable variance preferences between individuals, but testing this idea proved difficult. We could not find meaningful or affordable incentives to serve as alternative choices for our participants. We could use "pretend" or "role-play" scenarios (e.g., "Pretend you could always find 50 cents in one drawer or nothing or $1.00 in another. Which drawer would you open?"). But we questioned whether such scenarios would actually capture behavior of real-life events and decisions.

This perceived barrier opened the door for me to become involved in animal research. At that time in the history of motivation psychology, the majority of research was conducted with rats. I had a strong desire to also undertake studies using lower animals. I wondered if rats might exhibit disparate preference for variance. For example, given a free choice, would some rats consistently choose to receive five pellets of food, as opposed to an alternative choice where either one or nine pellets would be available? Would the former be labeled high need for achievement rats? And might some others consistently select the alternative where either one or nine pellets would be received, akin to the behavior in achievement settings of low need for achievement humans? When rats are hungry, these would be meaningful decisions, and we could afford to give away food pellets!

We set up a small animal laboratory, but it was soon apparent that crafting research with infrahuman participants is not easy. Should we always have the same value alternatives (e.g., five versus nine or one) or include other amounts as well (for example, two versus three or one)? Should the trials be spaced because consuming nine pellets of food might decrease hunger? Must the left- versus right-side alternatives be varied because rats have turning preferences? And how should the choice point be created? Animal research, we quickly discovered, was not the royal road to data collection.

We answered the choice-point question by using what was known as a "gap" procedure. When making their selection, the rats had to jump over a substantial space or gap in the apparatus so that their decision was irreversible and required cost and commitment. Inasmuch as so many research questions were raised, we decided to start our study with only one rat and see if he developed a stable choice preference.

For reasons I cannot remember, we called our rat "Farfel," which is the name of a rather dry pellet of food. Farfel was very cooperative and eager to be put into the experimental apparatus. And why not? Whatever choice he made, he received some food reward. It was a rat's paradise.

What we failed to notice was that Farfel was becoming increasingly obese. One day, as he reached his choice decision, he failed in his jump over the gap and fell to the ground. He ran (or waddled) through the psychology building into research oblivion. Perhaps his offspring still inhabit the building and, if we were good sleuths, we could discover if choice preferences are inherited. And that, to my lifelong disappointment, ended my career as an animal psychologist!

What I learned from this project was that the experimenter must consider the research procedure from the perspective of the participant. Had we undergone the experiences of Farfel, we would have anticipated his bodily transformation. In my subsequent research, I always was the initial participant in any study that I proposed or was initiated by my students. In so doing, I was able to undergo the experience of my research participants and discern if there were unnoticed problems.

Furthermore, if the experiment was unsuccessful when I was the subject, then I anticipated it would not succeed on others. Of course, if the experiment involved children at early stages of development, or individuals from other cultures, or examined unconscious processes, then this might not be the case. But I believe the scientific theory being tested must account for the behavior of the scientist as well as the behavior of the research participant. Hence, in many research studies, personal partaking is necessary.

CRITICAL THINKING QUESTIONS

1. What can you do, as the experimenter, to ensure that the participant perceives the experiment as you intended?

2. What are the methodological advantages and disadvantages of human as opposed to infrahuman participants?

3. As an experimenter, what ethical principles should you follow in regard to infrahuman subjects? Is it moral to cage chimps, or even rats, to use as research subjects?

PART

II

PREMATURELY JUMPING TO CONCLUSIONS

26 JUMPING TO THE WRONG CONCLUSION
A Lesson About People and Learning

Eva L. Baker
University of California, Los Angeles

In my educational research history, I have conducted many studies that compare the effects of different interventions on student learning and performance. When I recall mistakes I have made (and most of them have been mistakes in my management of teams), none involves procedures in these experimental studies. I was blessed to be taught by some of the wisest and most skilled teachers and mentors in educational research. I also did empirical studies in the course of developing assessments, and I will describe a mistake I made by jumping to conclusions when creating a new measure of history performance.

Now, a bit of background is in order. Choosing and using the right outcomes to determine the efficacy of various treatments can be very challenging. For instance, it is often the case that standardized tests are commonly used as dependent measures in research even when the treatment under study is likely to affect only a small portion of content or skill measured, a situation that results in finding no differences although differences may actually be there (a Type II error). I became interested in developing new and better outcome when I discovered that important classroom instructional differences, ones I could verify by talking to students, did not show up on their standardized test performance. Because public policies focus much of their attention on testing students for "accountability," educational effectiveness in general (rather the effects of an experimental treatment) is also judged by test results. By gauging student progress on examinations taken in different grade levels and for different topics, or by looking at changes of performance by groups of students at a particular grade level (Did Grade 4 math performance improve over the last five years?), test results feed directly into policy decisions about where to spend money and what to recommend to improve teaching effectiveness. But remember, if the measures are inappropriate or insensitive, like using a yardstick to measure liquid volume, policy and instructional users of results will make mistakes.

I had decided to develop better measures of learning to address this systemic problem. I chose the general topic of history, thinking that if we had better examinations of historical thinking, we would likely get more history taught in school. My own undergraduate areas were English and history, so I felt reasonably comfortable using assessment of student writing to show students' understanding of history content.

There are still a few more things that you need to know here. First, studies of writing have shown that people usually write poorly on topics for which they have had little background or exposure. For instance, most students cannot respond well to questions about "their summer vacation trip" if they have never had such an experience. I know that content knowledge plays a big part in my own writing; when I'm uncertain about topics or meaning of the content I'm addressing, my fluency and clarity fall apart. In our assessment studies, we realized that much of history content was treated at a very superficial level in texts; after trials with students who had supposedly learned information in their American history courses, even those in advanced placement courses, we learned that we could not rely on students' memory of content to guide their essay development. But our goal was not memorization; we wanted students to analyze and explain the meaning of important historical episodes. To do so, we gave students a primary sources—historical texts to read and write about within the assessment session. These texts usually presented opposing positions. For example, we began with texts from a debate by Lincoln and Douglas in the 19th century. In their assessment session, students read the speeches and were asked to imagine that the paper was directed to a friend who had missed school on the day the topic was treated. They were to explain to their friend the context and content of the debates, the positions and approaches taken by each speaker, and to summarize the major differences of the debaters.

As we progressed, we began by creating a general scoring scheme based on comparing essays by history experts, professors, or graduate students, with those of novices, who knew very little about the topic. The scoring approach was based on how experts wrote. For instance, the experts constructed focused rather than global essays, where they discussed one or two major principles or themes instead of many. They cited examples from the provided texts and also brought in other knowledge to make their arguments. They avoided anachronisms and major mistakes in interpretation. Writing by content, novices showed a different pattern. In contrast to experts, novices tried to cover all content, and they did not choose limited themes or principles to organize their paper. Examples were rarely used to bolster their arguments. Their essays also demonstrated major errors; a favorite one asserted that Lincoln obtained advice from a conversation with George Washington, a man who died about 60 years before the debates.

Our goal, then, was to develop a new model of content-focused essay examinations where the task and scoring scheme could be generalized across many different topics in American history. We wanted a common model to make assessment development more efficient and to assure that students were asked comparable questions on different content. The task given to students would always provide opposing positions illustrated in real speeches or letters by historical figures. All essays would be scored using the expert model consisting of principles, examples, and avoidance of mistakes. To be successful and practical, teachers had to be trained to rate essays using the scheme correctly, and a high level of agreement among raters was needed to make sure the essay test results could be trusted.

We began to develop assessments for other topics and found comparable results for the topics of American colonial history and the Great Depression era. Because we intended to include major social and political issues, and because our next try-outs were scheduled in Hawaii, we developed one particular Hawaiian history topic, on annexation of the territory argued by Queen Liliuokalani and Senator [Sanford] Dole. We also chose the topic of Chinese immigration and the Chinese Exclusion Act in the late 19th century. It was the Chinese immigration topic that led me to make a substantial error in my interpretation of findings.

For Chinese immigration, we tried out alternative relevant texts and then conducted a trial where we collected data from multiple classrooms of tenth grade students. An independent set of teachers was trained to use the scoring scheme and scored student essays, followed by our analysis of the data. Before we could make judgments about student performance, we had to check the agreement among teachers on rating identical essays.

We discovered that there were no longer high levels of agreement among the teachers scoring essays, a clear failure of the generalizability of the assessment model. I was devastated. To explain the results, I assumed that one of two things had happened. Either the scoring scheme was inappropriate for the topic or the training by our team staff of teachers failed. I became convinced that the teacher rater training had failed, for, I reasoned, good training would result in the same levels of agreement we had found for earlier assessments. I interrogated the trainers on my team to find out what the training had skipped or changed. Had anything unusual happened? Were the teachers similar to others we had worked with? When nothing emerged, I imagined that they were not being fully truthful. I became despondent, concerned about our team, and worried that the overall approach was likely flawed. All of our efforts over the preceding three years could have been wasted. How was I going to explain this failure to the funding agency? In which direction should I revise my thinking? How could I ever again trust the trainers? I turned the findings over many times during the next weeks, until one morning the obvious source of the problem became clear. Can you think of what it was?

I found another, better, more plausible explanation for the failure to find agreement among the raters. It was very simple and related to what I already knew about learning by students. Remember that students cannot write well if they do not know much about what they are trying to explain. The same principle applied to teachers—who we forget are learners also. They were learning to score essays on a topic that they did not fully understand, so it was inevitable that they would not agree with one another. As they read student papers, they would be unclear, in different ways, about what was right and which were relevant principles, appropriate examples, and mistakes or errors. How could we not expect lack of agreement on this topic?

After checking the plausibility of this explanation out with my staff, we created and administered to a sample of teachers, including our prior raters, a relatively short test about major ideas, controversies, and facts surrounding the Chinese Exclusion Act and the general orientation of Americans to immigrants from the last part of the

19th century to the first decades of the 20th century. We found that, on the whole, these teachers knew very little about the topic. They reported that they had not learned much about the issue in college classes, and that the topic was at best very lightly treated in the high school texts. They reported that they never—at least at the time—read or brought additional material about the topic into their classes.

To attempt to solve the problem, we decided routinely to assess teachers' content knowledge prior to rating and to provide teachers background material to support their understanding of topics in our essay history assessments. These two actions fixed the problem. I made apologies to the trainers.

So, my mistakes were in three parts. First, I forgot to apply to teachers the principle of content knowledge and competence as I had always done with student performance. Second, my first thought was to blame others for poor data, and third, I rushed to the conclusion that the entire line of work was doomed. I am sure I will continue to make errors of interpretation, but in assessment of content, this type of problem may be avoided in the future. It appears that newer, automated essay scoring can draw upon relevant vetted databases of content knowledge, and with luck, the systems will improve their understanding of meaning.

CRITICAL THINKING QUESTIONS

1. Student answers to open-ended assessments must be scored. Why is agreement among raters important?

2. How does content (declarative) knowledge interact with procedural knowledge and problem solving?

3. Other than failure of training and lack of content knowledge by raters, can you think of other explanations for the lack of agreement found for the topic of Chinese immigration history?

PART III

FOLLOWING A GARDEN PATH

27

WHY DIDN'T I SEE IT EARLIER?

Maya Bar-Hillel
The Hebrew University

We live our life one day after another, and hence our research, too, unfolds in time. My tale is about how the arbitrary order in which I encountered some of the effects I will discuss led me, for many years, down a garden path. Stickiness in belief revision, which is a form of confirmation bias, plus striving for parsimony, which is a form of theoretical elegance, hampered for years my ability to understand position effects in simultaneous choice (namely, choice from a set of options that are all presented at the same time, like a salad bar).

My graduate student, Yigal Attali, worked at Israel's National Institute for Testing and Evaluation (which is like America's ETS, the firm that produces the SATs and the GREs). Vaguely based on a mix of intuition and experience, he had a hunch that test-takers with no idea what the correct answer to a multiple choice (MC) question is gravitate to the middle of the offered answers more often than to the first or the last of the possibilities. Psychometric theory, in contrast, predicts that guessing respondents choose an answer at random.

A series of clever experiments and sophisticated analyses of data from real tests proved that Yigal's hunch was correct. But far more interesting was his serendipitous discovery that the people who invent the MC questions have a tendency to place the correct answer in the midst of the distractors they make up. These people, usually with advanced degrees, should have known better. According to game theory, in hide-and-seek situations, such as MC tests, the correct answer should be placed in a randomly chosen position. That is the only strategy that cannot be exploited: No matter how the test-taker guesses, every guess has the same probability of being correct. The test-takers' bias might be a response to the test-makers' bias. But where does the latter come from?

We could think of no good answer, but when searching the literature, we found many other studies of simultaneous choice from identical options (picking a can of soup from a supermarket display of identical cans; picking which roll of toilet paper to use in a bathroom stall; picking a chair to sit on when waiting for an experiment to begin; picking a questionnaire from three stacks of questionnaires; picking a number to bet on in a lottery; etc., etc., etc.). These seemed to resemble our test-makers' decision where to place the correct answer, which was also a choice from options that differed only in their position. In all these studies, the authors reported a *middle bias*—middle options were chosen disproportionately compared to those on the edges.

Besides a shared effect, these studies shared a lack of theory. At the end of our search, we still had no single explanation for the middle bias, but we sure had a lot of company! Middle bias was also reported when the simultaneously presented items were not identical (e.g., in store layouts). There it was called the *center-stage effect*.

We published our findings without explanation but with a generalization: For some reason, simultaneous choice was consistently subject to a middle bias.

Some years later, another student, Eran Dayan, studied choice from restaurant menus. We didn't expect novel results; we just thought it would be cool to show middle bias in an inherently interesting everyday context. Since menu items are not identical, the bias would have to be shown by comparing the popularity of any given menu item when it is placed in the middle of the menu options, versus when it is placed at the beginning or end of the list. There was indeed a position effect in menu choice—but to our surprise, it was the reverse of the expected middle bias. Being first or last on the menu conferred an advantage—not large but persistent—over being placed in the middle!

Eran's results could not be dismissed as a fluke. He had dozens of observations in a lab experiment, as well as in a real restaurant where real patrons were making real orders. He had data about choosing drinks, deserts, or entrees. For each setting and each category, and not just on average, the middle was *dis*advantaged. We had to take it seriously. But why was menu choice an exception?

I then had an epiphany: Menu choice was not really simultaneous choice. Although menus are presented simultaneously to one's eyes, they are presented sequentially to one's mind. They must be read and processed, rendering the presentation serial. In the sequential world, "position" is not in space but in time. And position in time is famously governed by the ubiquitous serial-position effect—which gives an advantage to being first or last, at the expense of the fuzzy middle. The psychology of the serial-position effect is well understood. It is menu choice, I realized, that conforms to a well understood rule, and MC questions, which must also be read and processed in a serial fashion, are the exception.

Exception? The literature was replete with middle bias; MC tests exhibited a middle bias; and yet were MC tests the exception? What was going on?

To cut a long story short, the data forced upon me the very belated realization that not in all simultaneous choices was a middle bias due to the same psychology, and not all serially processed choice sets were governed by the same psychology.

Simultaneous choice was subject to at least two major dichotomous considerations, which jointly could predict what effect position would have. First, it matters whether serial processing is required or not. Evidently identical cereal boxes on a supermarket shelf require no serial processing. They differ only in the position that they occupy. Other options, such as answers to a MC question, or a list of foods to order from, or a pull-down menu in an Internet site, clearly *do* require serial processing. When "middle" is in physical space and choice is implemented by reaching for it, the middle has the advantage of getting more visual attention, and reaching for it is easier, because it is often closer to where one is standing vis-à-vis the display, and it is less sensitive to careless reaching than the edges. This account cannot possibly explain middle bias in MC tests.

For that, a second consideration is required. If the choice involves strategic considerations, if it is a move in a two-sided game, then strategic considerations trump the advantages that accrue to the so-called *choice architecture*. In competitive hide-and-seek contexts, formally known as *zero-sum games*, choice is biased *against* salient options or salient positions; salient positions are not good hiding places. In contrast, in cooperative contexts, also known as *win-win*, salience is advantageous.

Nobelist Tom Schelling provided a famous example. Yale students were asked to imagine they had made an appointment to meet another Yalie in Manhattan the next Sunday but forgot to state a precise time and place and there was no way for them to communicate (this is a 1950s example). It was critical for them to meet—but HOW?? This is simultaneous choice: All spots in Manhattan, and all hours, are simultaneous candidates. Almost all respondents chose noon, and most chose the Grand Central information booth—arguably the most salient of Manhattan landmarks at the most salient time of day.

It took me over 10 years and several false starts (corresponding to several papers), to figure this out, simply because mere chronology misdefined "rule" and "exception."

REFERENCE

This chapter is based on the following paper:

Bar-Hillel, M. (2015). Position effects in choice from simultaneous displays. *Perspectives on Psychological Science, 10*(4), 419 – 433.

CRITICAL THINKING QUESTIONS

1. If you were being interviewed for a job, where would you like to be in the sequence of interviewees: First, last, or somewhere in the middle? How does this follow from the paper, if indeed it does at all?

2. In a simultaneous presentation of just two options, there is no "middle." Can you speculate whether there is an advantage or disadvantage to being first versus second?

3. There are famous position effects on the IQ of children born into a family. First-borns tend to be smarter than their siblings, followed by second-borns, then third-borns, and so on. Do you see any relationship between these position effects and the ones reported in my little essay? If so, what is it? If not, why not?

28 LOSING TIME

Charlotte J. Patterson
University of Virginia

Sometimes, the worst mistakes we make are not things that we do but things that we fail to do. Certainly, that was true for me. Or maybe it would be more accurate to say that I wish I had done the right thing sooner. Here is my story:

A few years into my career and happily settled into an academic position at a large university, my research was focused on issues in children's social development. I was teaching child development and studying ways that families and peer groups affect children's social and emotional growth. My research was getting published in top journals. It was challenging, and I enjoyed it—but something felt wrong. I kept wondering if "anyone" could have done my work. I knew that it took years of training to succeed at the research that my colleagues and I were doing, but the work did not seem to draw on anything in particular about me, either as a person or as a psychologist. I was not satisfied.

What was particular about me, as an academic psychologist, was that I was also happily settling into a lesbian relationship. After falling madly in love with a woman, I was increasingly finding that I wanted to spend my life with her, and I was hoping that she felt the same way. Luckily for me, she did. We began to talk about having children together. In those days, very few lesbian couples were doing that, and we wondered what that might be like for us and for the children we hoped to bring into the world.

There is an old saying about academics that goes like this: Question—How does an academic learn anything? Answer—Reads about it in a book. So, as a true academic, I went to the library. (Believe it or not, people actually did that, in those days.) I wanted to find out what psychologists had learned about lesbian and gay couples and about their children.

At the library, my experience was disappointing. Except for the work of a few gutsy pioneers, there was almost no psychological research on sexual orientation at all. Only a small handful of articles in professional journals focused on sexual orientation in family lives, and an even smaller number were focused on parenting or child development. What was worse, some work had been done from standpoints that seemed ignorant, discriminatory, or even downright bigoted. This was not what I had been hoping to find.

A short time later, as I was walking into my office one day, I had an idea. It dawned on me that perhaps I myself could contribute something to psychological understanding about sexual orientation. Although I had kept pretty quiet about my sexual orientation in professional circles, I had been coming out to family and friends for some time. I knew other people in the LGBT community and had heard many stories. Perhaps I could draw on my experience and training, conduct research on lesbian mothers and their children, and in this way, make a difference.

Thinking of this, I was excited but also felt scared. In those days, most same-sex couples could not even imagine that our relationships might one day be recognized as legal marriages. Lesbian and gay psychologists almost always stayed in the closet. There were whispers about certain people, of course, but I did not know anyone in developmental psychology who was openly lesbian or gay. Citizens in many states had recently been asked to vote on measures that would prevent lesbian or gay people from being teachers in public schools. Would parents or school administrators allow an openly lesbian psychologist to work with their children? And if not, how could I hope to pursue the career that I had planned?

At that time, if a person published scientific research on lesbian or gay issues, most readers assumed that the author must be lesbian or gay. After all, the argument went, who else could possibly be interested in such a marginal topic? So, if I published anything about sexual orientation, it would probably be seen by colleagues as a coming-out gesture, even if my identity was not explicitly acknowledged in the work. Was I ready to be known as "that lesbian psychologist"?

Considering questions like these, I felt indecisive. I had invested years of my life in training for the career that I hoped to have as a developmental psychologist. Could I really hope to succeed if I insisted on studying a stigmatized topic like sexual orientation? On the other hand, why would I want a career that required me to hide my own identity in order to pursue it? Looking back now, it seems to me that I wasted far too much time, going back and forth like this.

Eventually, I woke up one day and felt clear. I decided that I would focus my research on lesbian mothers and their children and work toward bringing the study of sexual orientation into the mainstream of developmental psychology. I wanted to learn more about children with lesbian and gay parents. I resolved to see lesbian mothers and their children not only noticed but discussed in every child development textbook openly and without prejudice. I knew that I had a contribution to make.

When I studied the research literature on child development in lesbian mother families more seriously, I discovered that there were a few good psychological studies, some in sociology, a handful in psychiatry, two or three in social work, and so forth—but though the results shared commonalities, they had not been assembled into a unified, coherent set of findings. I decided to write a review article that would bring together all of these research findings. My review suggested that lesbian mothers were mentally healthy and that their children were developing well. A brave editor took a chance on me, and the article was published in *Child Development*, the leading journal in my field (Patterson, 1992). Except for HIV work, this was the first time that an article on sexual orientation had ever appeared there. My article was even written up in the *New York Times*. I began to conduct empirical research on children born to lesbian women (Patterson, 1995). The results of this work—that children were developing well—do not sound like news today, but they did then, and my findings were noted in newspapers across the country. In this way, a new direction in my career was launched.

The role of sexual orientation in human development and family lives has remained the central topic of my research and professional work ever since (Patterson, 2006, 2009, 2016). Now that times have changed, there are many more of us who do this work, and we study many different questions about child growth and development in many kinds of families. This has turned out to be the most successful and most gratifying line of work that I have pursued. Looking back, I wish that I had started it sooner.

Why did it take me so long to pursue this field of study? Put simply, I was afraid. Finding the courage to study what I care so much about took me a long time, but I am glad that I finally did. My advice to younger people is to follow your heart, and pursue research that you care very much about, as this is how you will do your best work. Do it sooner, rather than later. If you are lucky, as I have been, you will also have a lot of fun along the way.

REFERENCES

Patterson, C. J. (1992). Children of lesbian and gay parents. *Child Development, 63,* 1025–1042. http://dx.doi.org/10.2307/1131517

Patterson, C. J. (1995). Lesbian mothers, gay fathers, and their children. In A. R. D'Augelli & C. J. Patterson (Eds.), *Lesbian, gay and bisexual identities over the lifespan: Psychological perspectives* (pp. 262–290). New York, NY: Oxford University Press.

Patterson, C. J. (2006). Children of lesbian and gay parents. *Current Directions in Psychological Science, 15,* 241–244.

Patterson, C. J. (2009). Children of lesbian and gay parents: Psychology, law, and policy. *American Psychologist, 64,* 727–736.

Patterson, C. J. (2016). Parental sexual orientation and child development. *Child Development Perspectives, 11,* 45–49.

CRITICAL THINKING QUESTIONS

1. What are some of the qualities that make a particular kind of research interesting?

2. How important is personal connection when choosing an area of research to pursue?

3. In what ways could it be an asset to have personal connection to one's research topic, and in what ways could it be a problem?

PART IV

USING MEASURES OF DUBIOUS RELIABILITY/ VALIDITY

29 VIRGINITY IN MATE SELECTION

David M. Buss
University of Texas, Austin

When I first started studying evolution-based hypotheses about sex differences in mate preferences, I discovered a research instrument that had been developed by sociologists in the 1930s. Happily, it contained four questions that corresponded well (or so I thought) to several key hypotheses I wanted to test about evolved preferences in choosing a long-term committed mate. One centered on the importance of resources, hypothesized to be more important to women. The relevant item was "good financial prospect." Two others centered on hypothesized cues to fertility—young age and physical appearance—hypothesized to be more important to men than women in mate selection. The instrument contained the item "good looks," a reasonable proxy for attractive appearance. And it asked participants whether they wanted their mate to be younger, the same age, or older, and to specify by how many years. Again, this seemed reasonable for getting at a preference for youth, a hypothesized cue to female fertility.

Another hypothesis focused on a sex difference in an adaptive challenge that men face, but no woman has ever faced over human evolutionary history—the problem of genetic relatedness to offspring, or in the male case, the problem of paternity uncertainty. This stems from a fundamental fact about human reproductive biology—fertilization occurs internally within women, not within men. So, women can always be 100% confident in their maternity of whatever children emerge from their bodies. Men cannot. Some cultures use the phrase "mama's baby, papa's maybe" to capture this sexual asymmetry.

The instrument I used contained what I though was a good way to see whether men had an evolved mate preference to solve this adaptive challenge—the item "chastity." In talking with people, I discovered that the term is somewhat ambiguous and used in different ways. Some thought it meant not having sex before marriage; some thought it meant remaining sexually faithful during marriage; still others thought it just meant the opposite of being "lustful." So, I made a decision to modify the question to clarify it. I modified the question to read *"chastity (no prior experience in sexual intercourse)."* This had the advantage of clarifying its meaning so that different participants would not interpret it in different ways. But this decision turned out to be a mistake, or at least a partial mistake.

The reason it was a mistake is that I had not thought through the logic of my hypothesis carefully enough. Importantly, for a mate preference to have evolved, it must involve a quality that our human ancestors could have actually observed or assessed in some way. Unlike qualities like age (roughly reliably assessed via appearance such as smooth versus wrinkled skin and behavior such as a sprightly versus a stooped, slow gait), physical attractiveness, and resources—qualities that can be evaluated with at least some accuracy, albeit imperfectly—virginity is not a quality that our ancestors could have observed or assessed reliably. There are no observable physical or behavioral cues to virginity. Even tests such as palpating the hymen are inherently unreliable; women vary tremendously whether they have an intact hymen, and many causes other than sexual intercourse can rupture an otherwise intact hymen (think horseback riding). In short, there are no reliable physical or behavioral cues to virginity that could have provided the statistical basis for selection to favor a male adaptation to prefer virginity per se.

Second, upon deeper thought, I realized that what's really relevant to men for solving the problem of paternity uncertainty is not whether a potential mate is a virgin but rather whether she remains sexually faithful after commitment or marriage (although observable sexual conduct prior to marriage might predict both pregnancy and the likelihood of infidelity after marriage). So for these two key reasons, the method I ended up using to test one of my key hypotheses was woefully inadequate for the task. The method was poor because I had failed to think deeply enough about the logic of hypothesized adaptations to solve the paternity uncertainty problem.

When the results of my 37-culture study (N = 10,047) came in after five years of data collection, the results revealed the error in my method (Buss, 1989). In contrast to the universal support for hypothesized sex differences in desire for resources, attractiveness, and youth, the results for virginity were all over the map. Literally. Of the 37 cultures, 62% showed the hypothesized sex difference, with men valuing virginity more than women in mate selection. However, 38% of the cultures showed absolutely no sex differences. Interestingly, there were no reversals—no cultures in which women valued virginity in potential mates more than did men.

Moreover, cultures differed tremendously in how much value they placed on virginity. It was seen as "indispensable" in a mate in mainland China, with no sex difference. In contrast, it was seen as "irrelevant" in Sweden, also with no sex difference. Other cultures fell in between these cultural extremes. Because many, although not all, psychological adaptations are hypothesized to be universal or universally sex-differentiated, discoveries of tremendous cultural variability *at the psychological level* appear to falsify or at least call into question the hypothesized adaptation.

Although my use of "chastity (no prior experience in sexual intercourse)" was a mistake, it turned out to be a mistake that led to novel discoveries in subsequent research. Although a mate preference for virginity per se does not seem to be an evolved adaptation, men do appear to have at least two other adaptations to solve the paternity uncertainty problem. One is a mate preference for sexual fidelity (and cues to sexual fidelity) in a long-term mate (Buss, 2016). A second is the emotion of jealousy, which in men seems to be heavily focused on the sexual aspects of infidelity—precisely the aspects that would have jeopardized a husband's genetic paternity (Buss, 2000, 2018).

Another benefit of my mistake is that the value people place on virginity in a mate turned out to be a wonderful marker of *cultural evolution*, which occurs more rapidly than biological evolution. For example, we have documented dramatic cultural evolution in urban China, where the value placed on virginity has gone from "indispensable" in the mid-1980s to merely "desirable, but not indispensable" a quarter of a century later (Lei, Wang, Shackelford, & Buss, 2011). In Brazil, it has gone from "desirable" in the mid-1980s to largely irrelevant in 2014 (Souza, Conroy-Beam, & Buss, 2016). Both cultures have experienced dramatic cultural evolution around norms of sexuality. In contrast, virginity has remained 'indispensable" in India, a culture in which arranged marriages remain prominent (Kamble, Shackelford, & Buss, 2014). These discoveries, in turn, led me to focus research attention on the cultural evolution of human mating.

So, what originally turned out to be a research mistake eventually led to deeper and more nuanced theorizing about psychological adaptations, novel empirical discoveries in subsequent research, and a new research focus on cultural evolution.

REFERENCES

Buss, D. M. (1989). Sex differences in human mate preferences: Evolutionary hypotheses tested in 37 cultures. *Behavioral and Brain Sciences, 12*, 1–14.

Buss, D. M. (2000). *The dangerous passion: Why jealousy is as necessary as love and sex.* New York NY: The Free Press.

Buss, D. M. (2016). *The evolution of desire: Strategies of human mating* (revised and updated). New York, NY: Basic Books.

Buss, D. M. (2018). Sexual and emotional infidelity: Evolved gender differences in jealousy prove robust and replicable. *Perspectives in Psychological Science, 13*, 155–160.

Kamble, S., Shackelford, T. K., Pham, M. N., & Buss, D. M. (2014). Indian mate preferences: Continuity, sex differences, and cultural changes across a quarter of a century. *Personality and Individual Differences, 70,* 150–155.

Lei, C., Wang, Y., Shackelford, T. K., & Buss, D. M. (2011). Chinese mate preferences: Cultural evolution and continuity across a quarter century. *Personality and Individual Differences, 50,* 678–683.

Souza, A. L., Conroy-Beam, D., & Buss, D. M. (2016). Mate preferences in Brazil: Evolved desires and cultural evolution over three decades. *Personality and Individual Differences, 95,* 45–49.

CRITICAL THINKING QUESTIONS

1. Can you explain why evolution by selection is unlikely to have forged a mate preference for virginity?

2. Can you identify cues available to our human ancestors that might have predicted sexual infidelity and hence compromised paternity?

3. Why do you think the importance people place on virginity has declined in China and Brazil but remained indispensable in India?

30 NEW FIELDS, NEW ERRORS
Breaking Rules Every Researcher Should Know

Robert A. Baron
Oklahoma State University

Let me start with an admission: I have had an unusual (some might say "weird") career. I began in social psychology, my first and most lasting love, moved into industrial and organizational (I/O) psychology, and from there into a branch of management known as organizational behavior. Now, I have found a new identity in the field of entrepreneurship—partly because I started and ran my own company, one that was based on my own research. The point of these ramblings is to indicate that I have made errors as a researcher in *all* these fields. So, in a sense, I could be judged "guilty, guilty, guilty" and again "guilty." Because these fields focus on very different topics and use sharply contrasting methods of research, I have found new ways to err in each of them. Looking back, though, one of my worst transgressions against sound research methods occurred when I first began to collect data in the field of entrepreneurship.

When I entered that field, I was truly a novice—but in a way, so was the field itself; it had only come into existence as an academic field in the 1990s. Right from the start, though, I viewed my major task as that of helping to import the principles, findings, and methods of psychology—and especially social psychology—into this new but rapidly growing field. Consistent with the self-established mission, one of my earliest studies focused on counterfactual thinking. Would entrepreneurs be more or less likely to engage in such thought than other persons? My initial guess was that they would engage in a lot of counterfactual thinking as they sought to learn from their early mistakes. But how could I investigate this issue? Entrepreneurs, as I learned from my own experience, are exceptionally busy people and have little time (or patience) for serving as participants in our research. This means that a researcher has to be very inventive in (1) finding them and (2) somehow enlisting their help. Obviously, they can't be told to make an appointment to serve as a subject in a research project. How, then, to collect data from them?

My first thought was that if they won't come to us, why don't we go to them? I was familiar with the general rules for conducting field research, but somehow, I lost sight of them in conducting the actual study. I had an excellent graduate student (in business, of course, not psychology!) working with me, and together, we decided that she would visit a number of local businesses and ask the owners to complete a very brief questionnaire on which they simply indicated how often they think about things they didn't do but wish they did and things they did do but wished they hadn't done. Our reason for focusing on these negative counterfactuals was because we predicted that entrepreneurs would engage in them frequently, since almost all suffered major setbacks and disappointment in their efforts to create something new and, as they hoped, better, than what currently exists. Uber, despite its recent troubles, is a good example of this process.

So far, so good. But then, I fell into major, and serious, errors. First, we didn't distinguish clearly between entrepreneurs and persons who were *not* entrepreneurs. Just owning their own business does not make individuals entrepreneurs: If they are doing pretty much what other business owners are doing, they are not trying to create something new. So, we really didn't have two clearly distinct groups for making the comparisons we wanted to make. Second, we didn't establish the reliability or validity of the brief scales we used. Did they really measure counterfactual thinking? I hoped so but didn't actively seek to determine if these hopes were fulfilled. In addition, we failed to collect data on the age, education, business experience, or even the success of these persons. In other words, we identified two samples (entrepreneurs and nonentrepreneurs), but we had no information on whether they differed in many other ways. If they did, then any differences in their reported tendencies to engage in counterfactual thinking might stem from these other factors, not from their identity as entrepreneurs. For instance, it's possible that people with lots of previous business experience (e.g., they owned another business in the past) would be more likely to engage in counterfactual thinking because they would recognize the importance of learning from previous mistakes. Who knows? We didn't collect the data needed to assess this and many other possibilities.

The findings of the study—if they can be believed!—indicated that, in fact, entrepreneurs were *less* likely than other persons to engage in counterfactual thinking. Basically, they were concerned about the future, not the past, and they tended to focus on that rather than on what happened in the past.

This raises a key question, at least for me: Did *I* learn from these mistakes? I think that I did and that as I conducted more studies designed to import social psychology into the field of entrepreneurship, I did a better job of developing the measures I used carefully. I also learned that some useful data could be gathered from financial records and other secondary sources rather from entrepreneurs themselves. But the bottom line is, I think, that I'm still learning, and although I have been an entrepreneur myself, I continue to try to recognize, and avoid, the mistakes I made in the past. There is an old saying I like very much that goes something like this: "Experience is what teaches you that you are now, or about to, make the same mistake again." I try to keep it in mind as I contemplate and plan new research projects.

CRITICAL THINKING QUESTIONS

1. Should the rules for conducting excellent research be the same in all fields? Why?

2. Can theories in one field be imported into another even though the topics the two fields study are very different?

3. How can researchers in one field avoid "reinventing the wheel"—that is, doing research that has already been conducted in a different field?

31 HOW DO WE COMPARE SENSORY OR HEDONIC INTENSITIES ACROSS GROUPS?

Linda M. Bartoshuk and Derek J. Snyder
University of Florida

Our laboratory studies the health impact of differences in taste perception. We measure these differences by asking people to rate the intensity (i.e., how strong is it?) and palatability (i.e., how much do you like it?) of food-related stimuli.

Our early studies focused on taste modifiers. For example, lemons taste sour, but if you taste a lemon and then eat miracle fruit (an African berry that can be purchased online), the lemon will taste sweet and less sour. S.S. Stevens (1955) advocated using intensity ratings with ratio properties (i.e., a sensation twice as strong is assigned a number twice as large), so we used this method, called "magnitude estimation," to quantify before-after comparisons.

By the 1970s, we were interested in studying genetic variation in taste. Certain chemicals are tasteless to some people but elicit strong taste in others. Fox (1931) accidentally discovered this "taste blindness" while preparing PTC (phenylthiocarbamide) in the laboratory; some flew into the air, and a colleague inhaled it and complained that it tasted bitter, but Fox tasted nothing. Subsequently, Fox and Blakeslee (a prominent geneticist of the day) distributed PTC capsules at the 1931 meeting of the American Association for the Advancement of Science (Blakeslee & Fox, 1932), instructing attendees (N=2550) to taste it and pull one of four levers on a voting machine. The results were as follows: 28% found PTC tasteless, 65.5% tasted bitterness, 2.3% tasted sourness, and 4.2% perceived another taste. Fox's 2-year-old child swallowed several capsules and was "temporarily incapacitated" with seasick-like symptoms, which led the authors to note, "The harmlessness of PTC when taken in moderate quantities, is therefore well established" (Blakeslee & Fox, 1932, p. 97). Today, we are a bit stricter about toxicity. We use PROP (6-n-propylthiouracil), a chemical relative of PTC, in our research because it is used medically (PROP suppresses thyroid function), so we can limit exposure to a fraction of the clinical dose.

Studies of PTC taste blindness were conducted all over the world. The *Journal of Heredity* even inserted a piece of paper impregnated with PTC into the issue describing the Blakeslee-Fox demonstration. To our delight, we found the original PTC paper intact in a library copy of the journal. Thanks to extraordinary will power, we left it there. However, we did copy it by soaking small pieces of filter paper in a saturated solution of PROP.

Taste blindness proves that differences in taste perception exist, but how large is the difference? Here, we were not satisfied with just classifying people as tasters versus nontasters; we wanted to know how bitter PROP was to the tasters, but we hit a snag. In the absence of mind reading, we cannot compare conscious experiences. To attempt such comparisons, we devised a new method, "magnitude matching," in which subjects matched PROP bitterness to the loudness of a tone (Bartoshuk et al., 2004). We identified three different groups. Nontasters of PROP matched the bitterness to the weakest tone. About half of the tasters matched the bitterness to a louder tone, but the other half matched the bitterness to a tone that was even louder still. If taste perception is not related to loudness (and we believe that it is not), we can conclude that these three groups experience different degrees of bitterness from PROP. We called individuals experiencing the greatest bitterness "supertasters." Working with an expert in taste anatomy, Inglis Miller, we found that supertasters have the most fungiform papillae, the structures that house taste buds (Bartoshuk, Duffy, & Miller, 1994).

Supertasting caught on among researchers and the broader culture, but some colleagues failed to replicate our results. Around this time, Derek Snyder joined the laboratory and decided to do his undergraduate thesis on the oral burn produced by chili peppers. Because supertasters express more taste buds and taste buds are surrounded by nerve fibers mediating pain, we expected that chilis would burn supertasters the most. Unexpectedly, this study would change our entire approach to measurement.

THE MISTAKE

In 1993, a colleague, Barry Green, devised a new scale for measuring oral sensations called the Labeled Magnitude Scale (LMS) (Green, Shaffer, & Gilmore, 1993). The LMS is a vertical line labeled "barely detectable" near the bottom, then weak, moderate, strong, very strong (all at points determined empirically with magnitude estimation), and "strongest imaginable" oral sensation at the top. Using the LMS, we found that supertasters perceive a bit more burn from capsaicin, but the effect was disappointingly small. Eventually, it dawned on us why: Labeled scales cannot show the full effect of supertasting because they assume that the labels mean the same intensity to everyone—but the labels denote greater taste intensities to supertasters because they live in a more intense taste world. For example, we now know that when supertasters say they experience a "very strong" taste, they are experiencing nearly twice the taste intensity that others experience (Snyder, Fast, & Bartoshuk, 2004). Now we understood why others had failed to replicate our work. They used labeled scales that cannot produce valid comparisons across people.

Despite this problem, we hated to give up labeled scales because subjects find them easy to use. Instead, we asked, could we produce a labeled scale that would make valid group comparisons? Working with Green, we stretched the LMS to its maximum by changing the top label to "strongest imaginable sensation *of any kind.*" When 100 subjects rated PROP bitterness with our new scale, which we called the general Labeled Magnitude Scale (gLMS), we identified supertasters just as reliably as we did with magnitude matching. The gLMS worked because, for most people, taste is never the most intense sensation, so the top label is independent of taste, just as sound was in our magnitude matching experiment.

The evolution of our labeled scale continues. We omitted the word *imaginable* as well as the intermediate intensity descriptors (Snyder, Puentes, Sims, & Bartoshuk, 2008), and we found that you only need to label the bottom of the scale as "no sensation" and the top as the "strongest imaginable sensation of *any kind*" to produce valid, reproducible data. We call this scale the Global Sensory Intensity Scale (GSIS), and we have extended this thinking to hedonic scaling (i.e., liking/disliking) with the Global Hedonic Intensity Scale (GHIS) (Kalva, Sims, Puentes, Snyder, & Bartoshuk, 2014). Our persistence in explaining this logic has led to growing acceptance by colleagues and the field at large.

Our mistake in how we asked subjects to respond led to an important insight. Any group comparisons using labeled scales are potentially compromised unless the investigators can show that the labels denote the same intensities to each group. The only change we would make if we faced this mistake today is that we would have made it sooner. Our story illustrates the benefit that accrues from being wrong and considering why: When something does not come out as you expect, this failed expectation can provide a window onto the next discovery.

REFERENCES

Bartoshuk, L. M., Duffy, V. B., Green, B. G., Hoffman, H. J., Ko, C.-W., Lucchina, L.A., . . . Weiffenbach, J. (2004). Valid across-group comparisons with labeled scales: The gLMS vs magnitude matching. *Physiology & Behavior, 82,* 109–114.

Bartoshuk, L. M., Duffy, V. B., & Miller, I. J. (1994). PTC/PROP tasting: Anatomy, psychophysics, and sex effects. *Physiology and Behavior, 56,* 1165–1171.

Blakeslee, A. F., & Fox, A. L. (1932). Our different taste worlds. *Journal of Heredity, 23,* 97–107.

Fox, A. L. (1931). Six in ten "tasteblind" to bitter chemical. *Science News Letter, 9,* 249.

Green, B. G., Shaffer, G. S., & Gilmore, M. M. (1993). A semantically-labeled magnitude scale of oral sensation with apparent ratio properties. *Chemical Senses, 18,* 683–702.

Kalva, J. J., Sims, C. A., Puentes, L. A., Snyder, D. J., & Bartoshuk, L. M. (2014). Comparison of the hedonic general Labeled Magnitude Scale with the hedonic 9-point scale. *Journal of Food Science, 79*(2), S238-S245.

Snyder, D. J., Fast, K., & Bartoshuk, L. M. (2004). Valid comparisons of suprathreshold stimuli. *Journal of Consciousness Studies, 11,* 40–57.

Snyder, D. J., Puentes, L. A., Sims, C. A., & Bartoshuk, L. M. (2008). Building a better intensity scale: Which labels are essential? *Chemical Senses, 33,* S142.

Stevens, S. S. (1955). The measurement of loudness. *Journal of the Acoustical Society of America, 27,* 815–829.

CRITICAL THINKING QUESTIONS

1. If your friend says that a glass of lemonade is very sweet and you say it is only moderately sweet, does that mean that your friend experiences greater sweetness from the lemonade than you do?

2. How could we determine whether women or men experience the most intense pain?

3. Can we compare the intensity of happiness of people around the world?

32 SCIENCE MARCHES ON ITS MEASURES

Larry E. Beutler and Samarea Lenore
Palo Alto University

No phenomenon can be reliably studied if it cannot be measured. The advancement of psychological science, like any other science, depends on how validly and reliably we can measure the phenomena that we study. However, nearly half of the published studies in psychology create at least one test of their own making. That means that many of the measures used in psychological research depend wholly on face or content validity. My story is one of not taking the time to use the best measure available. It is a story of how accepting that self-made measure led to an erroneous conclusion.

There are often circumstances within the research or clinical environment that limit the amount of time or resources available to be assured of optimal measurement. In challenging circumstances, it is very easy to "settle for" a measure that is easy to administer and has the right name and then to place unwarranted faith in the results. It is from circumstances like this that unrecognized errors frequently occur. And it was from a circumstance like this that I learned to take the time that it takes.

Over a period of three decades, my research group and I had been trying to identify, from extant research literature, a set of basic, cross-cutting principles that characterize and distinguish effective psychotherapy. We asked the question, "What are the key plans and actions that, when used, are consistently associated with improvement?" The idea was that, once identified, we could train psychotherapists to use these cross-cutting principles to guide them and would reduce their reliance on abstract theories of psychotherapeutic change. We took care and time to review thousands of research studies and carefully catalogued what patient, therapist, and treatment factors were present in each study as correlates of improved functioning, lowered symptoms, and better social adjustment (Beutler & Clarkin, 1990). Once we had catalogued all contributors to a good outcome, we began a reiterative process of narrowing the list down by grouping constructs with synonymous meanings or redundant terms and deleting those that had not been replicated several times.

At this point, we began to cross-validate our initial findings through a series of randomized research trials of some of these early principles (e.g., Beutler et al., 1991; Beutler, Mohr, Grawe, Engle, & MacDonald, 1991). Finally, we worked with a heterogeneous group of scholars and practitioners to reword each correlate that met our criteria, and then restated the correlation into a "principle of change" that expressed the results of a preponderance of evidence. These principles took the general form of an "if-then" format—for example, "when a therapist does X, the likelihood of Y (outcome) increases."

Over the intervening 12 years, we identified a dozen empirically derived principles that met our criteria of replicability, efficacy, and endurance (Beutler, Clarkin, & Bongar, 2000), and our research became more complex as we expanded the range of problems to which the principles could be applied. It was at this point, when we were initiating a very complex study of patients with co-occurring chemical dependency and depression, that we came to the problem of measurement. We were studying three variations of psychotherapy, including one that was specifically incorporating our core principles. The other treatments included one that employed a different set of principles that countered our own list. The third treatment was a form of cognitive therapy that was the usual treatment for these kinds of individuals. As the community standard, we hoped that our treatment would outperform it, or at least equal this standard.

The first thing we had to do in the study was to train all our therapists to ensure that they were proficient in the use of one of the three treatments. Thus, we developed a training curriculum for all three conditions, in which experts in those modalities worked with community therapists until they were considered to be skilled. Then we began assigning cases to therapists in each of the three groups. As each therapist conducted his or her preferred therapy, we knew that the results would be valuable only if we had evidence that all therapists complied with the treatment guidelines and manual for their form of intervention.

There were two ways we could measure therapist compliance. One was to construct a rating sheet, pretty much the way each of the other two therapies had done, in which we ask the supervisors how well each therapists complied with each of the principles. Supervisors routinely met with all therapists weekly, and following one of these sessions, they would simply fill out the 12-point rating sheet to indicate how well the therapists complied with each principle. The other method of rating was more arduous. It required blind raters to rate discrete therapist behaviors from DVDs, using an already validated instrument. The list of behaviors to be rated was extensive, but it had been constructed in order to rate many different types of psychotherapy and would provide compliance information on all three therapies.

Of course, you know what we did. We used the simple questionnaire. In the report of findings (Beutler et al., 2003), we indicated that all treatments were essentially equally effective. We went on to test the principles and noted that it didn't matter what type of therapy was being practiced; to the degree that therapists complied with our core principles, their patients did 30% better than those of therapists who did not comply. That finding was important, but when we got around to looking at compliance with each treatment, including our principle-based one, using the more time-consuming rating procedure, we found that therapists using our treatment principles were more compliant with the treatment than others, and the treatment (ours) with the highest compliance got the higher outcomes. How I wish we had known that our treatments had higher compliance than others at the time we published the study. We put so much time and effort into designing the study and carrying it out and so little into assessing the very things that were important to us. The cost was significant of taking the easy way rather than taking the time the study needed to take.

REFERENCES

Beutler, L. E., & Clarkin, J. F. (1990). *Systematic treatment selection: Toward targeted therapeutic interventions.* New York, NY: Brunner/Mazel.

Beutler, L. E., Clarkin, J. F., & Bongar, B. (2000). *Guidelines for the systematic treatment of the depressed patient.* New York, NY: Oxford University Press.

Beutler, L. E., Engle, D., Mohr, D., Daldrup, R. J., Bergan, J., Meredith, K., & Merry, W. (1991). Predictors of differential response to cognitive, experiential- and self-directed psychotherapeutic procedures. *Journal of Consulting and Clinical Psychology, 59*, 333–340.

Beutler, L. E., Moleiro, C., Malik, M., Harwood, T. M., Romanelli, R., Gallagher-Thompson, D., & Thompson, L. (2003). A comparison of the Dodo, EST, and ATI indicators among comorbid stimulant-dependent, depressed patients. *Clinical Psychology & Psychotherapy, 10*, 69–85.

Beutler, L. E., Mohr, D. C., Grawe, K., Engle, D., & MacDonald, R. (1991). Looking for differential effects: Cross-cultural predictors of differential psychotherapy efficacy. *Journal of Psychotherapy Integration, 1*, 121–142.

CRITICAL THINKING QUESTIONS

1. What question guided the research on principles of psychotherapy?

2. What are the two ways of measuring compliance in research on psychotherapy?

3. What is the conclusion reached by the author?

33 RELIABILITY IS NOT READINESS

C. J. Brainerd
Cornell University

My biggest research mistake occurred some years ago, when I used a confounded measure of children's readiness to learn to investigate their ability to learn some basic logical and scientific concepts. In retrospect, there were two reasons for this error. One was groupthink—so many others were doing the same thing. The other was conceptual bias. I was seduced by a hypothesis that was in fashion at the time, and the experience taught me just how insidious confirmation bias can be.

Developmental psychologists have soft spots in their hearts for the idea that the unfolding of psychological traits during infancy and childhood is innate, which one of our late brethren, Sheldon White, aptly summarized as "the view of human development as a progression through maturational schedules." Our history is brimming with examples, but imprinting and critical periods are the staple ones in freshman psychology. When it comes to teaching things to children (colors, numbers, word meanings), this idea takes the form of the *readiness hypothesis*. According to readiness, children are unable to learn those things until maturation has delivered the prerequisite learning abilities to them. Again, there are many examples in our history, but the one that motivated my mistake is another staple of freshman psychology: Piaget's theory of cognitive development.

Everyone knows that Piaget proposed a theory in which the understanding of basic logical, mathematical, and spatial concepts develops through a sequence of invariant, culturally universal stages. His theory was none too friendly to the notion that children first learn those concepts through adult instruction, which Piaget called the "American idea." He claimed that on the contrary, concept learning "is subject to the general constraints of the current developmental stage," that it will "vary very significantly as a function of the initial cognitive levels of the children," and that "teaching children concepts that they have not acquired in their spontaneous development . . . is completely useless."

In short, it will be very hard to teach children Piagetian concepts that they do not already understand—the most famous example, on which most research focused, being conservation concepts. Conservation concepts refer to our understanding that the quantitative properties of objects do not depend on their visual appearance and are not affected by changes in appearance. For instance, consider two rows of marbles, such that (a) each contains ten marbles and (b) one row is twice as long as the other.

If an adult and a 5-year-old are asked whether the rows have the same number, the adult will count them and say yes, but the child will quickly say that the longer row has more. Piaget studied many varieties of conservation (e.g., length, weight, area, volume), and during the 1960s and 1970s, several researchers tried to confirm his hypothesis that it would be hard to teach them to children who did not already understand them. The procedure had four steps, the last of which was the mistake.

1. A battery of conservation pretests was administered to children, to identify three groups of subjects: no knowledge (fail all tests), partial knowledge (pass some tests, fail others), and full knowledge (pass all or nearly all tests). The first two groups were retained for a training phase; the second group being "ready to learn" and first group not being ready.

2. Children in those two groups were randomly assigned to learning and control conditions, with the former receiving some sort of concept training and the latter receiving a placebo.

3. After that, a battery of posttests was administered, and subjects were reclassified according to which of the three knowledge levels they now belonged to. The training procedure was deemed to be effective if the classifications were higher for children in the learning condition than children in the control condition.

4. For children in the learning condition, the readiness hypothesis was said to be confirmed if posttest knowledge levels were higher for children who began in the partial-knowledge state than for children who began in the no-knowledge state.

The last step, the readiness measure, was implemented by several authors, who published experiments that supposedly showed that the readiness hypothesis had been confirmed because after learning, posttest knowledge levels were higher for children who began with higher knowledge levels (Inhelder, Sinclair, & Bovet; 1974; Strauss & Rimalt, 1974). As the author of the very first experiment put it, "The group most likely to profit from training is . . . the group who passed one pretest [partial knowledge] as compared to the groups that passed no [no knowledge] or two pretests [full knowledge]" (Beilin, 1965, p. 335). I was one of those authors: "the trainability of the present *Ss* depended on their pretraining stage" (Brainerd, 1972, p. 117).

The mistake is that the relation between children's pre- and posttest knowledge levels may have *nothing to do* with readiness to learn. As long as the two tests are reliable, pre- and posttest knowledge will be positively correlated, except in one extreme situation. Another way of saying this is that children with higher pretest knowledge will naturally have higher posttest levels because they were higher to begin with. The only way that this could fail to happen is if learning completely violated the readiness hypothesis, such that children who start with no knowledge learn vastly more than children who start with partial knowledge; that is, when a little knowledge is a bad thing. Thus, using the correlation between pre- and posttest knowledge levels to measure readiness is decidedly biased in favor of the readiness hypothesis because the correlation will be positive even if no- and partial-knowledge children learn at the same rate.

Realizing this, I wrote an article that reviewed all the experiments that had used that metric, in order to see if a valid measure would support the readiness hypothesis (Brainerd, 1977). The obvious measure is to calculate the amount of pre-post knowledge *improvement* for children in the learning condition, which has to be greater for partial-knowledge children. When I did that, however, the amounts of improvement for no- and partial-knowledge children were virtually the same. Startlingly, then, several experiments—13 in all—that were thought to have confirmed Piaget's readiness hypothesis had completely cut the ground from under it. The lesson is that it is good to be skeptical about hypotheses, even those that everyone seems to accept.

REFERENCES

Beilin, H. (1965). Learning and operational convergence in logical thought development. *Journal of Experimental Child Psychology, 2*, 317–339.

Brainerd, C. J. (1972). The age-stage issue in conservation acquisition. *Psychonomic Science, 29*, 115–117.

Brainerd, C. J. (1977). Cognitive development and concept learning: An interpretative review. *Psychological Bulletin, 84*, 919–939.

Inhelder, B., Sinclair, H., & Bovet, M. (1974). *Apprentissage et structures de la connaissance.* Paris: Presses Universitaires de France.

Strauss, S., & Rimalt, I. (1974). Effects of organizational disequilibrium training on structural elaboration. *Developmental Psychology, 10*, 526–533.

CRITICAL THINKING QUESTIONS

1. Can you think of any examples of things that happen during human development that are true instances of readiness?

2. Why do you think that it is just as easy for children who know nothing about conservation concepts to learn them as it is for children who already know something about them?

3. Why is pre- to posttest improvement in conservation concepts a valid measure of children's readiness to learn?

34 THE IMPORTANCE OF BEING THERE

Gary P. Latham
University of Toronto

Organizational psychologists are trained to predict, explain, and influence behavior in organizational settings. Among our long-standing interests is the selection process, namely, the development of selection tests that will enable an employer to accurately predict prior to hiring who is going to perform effectively on the job.

To decide whether a selection technique is useful, we organizational psychologists take the following four steps. First, we do a job analysis to identify the knowledge, skills, and behaviors that are critical to performing the job. Second, we actively encourage people from all sectors in society to apply for the job. Third, we assess the reliability of the selection instrument developed on the basis of the job analysis. Interobserver reliability is assessed when the test (e.g., an interview, an assessment center) consists of observations by the hiring managers. It is defined as the extent to which there is agreement between two or more observers (e.g., interviewers) who make their assessments of an applicant independently. Fourth, we determine the validity or accuracy of the selection technique in predicting job performance.

A test is defined legally as any procedure used to make decisions as to whom should be hired, promoted, demoted, admitted to a training program, laid off, or terminated. The selection test most frequently used to hire employees is the selection interview, specifically an unstructured interview.

The problem with an unstructured interview is that it lacks reliability and validity. This is because different questions are asked of different applicants, the questions are often not job related, and even when the questions are job related, the different interviewers cannot agree as to who is an acceptable/unacceptable applicant. The problem is the lack of structure.

What to do? The likelihood of convincing us psychologists, let alone the public, to refrain from using an interview to select people is low to zero. Hence, I decided to fix it. Working with my colleagues (Latham, Saari, Pursell, & Campion, 1980), I developed the Situational Interview (SI). An example of an SI question is shown in Table 34.1.

TABLE 34.1 ■ A Situational Interview Question
You, as the purchasing manager, often negotiate and mingle with suppliers. You frequently speak with Pat, the sales manager of one of your largest suppliers. In fact, you both share a common interest in sports. In one particular conversation, Pat has invited you to an athletic event next week. In the same breath, Pat asks you about the offers that were submitted to you last week by other suppliers as part of a sealed-bid process. More specifically, you are asked what the price must be to win the bid. Pat's company has been able to supply parts with very good quality to you in the past. Giving this information to Pat will enable you to drive down your costs, one of your primary mandates as a purchasing manager. What would you do in this situation?

In addition to the fact that the SI is structured, this interview method has the following advantages:

First, it is based on goal setting theory—intentions predict behavior (Latham & Locke, 2018). Empirically based approaches with a theoretical framework usually are more effective than atheoretical approaches.

Second, all the questions asked of the applicants are job related. They are derived from a job analysis. Each interviewee is asked the same job-related questions.

Third, the items from the job analysis are turned into "what would you do in this situation?" Hence the name, situational interview.

Fourth, to increase the likelihood that an applicant will state his or her intentions in response to a situation, there is a dilemma that "forces" applicants to explain what they believe they would do rather than give a socially desirable answer, an answer the applicant believes the interviewer wants to hear (see Table 34.1).

Fifth, a behavioral scoring guide is developed for a 1-, 3-, and 5-point answer. The behavioral scoring guide reflects the organization's values. Hence a 5-point answer in one organization may be scored a 3 in another organization. The use of a behavioral scoring guide minimizes interviewer bias and facilitates interobserver reliability.

Sixth, a pilot study is conducted to weed out useless questions. That is, if everyone gets the answer right, there is no variability, so the question is thrown out. Similarly, if everyone gets the answer wrong, the question is thrown out because, in both cases, the question does not differentiate high from low performers.

Finally, scores on the SI are correlated with an individual's job performance one year later. In our first study, the interobserver reliability among the interviewers was high, and the validity coefficient in our study was significant. The SI proved to be worthwhile regardless of whether an applicant was Black or White, male or female (Latham et al., 1980).

The company where I was employed as the staff psychologist now wanted to use the SI in a different domain, selecting newsprint employees as opposed to selecting employees for work in a pulpmill. What could go wrong? We now had evidence this interview method works. But it didn't.

What went wrong? The above steps for developing an SI were followed to the tee, or so we thought. We then correlated the scores on the SI with the employee's performance on the job. To our shock and dismay, the correlation was not significantly different from zero. How could this be? We had naively believed using the SI was foolproof.

We psychologists were present in performing each of the above steps. But we were absent when managers asked the interviewees the SI questions. In our discovery process for the low interobserver reliability and nonsignificant validity coefficient, we learned that the managers asked each question in a uniform, consistent manner. So far, so good. Then in their rush to judgment, they ignored the scoring guide for assessing each answer. Consequently, we had them rescore each interviewee's answers using the scoring guide. Eureka! A significant validity coefficient was once again obtained (Latham & Saari, 1984). The moral to this story is straightforward. Foolproof procedures in science seldom exist. To minimize the probability of being fooled, be present when the data are being collected.

REFERENCES

Latham, G. P., & Locke, E. A. (2018). Goal setting theory: Controversies and resolutions. In D. Ones, N. Anderson, C. Viswesvaran, & H. Sinangil (Eds.), *Handbook of industrial, work & organizational psychology, Vol. 1* (pp. 103–124). Thousand Oaks, CA: Sage.

Latham, G. P., & Saari, L. M. (1984). Do people do what they say? Further studies on the situational interview. *Journal of Applied Psychology, 69,* 569–573.

Latham, G. P., Saari, L. M., Pursell, E. D., & Campion, M. A. (1980). The situational interview. *Journal of Applied Psychology, 65,* 422–427.

A SCORING GUIDE

The behavioral scoring guide to the question about the purchasing manager and the sales manager is as follows:

5 points = highly acceptable. I would politely explain to Pat why I can't release the bid information, nor accept an invitation to attend the athletic event, because of the policy of my organization and the logic behind that policy. I would also explain how much I value the relationship between our two organizations.

3 points = acceptable. I would tell Pat that I am unable to provide the information or attend the athletic event. (No explanation is given.)

1 point = unacceptable. I would release the information and attend the event. Success in this job is all about personal relationships that increase my bottom line.

CRITICAL THINKING QUESTIONS

1. Why were my coauthors and I so confident that we would easily replicate our findings?

2. Are there compelling arguments today for journals to publish conceptual replications?

3. What should my coauthors and I have done differently to increase the probability of a significant validity coefficient if it had proven to be impossible for us to be present during the interview process?

35 FAILURE TO CONDUCT A PILOT STUDY

Frank C. Worrell
University of California, Berkeley

MY BIGGEST MISTAKE

I am very interested in how adolescents' thoughts about themselves—that is, variables such as self-concept, ethnic identity, and time attitudes—affect their educational and psychological functioning. These variables are sometimes referred to as psychosocial constructs, as they reflect an individual's psyche, but also have an impact on their functioning in different social contexts, such as school. Psychosocial constructs are typically measured using questionnaires. Early in my career, much of my research involved examining the scores on questionnaires assessing latent constructs (e.g., self-efficacy, self-concept) to determine if these scores were psychometrically sound or *valid*, that is, consistently measuring what they were supposed to be measuring. If an instrument's scores are not valid, any conclusions based on those scores are unlikely to replicate. Moreover, from the point of view of a junior scholar, validity analyses can also be published, resulting in a win-win situation. If an instrument works, then one gets a publication showing that the scores are working as the authors claim, and one can use the instrument in future studies. However, if the instrument's scores do not stand up to scrutiny, you have made another contribution to the field and have also saved yourself from using an instrument that may not allow you to draw conclusions.

Unlike an instrument like a ruler or compass, psychological instruments do not necessarily work the same way in all groups. Thus, it is important to examine the evidence of the construct validity of the scores that you want to use in samples from the population that you want to generalize to. For example, scores may be consistent or reliable in a sample of gifted adolescents but not reliable in a sample of at-risk adolescents (Worrell, 2000). Two of the more common forms of construct validity evidence that are examined include (a) internal consistency reliability, which tells you if participants are responding in the same way to the multiple items measuring the same thing on your questionnaire or survey, and (b) structural or factorial validity, which tells you if the items measuring the same thing on your survey are hanging together as a group.

What Happened

One of the constructs that I was interested in was self-concept, particularly as measured by the Self-Perception Profile for Adolescents (SPPA; Harter, 1988). The factorial validity of SPPA scores had not been examined in academically gifted students, a group that I study. The instrument consists of 45 items and assesses nine different aspects of self-concept with 5-item scales: global, scholastic, social, athletic, physical appearance, job, romantic appeal, behavioral, and close friendship. The SPPA requires you to choose *one of four* options for each question, but it differs from most instruments in the way the items are presented. Instead of getting one item with four responses, the items are presented with two statements (see the sample item from the SPPA below).

Really True for Me	Sort of True for Me				Really True for Me	Sort of True for Me
☐	☐	Some teenagers like to go to the movies in their spare time.	BUT	Other teenagers would rather go to sports events.	☐	☐

First, the respondents have to decide whether the statement on the right or the left is most like them. Thus, in this example, the respondents need to decide if they prefer movies or sports more. If the respondents prefer *movies* more, they should choose one of the two responses (i.e., *really true for me* or *sort of true for me*) on the left and no response on the right. However, if the respondents prefer sports over movies, they should choose one of the two responses on the right and none on the left. As can be seen, it is easy for a respondent to think that he or she needs to choose a response from both the movie side and the sports side, resulting in two responses to one item, which invalidates the item.

In 1995, I administered the instrument to sample of 414 students and wrote up a paper on the reliability and structural validity of the scores on 248 (59.9%) of the participants. The article was published (Worrell, 1997), and I contended on the basis of my study that only four of the eight factors were working as they should, and that the other four factors were not working. I made several errors in this paper, but the primary one was the failure to follow a fundamental rule of survey research—that is, conducting a pilot study. If I had conducted a pilot study, I would have discovered that a substantial number of respondents were not completing the measure appropriately, and I would not have had a study with 40% missing data. Thus, the upshot was that 40% of the responses were uninterpretable, and as the data were collected anonymously, there was no way to go back to the participants and get them to correct their responses.

The primary reason for this error, I believe, was an assumption that I made about the students being able to complete the forms because they were gifted and because I had used the SPPA in a previous study. However, in the previous study, participants completed the questionnaires individually or in small groups under my direct supervision. I generalized from this experience without thinking it through. I learned that it is critical to consider each aspect of a study, including how data will be collected and to conduct a dry run to see how participants respond to items. Even though much of my data collection today is done via web portals like SurveyMonkey and Qualtrix, I go through the surveys myself and get students and potential participants to complete the questions and provide feedback about their experiences. In sum, you should *never assume* that you know how participants will respond to survey items, and you should *always solicit input* in advance from individuals who are similar to the ones you are planning to ask to participate in your study.

REFERENCES

Harter, S. (1988). *Manual for the Self-Perception Profile for Adolescents*. Denver, CO: University of Denver.

Worrell, F. C. (1997). An exploratory factor analysis of Harter's Self-Perception Profile for Adolescents in academically talented students. *Educational and Psychological Measurement, 57*, 1016–1024. doi:10.1177/0013164497057006010

Worrell, F. C. (2000). The reliability and utility of self-concept instruments with at-risk populations. *The Journal of At-Risk Issues, 7*(1), 31–41.

CRITICAL THINKING QUESTIONS

1. Do you think the missing data had an impact on the conclusions being drawn?

2. What other aspects of the study would have been affected by the missing data?

3. In addition to conducting a pilot study, are there other things that can be done to minimize the amount of missing data in a study?

CARELESSNESS

PART

V

36 SMALL CHANGE— BIG MISTAKE
Check and Check Again

Daniel R. Ilgen
Michigan State University

As an organizational psychologist, I have always been interested in work behaviors. In the work domain, concerns with human performance dominate all others. Defining and measuring performance, setting goals and standards, evaluating actions with respect to standards, or comparing people's performance at one time and/or across time are just a few of the ways in which work performance is addressed. Early on, we focused on information actors received about the nature and quality of their performance of a task/job, leadership, or any other behaviors impacting the goals and objectives of their work (Ilgen, Fisher, and Taylor, 1979; Taylor, Fisher, & Ilgen, 1984). Such information is critical for many aspects of work, yet it is fraught with opportunities for misperceptions, inaccuracies, biases, and other breakdowns in the veridicality between what is and what is believed to have been the actors' level of performance.

In most models of work performance, performance feedback is embedded in a dynamic sequence initiated by the actors' behavior and culminating in judgments about the extent to which that behavior fits expectations/goals/standards for it. The feedback is typically expressed in terms that lie along a positive-to-negative continuum (good to poor). Much of the literature is based on laboratory studies or responses to simple opinion surveys. When an opportunity arose to design a study that would overcome many of the weaknesses of existing performance feedback research, we jumped at it.

We received permission to sample active duty Air Force personnel who were assigned to small air defense teams working in missile silos spread out along the border between the United States and Canada. Team tasks and positions were similar across teams-as were the hierarchical relationships among positions and people. Our interest was in the impact of performance feedback to team leaders from their subordinates and from objective task indicators, such as data on the speed and accuracy of responses in simulated exercises. A critical challenge was to assure voluntary consent and protect the confidentiality of all responses while, at the same time, identifying members for data analytic purposes.

An attempt to strengthen confidentiality led to our big mistake. First, all respondent identification information was coded in a way that only we researchers could decode. We placed that information on the cover of the survey instrument. Envelopes addressed to be mailed directly to our university were attached to the survey. Somewhere near the end of piloting the measure, we decided to move all respondent identification information from the cover of the questionnaire to its last page in case a subject might leave a completed or nearly completed instrument lying around prior to sealing it in the envelope for mailing. The final edits were given to the clerical staff. Someone proofed the changes. Data were collected in the field and return envelopes mailed back to us directly from participants. Several weeks passed before we coded the data. We immediately discovered that the identification information removed from the questionnaire cover had not been placed on its last page. It was impossible to match responses to specific individuals and thus create the network connections needed to study performance feedback in the way the study was intended. It was a costly mistake in terms of time, travel, and, I suspect, the willingness of volunteers from this unique field sample to participate in research.

What if . . .

One obvious lesson from this experience is the need to check and recheck everything. But, this advice rings hollow in face of the fact that there is a litany of ways in which mistakes are made. No checklist can anticipate them all. But I have found it very useful to incorporate into *every* study's development a team meeting devoted exclusively to the question of failure. *What if* what we are planning fails? How might it fail? What are potential reasons for failure? What might be done to anticipate and avoid the failure?

In our feedback study, another proofing may have caught the problem. Yet proofing is boring and tedious while thinking about theory and practice ideas directs attention away from line-by-line proofing the next time through. When the research team forces itself to generate ideas only about failures that, too, can be a creative task! More important, frequently simple actions exist to avoid failures when researchers are open to considering them.

The "what if" question works even better when the discussion of the unexpected is directed at theoretical questions. As researchers, we are quite good at generating more arguments in support of our position. For errors, we must consciously force a failure frame-of-reference to create exploration of potential failures. What if the data do not support our expectations? If our hypothesis is that **a** will be greater than **b**, *what if* **b** is greater than **a**? I ask this question often in dissertation defenses. The first temptation is to say that cannot be and defend why it cannot. If forced to stick with the discussion of my alternative, sometimes we conclude the alternative is not worth considering, but far more likely is the reluctant conclusion that it may be possible, and that is followed by some ideas about what might be done to either reduce its probability or provide some understanding of why the reverse was observed. On many occasions, it has led to small changes that have reduced the need to fall back on the conclusion that "more research is needed" to follow up on data not fitting the anticipated hypotheses.

REFERENCES

Ilgen, D. R., Fisher, C. D., & Taylor, M. S. (1979). Consequences of individual feedback on behavior in organizations. *Journal of Applied Psychology, 64*, 349–371.

Taylor, M. S., Fisher, C. D., & Ilgen, D. R. (1984). Individuals' reactions to performance feedback in organizations: A control theory perspective. In K. Rowland & J. Ferris (Eds.), *Research in personnel and human resource management* (Vol. 2). Greenwich, CT: JAI Press.

CRITICAL THINKING QUESTIONS

1. How might we create a culture of safety for raising possible flaws in our research as projects are developed?

2. What are some strategies for reducing the chances of overlooking errors?

3. Select a published article in which the author(s) states in the discussion that "more research is needed." Are there ways that they could have benefited from asking the "*What if*" question? What are they?

37 LOSING MY DISSERTATION DATA

Reinhold Kliegl
University of Potsdam, Potsdam, Germany

An overarching theme of my research, starting 40 years ago, has been how individual differences in cognitive processes can help us gain a better understanding of how the mind works in general and how they relate to complex cognitive tasks in everyday life. In particular, rather than using psychometric tests, I have tried to measure these individual differences in experiments that were informed by theories about very specific cognitive processes. My biggest mistake occurred in 2009, relates back to the very beginning of my research, and speaks to the value of "old" data.

I carried out my research on individual differences in cognition in two quite unrelated domains. As a graduate student at the University of Colorado in Boulder (1977 to 1982), I worked in the field of eye-movement control during reading. We tried to link individual differences in experimental effects in orthographic and phonological processing (i.e., processes required to recognize words) to how disabled readers move their eyes during oral and silent reading of short paragraphs. With a move to the Max Planck Institute for Human Development in Berlin (1983 to 1993), my research shifted to cognitive aging with a focus on memory, especially working memory. I looked at individual differences in limits of mnemonic skills. We also determined for every individual in groups of young and old adults how much time they needed to achieve various levels of accuracy in experimental conditions varying systematically in the degree of cognitive complexity.

In 1994, I moved to the University of Potsdam, adding new interests in psycholinguistics (e.g., age differences in syntactic processes) and formal modeling in the timing of motor processes (e.g., how precise are concert and amateur pianists when they are asked to play a 2-over-4 rhythm in one hand and a 3-over-4 rhythm in the other hand?) to the research portfolio. This new research led to a general interest in dynamical models of timing. The problem was that data collected about hand movements during the production of rhythms were not optimal for this purpose; basically, we could not ask our pianists to produce the extremely large number of hand movements we needed for our nonlinear dynamical models. This motivated a return to reading as the main research focus. Eye movements during reading are very well suited to addressing questions about the timing and accuracy of cognitive processes and particularly those involved for reading, because people produce them effortlessly and with high temporal and spatial precision for a long period of time. Moreover, the combination of mathematical and computational modeling with recent advances in multivariate statistics afforded new opportunities to understand individual differences in experimental effects.

My "moves" between research topics were correlated with moves between institutions. Throughout these years, I had carried with me from Boulder to Berlin to Potsdam a computer tape with raw data of my master's and dissertation research on eye movements in reading. This tape contained data of 141 normal and 141 reading-disabled children varying in age from 6 to 15 years. We had collected eye movements from their reading of two paragraphs. The children had also participated in experiments to measure basic processes in word recognition and a very comprehensive psychometric assessment of intelligence and reading-related skills (among many other assessments). The tape also contained data from other experiments and computer programs I wrote for preprocessing and multivariate statistics of this unique set of data. One highlight was the use of simulation techniques to distinguish effects of local and global control of eye guidance during reading and individual differences in these effects. Space for storage was scarce in those days; in retrospect, it is quite amazing that, with very strong compression, everything fit on one tape even if tape capacity then amounted to less than 20 MB! I had considered myself very lucky that in Boulder and in Berlin there were computers that allowed me to read the tape. This made for a smooth transition and allowed me to carry on some unfinished work for the first couple of years in Berlin.

In 2011, I thought about a reanalysis of the eye movement data I had collected as a graduate student. The plan was to use our new analyses programs for saccade detection and use new statistical models (e.g., search the web for "linear mixed models with crossed random effects") to test hypotheses about parameters of eye-movement control during reading of paragraphs. Indeed, I am still not aware of a comparatively rich set of data comprising lexical decisions and eye movements in reading for such large samples. I was sure that advances in the analyses of eye movements and multivariate statistics would lead to the discovery of new correlations of experimental effects and eye-movement reading style. Unfortunately, I could not locate my computer tape anymore. Ironically, I must have lost it during the latest and shortest move in my career, just a couple of years ago, within the campus of the University of Potsdam, relocating to a building 200 m away from the former one. Attempts to recover the data from archives at my former institutions also failed—so far. This is a very deep disappointment. The loss of this tape denied me the opportunity at an attempt to achieve some closure on questions that have been with me for such a long time with data collected at the very beginning of my research career. It really still hurts just thinking about it.

What did I learn from the experience? There is an obvious answer, and it ties in with a current change in psychological research practice. The obvious answer is to make sure there are multiple copies of all your data. The most effective way to guard against data loss is to upload your data to a local repository at your department or university (e.g., http://read.psych.uni-potsdam.de/pmr2) or to a psychological repository such as the one provided by the Open Science Framework (https://osf.io). Such repositories also allow you to grant public access to the data. Data sharing is in the spirit of reproducible research, but, when viewed from a very practical perspective, every person downloading your data also generates a backup for you. I wish I had thought of it earlier.

CRITICAL THINKING QUESTIONS

1. What would be appropriate measures to guard against loss of data in your research context?

2. Would it be useful in your research context to revive some old data for addressing current theoretical issues?

3. Do you think advances in multivariate statistics might uncover significant effects where absence of evidence for effects was the primary verdict, say, 40 years ago?

38 PEERS, PROCEDURES, AND PANIC
A Careless Error That Offered a Lifetime of Benefits

Mitchell J. Prinstein
University of North Carolina at Chapel Hill

It was late on a Wednesday evening. The light from my faculty office was the only one shining in an otherwise empty and eerily silent psychology department. I had just completed my postdoctoral fellowship only two years prior, and I had hoped that the solitude on this winter night would allow me to make significant progress on a manuscript recently invited for resubmission.

This paper had been especially frustrating to write. I had written what I hoped was a paradigm-shifting theoretical analysis of prior work on adolescent aggression, and I had data from two empirical studies to support my hypotheses. The paper had been rejected from two journals already, undergone significant revision and reconceptualization, and now—finally—had attracted interest from a generous editor and two lukewarm reviewers. Just a few more minor revisions, I had thought, and this paper would be ready to mail, hopefully for final acceptance.

That's when I noticed my error. A reviewer had asked for clarification regarding the study procedures, and as I dug through old e-mails and dusty paper files containing details about our data-collection records, it hit me like a slap across the face. I had mistaken two datasets for one another and inadvertently coupled the methods from one study with the data from another. At best, my analyses were severely compromised; at worst, they were flat out wrong, and all of the months I had spent on this paper had been for naught.

The realization began as a pit in my stomach, one that I thought that I would be able to eliminate simply through diligent retracing of my steps. There was no way, I told myself, that I would make such a ridiculous error. As a young professor, I did not think my body of work could possibly have become substantial enough that I wouldn't remember the basic details of my own research. I was young, alert, energetic—I had never had a lapse in memory before. But as I dug deeper and deeper into my records, my denial became progressively less effective. Now the pit had become nausea, soon followed by cold sweats, and a panic-stricken series of scenarios began playing in my head. I had troubled three editors and at least nine reviewers with results that were simply wrong. How would I explain this to the journal that had invited a resubmission of this paper? Would I be regarded as a sloppy or careless scientist? Would my integrity be challenged among those whom I looked up to in the field? Were my hopes of eventual tenure gone?

The study was one involving a sociometric assessment, a procedure that involves the use of peers' nominations to measure youths' social behavior. Data from grade-wide rosters are tallied and then standardized to learn how much each focal child is selected by his or her peers as aggressive, victimized, or well-liked, for instance, as compared with others in the grade. Once each child's standardized score is computed, it can be imported into a different dataset and used as a predictor or outcome of other constructs that may have been measured using self- or teacher-reported questionnaires. I had collected sociometric data in every study I had been involved in since graduate school, sometimes using a gradewide nomination procedure and other times using an expert nomination procedure (i.e., a small subset of teacher-selected nominators). The distinction is always important to report but usually inconsequential for analyses. Unfortunately, that was not the case for this paper—which offered a contribution that relied heavily on its methodological approach and now seemed destined to become the most time-consuming contribution to the recycling bin down the hall that I had ever produced.

The ending to the story was not too dire. I stopped catastrophizing. Then I invited a trusted collaborator to help me consider what might be salvaged, explained my error to a very understanding editor, and reconsidered my findings in light of the data's true origins. The contribution of the study results was not nearly as innovative but worthwhile nevertheless, and the paper was ultimately published (in that same journal). Although the manuscript did not have the effect on my burgeoning career I had hoped for, my error paid important dividends for decades to come, as it has guided my work as an investigator in at least three ways.

First, perhaps most superficially, I learned that one cannot underestimate the importance of meticulous data management and record keeping. In the case of this particular paper, it became difficult to trace the origins of computed values in one dataset to the constituent files that had been used to derive these computed data points residing elsewhere on my crowded hard drive, thus leading to the mix-up. But the issue, as simplistic as it seems, has far more general application. In the many years since, there have been lapses of several years—sometimes spanning the switch between several computers—between the time I began and completed analyses. I have been asked to provide data for meta-analyses, requiring me to revisit archival datasets from studies completed years prior, and I have revisited my own work to reanalyze old data in light of new theoretical innovations that have emerged in the field. In each case, I am grateful that my mistake led to the development of a careful record-keeping system to help organize data files from dozens of studies, and hundreds of variables that have been computed, recoded, or restructured so I can more readily work with them again. I have found the same procedure to be equally useful with word processing files that often undergo several drafts, often with several contributors, and referencing dozens of studies. It is remarkable how much time the development of an organized system of record keeping in the early professional years can cumulatively save hundreds of hours of retracing steps over the course of one's career.

Second, more substantially, I learned the hard way that our careers usually are not based on a single paper, and tenure will not be earned from a single idea. Similarly, our contributions to the field are not likely to be stymied by a single mistake. So it probably makes sense not to worry too much about any one paper. This was a lesson I needed in the early stages of my career, when I felt the extreme pressure to publish and publicize, or perish. Too often I worried—how could I possibly earn a reputation to warrant six to ten strong promotion letters from luminaries in the field, when I was but one young researcher in a discipline crowded with hundreds of more talented young scholars? How would my work get the attention I hoped it deserved? That kind of thinking led me to look for quick ways to demonstrate my worth in the field, to feel dismay with each and every rejected paper, and to pin too many hopes on the fate of any one submission. Looking back, I believe it was this mistake that ultimately helped me recognize the sprint/marathon distinction and develop patience for the career that would take decades to unfold.

Last, my mistake represented a pivotal transition point for me when I realized that my identity as a postdoc had ended, and my responsibilities as a faculty member had begun. I had always heard that faculty were inordinately busy, constantly juggling far more than was reasonable, and that recognizing one's limits was the key to success. Until that point, at the age of 30, I had not realized how this would eventually apply to me as well. But this was the wake-up call that helped me recognize my limits—I couldn't do it all. It's a lesson I continue to grapple with each day, and it becomes more relevant with every year my stamina diminishes and my limits increase. Academia is a job that we never finish. We never go home and feel as if our work is truly done. We can always read more, write more, analyze more, and the more we add to our plates, the harder it is to give each task the attention it deserves. Conscientiousness, diligence, and drive are important. But among a perfectionistic group of scholars, it is easy to forget that sometimes it is also important to turn off the light and just go home.

CRITICAL THINKING QUESTIONS

1. Why does it matter that we report our methods precisely the way we conducted them in our research reports?

2. What work habits can you invest in now to pay dividends later? Is there a small habit or organizational strategy that you can employ today, to save you hundreds of hours over the next 30 years?

3. Our careers are not based on a single paper or idea but rather a collection of pebbles that we hope will eventually become a mountain of work that others will be able to build their own mountains on top of. How do you envision your research program? What pebbles are you working on now, and what do you hope will be the eventual contribution your career will make?

MULTIPLE MISSTEPS
The Twin Study That Should Have Been

Nancy L. Segal
California State University, Fullerton

I am fortunate to have landed in a twin research and teaching career that has been so professionally engaging and personally rewarding. My doctoral dissertation completed at the University of Chicago, "Cooperation, Competition and Altruism Within Twin Sets: A Reappraisal," was the launch of that career (Segal, 1982). From Chicago, I traveled to the University of Minnesota as a postdoctoral fellow and eventually research associate, affiliated with the Minnesota Study of Twins Reared Apart (MISTRA), a world-famous study both now and then (Segal, 2012). Nearly a decade later, I accepted a faculty position in the Department of Psychology at California State University, Fullerton, where I established a Twin Studies Center and library, and teach developmental psychology and behavioral genetics to undergraduate and graduate students (Segal, 2017). It all sounds great.

But early on I made a big mistake that cannot be undone, one that continues to darken my research spirits from time to time: *I failed to track the behavioral and physical development of the 104 young twin pairs I recruited for my doctoral research.* As of 1982, the mean age of the twins was 8.03 years (SD = 1.51) and ranged between 5.04 and 13.28 years—today the youngest twins would be 40, and the oldest would be 48. (One adult pair completed selected portions of the study for a total of 105 pairs, but was excluded from the age calculations.) Had I continued to follow these twins longitudinally I would have compiled a truly remarkable data source.

WHY THE MISSTEP?

I sometimes ask myself why I failed to maintain research contact with the twins and their families that I so carefully studied. (I have been in touch with several sets and some parents but on an informal basis. The twins in one such identical set, Dean and David Kopsell, are shown in Photos 39.1, 39.2, and 39.3). I suspect that this regrettable oversight was linked to my overwhelming excitement at the prospect of joining the Minnesota team, blinding me to the great opportunity I had crafted for myself in Chicago. I was a new PhD investigator, soon to be surrounded by some of the key players in the twin research world, such as Professors Thomas J. Bouchard, Jr. (director of the MISTRA), David T. Lykken, Auke Tellegen, and Leonard Heston, and wanted to be fully engaged in the activities of that project. In fact, during the early years, I shared responsibilities for scheduling and data collection for the separated sets that visited our lab for an entire week of psychological and medical assessment, leaving little time for much else. Looking back, that may have just been an excuse

Credit: Donna Kopsell, mother.

Photo 39.1 David (left) and Dean Kopsell at age 3.

Credit: Dr. Nancy L. Segal.

Photo 39.2 Dean (left) and David Kopsell at age 9 engaging in puzzle completion task as part of my dissertation research.

Credit: Paul Thomas.

Photo 39.3 David (left) and Dean Kopsell at age 45, at a professional meeting. Both twins received doctoral degrees in horticulture and are writing a textbook together on that subject.

because, in reality, I could have prepared and forwarded questionnaires and inventories to the young twins and their families from time to time without much effort.

There is another possible reason why I failed to take advantage of the sample I had assembled, namely, that exciting new research ideas and projects were becoming available. In Minnesota, I received a letter from a twin whose co-twin had died, informing me that little research had been done to understand the unique features of twin loss. This note and several others like it led to my study of bereavement, which now includes over 700 twin survivors (see Segal, 2011). My colleagues and I discovered a set of reared-apart triplets composed of an identical female twin pair and a male co-triplet, all of whom were affected with Tourette disorder. The symptoms of Tourette disorder include multiple motor and vocal tics lasting for more than one year, onset of the condition before age 18, and symptoms not attributable to the physiological effects of a substance, such as cocaine, or another medical condition, such as postviral encephalitis (American Psychiatric Association, 2013). Intensive study of these triplets—the first reared-apart multiple birth set to show this disorder—led to a case report published in a well-known medical journal (Segal et al., 1990). We also were excited to published the first four-group study of personality similarity that included identical and fraternal twins reared apart and reared together (Tellegen et al., 1988) and the first reared-apart twin study of periodontal disease, both of which commanded considerable attention (Michalowicz et al., 1991). Finally, the researchers from the MISTRA, myself included, were often interviewed by members of the media, sometimes requiring out-of-town travel. The bottom line is that there wasn't time to devote to a seemingly finished project when so many new ones were appearing.

LESSONS LEARNED

I have learned several lessons from letting my first twin study fade away. First, it is important to think about the potential value of a study—I thought it was finished, but in fact, it could have enjoyed a lively future. Second, there is always time for important things—my schedule in Minnesota was very full, but I had many weekends to myself and could have crafted some questionnaires to send to the twins and their families. Third, I should have consulted several senior faculty members about how to manage the different parts of my new career, which would have included projects such as my dissertation twin sample—had I scheduled such meetings, the topic would likely have come up in the course of the conversations.

OTHER OPTIONS

I wish I could rewrite my academic life history to include those 105 pairs of twins. If that had ever been possible I would have written a grant to support longitudinal data collection, or at least done an annual or semiannual assessment of the twins' behavior by mail; of course, such research would have been facilitated in more recent years by the Internet. It would have also been possible to have hired local testers to administer various protocols to participants in person, such as intelligence tests and life history interviews. In fact, I have put this procedure in place today with my studies of virtual twins, that is, same-age unrelated individuals reared together from birth (Segal, Tan, & Graham, 2015), young reared-apart and reared-together twins from China (Segal, Stohs, & Evans, 2011), and switched-at-birth twins from Colombia (Segal & Montoya, 2018).

RETHINKING COURSES OF ACTION

I hope that students and young professionals reading this essay will think carefully about the future life of projects that they feel are complete. They should ask themselves if additional analyses are possible from an existing data set or if minor modifications or additions might yield even an even better, richer data source for the future. Gathering information from participants is a time-consuming task, and yet, most researchers (myself included!) gather extra material that may not be central to a particular hypothesis or question at hand. Still, when the project seems complete, we tend to move on to a new issue that catches our attention. I am not suggesting that we forsake new opportunities or promising paths—I am suggesting that we find ways to balance what we have and what we hope to achieve.

REFERENCES

American Psychiatric Association. (2013). *Diagnostic and statistical manual of mental disorders* (DSM–5). Washington, DC: Author.

Michalowicz, B. S., Aeppli, D., Kuba, R. K., Virag, J. G., Klump, D. G., Hinrichs, J. E., . . . Pihlstrom, B. L. (1991). Periodontal findings in adult twins. *Journal of Periodontology, 62*(5), 293–299.

Segal, N. L. (1982). *Cooperation, competition, and altruism within twin sets: A reappraisal.* (Doctoral dissertation). Retrieved from WorldCat (OCLC Number: 17100586).

Segal, N. L. (2011). Twin, adoption and family methods as approaches to the evolution of individual differences. In D. M. Buss and P. Hawley (Eds.), *The evolution of personality and individual differences* (pp. 303–337). Oxford, UK: Oxford University Press.

Segal, N. L. (2012). *Born together—reared apart: The landmark Minnesota twin study.* Cambridge, MA: Harvard University Press.

Segal, N. L. (2017). Segal, Nancy L. In V. Zeigler and T. Shackelford (Eds.), *Encyclopedia of personality and individual differences.* New York: Springer doi:10.1007/978-3-319-28099-8_1810-1.

Segal, N. L., Dysken, M., Bouchard, T. J., Jr., Pedersen, N. L., Eckert, E. D., & Heston, L. L. (1990). Tourette disorder in a set of reared-apart triplets: Genetic and environmental influences. *American Journal of Psychiatry, 147*(2), 196–199.

Segal, N. L., & Montoya, Y. S. (2018). *Accidental brothers: The story of exchanged twins and the power of nature and nurture.* New York, NY: St. Martin's Press.

Segal, N. L., Stohs, J. H., & Evans, K. (2011). Chinese twin children reared apart and reunited: First prospective study of co-twin reunions. *Adoption Quarterly, 14*(1), 61–78.

Segal, N. L., Tan, T. X., & Graham, J. L. (2015). Twins and virtual twins: Do genetic (as well as experiential) factors affect developmental risks? *Journal of Experimental Child Psychology, 136*, 55–69.

Tellegen, A., Lykken, D. T., Bouchard, T. J., Jr., Wilcox, K. J., Segal, N. L., & Rich, S. (1988). Personality similarity in twins reared apart and together. *Journal of Personality and Social Psychology, 54*(6), 1031–1039.

CRITICAL THINKING QUESTIONS

1. If you could devise the ideal study, what would it be?

2. Are you the type of person who prefers to seize new opportunities, or do you prefer to stay in familiar situations?

3. If you saw a fellow student set aside a good project for a new one that appeared promising, what would you advise?

40 ALWAYS LATE
Causes and Consequences Far and Wide

June Price Tangney
George Mason University

I am always late.[1] Late for meetings, late with feedback for students, late getting back to collaborators, late submitting reviews, late getting started on papers and grant applications, late for dinner, late for dates, and—yes—late with this chapter.

"Always late" has been one of the biggest impediments to my research—and in preparing this essay, I realize that it has high costs across multiple domains of life beyond good science. My New Year's resolution is to drastically change this lifelong pattern, drawing on social-psychological research and some sound advice I give to students but don't always follow myself.

THE HIGH COSTS OF BEING LATE

Most relevant to this volume, my research has suffered in terms of both quality and quantity. Although I have yet to miss a grant deadline, I've waited too long to start. No doubt, the quality of my proposals (and when funded, the ensuing research) would have been enhanced had I had more time to read, think, and rewrite. The quality of my research has been adversely affected by out-and-out tardiness, too. Throughout the research process, I benefit immensely from the input of undergraduate and graduate students, alike. Too often, I've "unavoidably" arrived late for lab meetings, squandering away 10 to 15 minutes of this invaluable resource as we struggle, for example, to develop, pilot-test, carry out, or analyze a given study.

Regarding quantity, I'm embarrassed to admit that I'm too often the bottleneck in getting feedback to student and peer collaborators on multiauthored papers. It's particularly problematic for students and junior colleagues, where time is of the essence as they contemplate applying to graduate school, seeking post-docs, or landing a first job. The critical final phase of research—communicating scientific findings to colleagues and the public—grinds more slowly through the peer-review process than it should, as a consequence.

Beyond hindering the quality and quantity of research, "always late" has broader intrapersonal and interpersonal implications. At the intrapersonal level, running against and over deadlines increases my level of stress. It leaches the fun out of

---

[1] There are some exceptions. I am scrupulous about being on time to class, meeting clients, and getting letters of recommendation out.

meaningful work, turning efforts toward a valued goal into a stressful last-minute chore. Moreover, failure to meet obligations in a timely manner elicits painful feelings of shame, guilt, or both. In short, the "always late" lifestyle is not conducive to my psychological well-being. Equally important, there are potentially high interpersonal costs to being chronically late. Both personal and professional relationships will suffer to the extent that others interpret my tardiness as a sign of disinterest, disrespect, or a sense of self-importance.

WHY DO I PERSIST AT BEING LATE? SOME ANSWERS AND POTENTIAL SOLUTIONS

"I'm busy" doesn't cut it. Everyone's busy—even my retired mother complains that there are not enough hours in the day. Furthermore, many busy people are consistent at meeting obligations promptly and showing up on time.

One problem is the "planning fallacy" (Kahneman & Tversky, 1979)—the tendency to seriously underestimate the time it will take to do a task, despite much previous experience on similar tasks to the contrary. Like many people, I constantly allow myself to fall prey to the planning fallacy.

Here's an embarrassing example. I've been working at George Mason University for 30 years. One time, it took me a record 22 minutes to drive door-to-door. Traffic was perfect, stoplights were unusually well-timed, and I added a few mph here and there. Ever since, I've mentally allowed myself 22 minutes to get to work—banking on the most optimal outcome, ignoring the inevitable "regression toward the mean," random red lights, and other delays.

Here's another example that may resonate with many of you. Like many people, I begin each day with a "to do" list—a wildly optimistic "to do" list. I greet each day as if it were ushering in a new era, an era in which tasks are routinely accomplished in record time, no unanticipated impediments arise, and time itself is elastic. I don't think of time explicitly—two and one half hours to read an article, three hours to write a results section, three hours to prep a class, four hours to write a letter of recommendation. And I certainly don't analyze how long it took me on average to write each of the last 10 letters of recommendation. Every day, I set myself up for failure as I optimistically list all the things I *wish* I could get done or things I know I *should* get done. You can guess the outcome. It is shocking to realize that I have never once completed my daily list—not in 50+ years!

Recognizing these biases and getting realistic would go a long way toward minimizing the "always late" trap. I'd like to start each day with a do-able plan, not a pie-in-the-sky wish list. Research indicates that people are more realistic in planning tasks if they (a) think concretely about the steps in the task, (b) estimate the time it is likely to take to complete each step, based on past experience (not wishful thinking), and (c) factor in potential roadblocks or setbacks that will need to be circumvented (Kruger & Evans, 2004).

A second problem for most of us is the overwhelming array of potentially interesting and important tasks to take on, projects to join in on, and events to attend. In college, in growth-oriented places of employment, in academia, and I imagine in most sectors, there are far more worthwhile things to do than there is time to do it all.

Ironically, the diversity of options ends up being a curse to many of us who have a knee-jerk tendency to say "yes" to each incoming opportunity or request, to embrace it all with the enthusiasm of one who has endless time. Without intention, we become saddled with far more than a reasonable human being can accomplish while still maintaining work-life balance.

On the other hand, the diversity of options is a blessing if one thinks of life as presenting a menu, offering us with an opportunity to pick a fine dinner. Who would want to visit a restaurant with only a one or two attractive menu items to complete a dinner? The best restaurants offer a range of mouth-watering options, so enticing that it's hard to decide. Importantly, you can't pick everything on the menu. You have to decide on a reasonable number of items for a dinner and promise to come back another time to sample more. Life is a lot like restaurants, I've found. Well-matched, but ill-timed opportunities have a way of reappearing on subsequent "menus."

Treating life as a menu, rather than as a series of imperatives, requires (a) the ability to choose wisely and (b) the ability to say "no." Choosing wisely means periodically taking stock of one's values and goals and then using these values to guide which tasks to pursue and which to decline. Regarding the invaluable art of saying "no," I am just learning. Sometimes, just a gracious "Thank you for the invitation. I'm sorry I'm not available. Best wishes . . . " is sufficient. No need to make excuses. But to my mind, the best way to decline is to include suggested alternatives—others who would benefit from the opportunity, others with more relevant expertise, or others with passionate interest in the topic at hand. In this way, we can maximize the richness of everyone's menus, make value-informed choices, and order only what we can reasonably finish in a day, a week, a month, or a semester—all without keeping students, colleagues, and loved ones waiting.

REFERENCES

Kahneman, D., & Tversky, A. (1979). Intuitive prediction: Biases and corrective procedures. *TIMS Studies in Management Science, 12,* 313–327.

Kruger, J., & Evans, M. (2004). If you don't want to be late, enumerate: Unpacking reduces the planning fallacy. *Journal of Experimental Social Psychology, 40,* 586–598.

CRITICAL THINKING QUESTIONS

1. How has being late been costly to you in academic or work settings?

2. What, in your experience, are some of the other hidden costs of being late?

3. What does psychology tell us about people's accuracy in planning time to complete tasks?

4. What strategies might one try to minimize an "always late" lifestyle?

5. Do you think those strategies will work? Why, or why not?

WHEN RESULTS ARE TOO GOOD TO BE TRUE, THEY ARE PROBABLY NOT TRUE

Thomas S. Wallsten

University of Maryland

Gal Zauberman

Yale University

Dan Ariely

Duke University

This egregious research error occurred some 25 years ago. The experiment, which we will outline shortly, yielded surprising and very consistent results that completely undermined our understanding of the process we were studying—or so we thought until a reviewer of our submitted manuscript brought us up short. This brief essay describes what happened as best as we can recollect it now.

Complete disclosure requires stating up front that none of us has retained records or files of that research, which ultimately did not result in a published report. Each of us has changed location since the time of that work and has long ago disposed of our files associated with it.[1] Consequently, details of why we ran the experiment and precisely what (we thought) the outcomes were are somewhat hazy in our minds, and we will not attempt to reconstruct them here. But we all clearly remember the nature of our mistake and how we discovered it, or more precisely, how someone else discovered it and saved us from the embarrassment of publishing startling, yet clearly wrong and therefore irreproducible results.

We were interested in the effects of different response modes on human judgment in both conceptual and perceptual tasks. The topic is important because decision makers often rely on uncertain forecasts of experts or witnesses. Examples include a meteorologist forecasting precipitation, a physician making a diagnosis, an intelligence analyst writing a report in a national security context, or a witness testifying in a legal proceeding. In these and many other cases, the forecaster's, diagnostician's, or witness's judgment is based on conceptual information, that is, on knowledge, reasoning, or inference; on perceptual information, that is, on events,

---

[1] It is arduous enough to maintain back paper and electronic files of published research, without also dragging along evidence of one's errors and failures!

scenarios, or activities seen, heard, or otherwise experienced; or, and perhaps most often, on a combination of both conceptual and perceptual information. One question is whether the two types of information are processed in the same way. Another is whether the type of question asked influences how the information is processed, and if so, does it do so equivalently for both types of information? Papers that discuss this topic include Ariely et al. (2000); Juslin, Olsson, and Björkman (1997); Juslin, Winman, and Olsson (2003); and Wallsten (1996).

Our study focused specifically on differences that may occur as a function of full-scale versus half-scale responses in both conceptual and perceptual tasks. In the full-scale condition, participants read a statement that was either true (correct) or false (incorrect) and had to give their subjective probability that it was true. In a conceptual task, the statement might have been, "The current population of Detroit is greater than that of St. Louis." In the perceptual condition, the participant first briefly viewed two horizontal parallel lines, one slightly longer than the other, and then saw a statement that might have said, "The top line was longer than the bottom one." In either case, they responded with a probability ranging from 0% to 100%, representing their confidence that the statement was correct. Hence they used a full, 0% to 100%, scale. In the half-scale condition, participants would first answer a question, "Which city currently has the greater population, Detroit or St. Louis?" or "Which line was longer, the top or the bottom?" They would choose one alternative and then provide a subjective probability ranging from 50% to 100% that their choice was correct. Hence they used a half-scale.

Importantly, every conceptual problem appeared in its true and in its false version at separated points in the sequence; for example, participants saw "The current population of Detroit is greater than that of St. Louis" one time and at some other time saw "The current population of St. Louis is greater than that of Detroit." Similarly, the statement associated with every unique pair of lines referred once to the top line and another time to the bottom line being longer.

The primary dependent variable was response additivity. Judgments are said to be *additive* if the probabilities given to the true and false version of the same problem sum to 100%. Checking additivity was simple in the full-scale case but first required conversion to a full scale in the half-scale case. (See Ariely et al., 2000 for how that is done.)

Our analyses showed a large and remarkable interaction on the additivity measure of our two independent variables.[2] The result was so surprising that we checked and rechecked our analyses and did them in various ways. Finally, convinced that our result was real, we wrote the manuscript stating that more research is needed on the topic and submitted it to a journal. One reviewer could not believe our results and asked for our raw data so that he could analyze them himself. He found no interaction whatsoever!

---

[2]An interaction between two independent variables (IVs) occurs when the effect of one IV on the outcome measure (the dependent variable) depends on the level of the other IV. In our case, that means that either the full-scale response mode yielded additive judgments in the conceptual, but not in the perceptual condition, while the half-scale yielded the reverse, or the other way around. Regrettably, we don't recall the direction that we erroneously thought we had obtained.

With more examination, we finally discovered our error. We had collected the data on PCs and then converted them to a format readable by Apple computers. This was the early days of Apple computers, and this type of cross-platform data transfer was in its infancy. We had made a systematic conversion error. Therefore, regardless of how we analyzed our PC-collected data on the Apple computer, we reproduced the same error. The reviewer, in contrast, analyzed our data on his PC and had no such problem. We are grateful that he did so, saving us from embarrassment and the field from an erroneous and misleading error.

What did we learn? One lesson was to be very skeptical of unexpected results. If results are too startling given our current understanding of a phenomenon or are too good to be true, there is a good chance they contain an error. Another was not to rely unquestioningly on new (or for that matter well established) technology. We easily believed we might have made an analytic mistake, but it never occurred to us that the error might have arisen in the "simple" process of data transfer from one platform to another. When error checking, consider every step involved from creating the experiment through data collection, storage, and transfer through data analysis.

REFERENCES

Ariely, D., Au, W.-T., Bender, R. H., Budescu, D. V., Dietz, C. B., Gu, H., Wallsten, T. S., & Zauberman, G. (2000). The effects of averaging probability judgments between and within judges. *Journal of Experimental Psychology: Applied, 6,* 130–147.

Juslin, P., Olsson, H., & Björkman, M. (1997). Brunswikian and Thurstonian origins of bias in probability assessment: On the interpretation of stochastic components of judgment. *Journal of Behavioral Decision Making, 10,* 189–209.

Juslin, P., Winman, A., & Olsson, H. (2003). Calibration, additivity, and source independence of probability judgments in general knowledge and sensory discrimination tasks. *Organizational Behavior and Human Decision Processes, 92,* 34–51.

Wallsten, T. S. (1996). An analysis of judgment research analyses. *Organizational Behavior and Human Decision Processes, 65,* 220–226.

CRITICAL THINKING QUESTIONS

1. What does one learn from this event about the value of being open about one's research and of sharing one's data?

2. What mistakes did we make while checking our analyses and results?

3. What is the right way to test automated algorithms?

4. How could we have avoided our error?

PART VI

OVERRELYING ON OTHERS

42

OF COURSE OUR PROGRAM IS ERROR-FREE—NOT!

Mary Hegarty
University of California, Santa Barbara

You have spent months reading the literature and designing a study with your advisor. She has finally given you the go-ahead to run the study. You stay up late programming your experiment and schedule several subjects a day for the rest of the week. You are feeling very productive, finally! Then, at the end of the week, you download the data and find that there was an error in your program, and the data you collected are meaningless. Sound familiar?

This is an example of an error that was recently made in my lab. I was the advisor in this situation, and I had worked with a graduate students and an honors student to design a study about mental rotation of molecular models. Our study had to be run with students who had a particular level of knowledge of organic chemistry, and we had access to students with the this level of knowledge only a couple of times a year. We had spent months developing virtual molecular models and paid the participants $20 each for their participation. After running the study, we downloaded the data and found that the reaction-time data were collected correctly, but due to an error in the program, accuracy data had not been collected!

My biggest research mistake, which unfortunately is a recurring mistake, is to let junior researchers go ahead and run an experiment without checking that it is programmed correctly and that the data are being collected properly. In this instance, we lost the data, and we had to wait several months before we could run the study again (the honors student had graduated by then). In another instance of this error, we had run over 200 students through four hours of testing in a large multivariate study. We realized only after the fact that the program for one of the measures had a bug, and these data had not been collected correctly. We were able to recover the data eventually, but it was an extremely time-consuming process that again held up our research progress.

Why do we make these errors? I think there are several reasons. First, we want to make progress on our research. The process of designing a study can take months, and once the study is finally designed and all the stimuli are made, we want to collect those data as soon as possible. We never feel more productive than when we are collecting data! Second, we are overconfident in our ability write a bug-free program. Programming is an inherently error-prone activity. I cannot think of a time when

I or someone else wrote a program that did not initially have a bug in it. But even though we have been through this over and over, we still seem to believe that the next program we write will be perfect the first time. Third, in the case of our multivariate study, there were many new measures of navigation ability to be developed and piloted for our study, and we did not pay enough attention to one of the more routine measures (a measure of spatial working memory).

From making this mistake over and over, I have learned two things. First, I have learned that I and my students are overconfident in our ability to prepare experimental materials (including programs) without error. Second, I have learned that you cannot be too careful to pilot all aspects of an experiment before you run subjects.

I now try to check all experiments thoroughly before I let my students and research assistants collect the data. Typically, I insist that they run me as a pilot subject (which they hate!), and I take the time to run through the whole experiment, not just a few trials. I deliberately make errors and check that an error is recorded correctly on those trials. I try to pretend I am an unmotivated undergraduate student (or a member of whatever population the participants will be drawn from) and think about all of the things I might do to "break" the program. Then, I encourage my students to run some pilot subjects from the actual population they are testing and fully process the data to make sure all data are being collected properly. Only then am I confident that the experiment is ready to run.

Based on this recurring mistake, I have advice for both students and junior researchers. To students, my advice is to thoroughly pilot your research study before you run it. It is not enough to run yourself or a lab mate through a few trials (although it is always a good idea to run yourself through your own experiment). You need to run several participants through the whole experiment, and if your eventual participants are Psych 1 students, run some Psych 1 students as pilots! Then download your data. Sort and aggregate the data as necessary to get them ready for analysis and make sure that the data values are in the range that you expected. If trials are coded as 1 for correct and 0 for incorrect, make sure that the all of the values for trial accuracy are either 1s or 0s. If people seem to be spending between three and five seconds per trial, check that the reaction times are actually in that range and not giving you values that are far outside that range. Only if all this checks out should you go ahead and run your experiment.

For junior researchers, my advice is to train your students to be obsessive in checking their programs and other data-collection procedures but also to check them yourself. I can sometimes detect obvious errors in my students' data that they do not notice. This is typically not because they are careless but because they have less expertise. They do not know what values to expect, meaning that they do not notice when a set of data points are out of range. More generally, we all need to realize that programming experiments is inherently an error-prone process, and so some careful checking of our programs and other data collection procedures in advance can be a stitch in time that saves nine!

CRITICAL THINKING QUESTIONS

1. What are some of the ways that you can check that your data are being collected accurately in an experiment? Think about the types of measures you are collecting (accuracy, reaction times, etc.) and how you would check each of these.

2. Why is it a good idea to run yourself through your own experiments?

3. Why is it a good idea to also run pilot subjects from the actual population that will be tested in your experiment?

HIRING A WOMAN TO DO A MAN'S JOB

The Perils of Equal Opportunity Employment When Running (Ruining) Social Psychological Experiments

Julie T. Fitness
Macquarie University

There is a well-known phenomenon in medical circles known as "white-coat hypertension." This term refers to the effects of anxiety experienced by some people (and apparently, cats) when visiting a health professional, including temporarily elevating blood pressure to alarming levels. This means that blood pressure readings taken in clinical contexts may be quite unreliable, depending on the extent of patient stress evoked by the situation. Of course, social psychologists have long been interested in the power of the situation to influence human behavior, with some of the best known illustrations described in Milgram's studies in the 1960s on obedience to authority. However, while Milgram deliberately created a situation designed to place ordinary people under extreme stress and regarded his own role as an authority figure (wearing a laboratory coat) as integral to that situation, potential experimenter effects on participants' thoughts, feelings, behaviors (and even physiology) may not, ironically, be at the top of a busy social psychologist's list of things to think about. I discovered this the hard way, by doing what I thought was a favor for one of my graduate students that ended up putting his research program behind by about three months. (He forgave me—I think!)

Fifteen years ago I was supervising several student projects on the emotion of anger in different relational and cultural contexts. One of these projects was designed to test the functionalist position that, although typically regarded as a negative and undesirable emotion, anger could actually feel good and motivate potentially adaptive behaviors such as (in the case of this project) goal persistence. In the first study, advertised as an investigation of the effects of physical arousal on the way people recalled life events, 31 female and 13 male participants were tasked with placing one hand in very cold water for as long as they could bear it. Their persistence was measured in seconds. Afterward, they were asked to imagine, as vividly as possible, a situation in their lives that made them feel really angry (or sad, happy, or neutral). Following a manipulation check to ensure they were feeling their assigned emotional states, participants were asked to repeat the cold-water task with their other hand, for the sake of reliability. The results of this study were intriguing. The emotion inductions worked well, and feeling angry (as opposed to feeling sad, happy, or neutral) significantly increased persistence in the second cold-water task—but only for men, not women.

In the second follow-up study, the cold-water task was replaced with an effortful handgrip task to measure persistence, and only two experimental conditions were run: induced anger and no emotion. Thirty males and 25 females were recruited and run through the same procedure as before. However, this time their salivary cortisol and testosterone levels were measured before, during, and after the study, in order to explore whether the effect of anger on persistence might be mediated by an increase in these hormones (both of which had previously been shown to reduce pain sensitivity in men). As might be imagined, running this study was a complex, expensive, and labor-intensive task. Obtaining three saliva samples from each participant and then accurately recording and refrigerating each sample for later analysis required patience, accuracy, and time that was running away from us. Accordingly, after the experiment had been running for a couple of weeks, I hired an enthusiastic and conscientious young honors student to help run the studies.

Unfortunately, this quest for efficiency had what I should have realized would be a seriously confounding effect on the results of the study. To put it simply, the student running this project was a young man, and our new research assistant was an attractive young woman who ended up running two thirds of the experiments. She followed a strict experimental protocol and was blind to the study's hypotheses. However, the results were compromised. Specifically, and in line with Study 1, the neutral anger-inductions were successful. However, the positive anger-persistence association that had been previously found for men disappeared. Both the angry and nonangry men persisted equally as long and significantly longer than the women. Careful examination of the data revealed that, regardless of anger, men were more motivated than women to persist with the handgrip task when interacting with the female, as opposed to the male, experimenter. This confound also rendered the salivary testosterone and cortisol data for men uninterpretable.

A poststudy literature search found a rich, albeit old, body of work that had looked specifically at the potential effects, not just of experimenter expectations (about which I had been soundly trained), but of experimenters' biosocial characteristics, including sex, physical attractiveness, even dress, on participant behavior (e.g., see Barnes & Rosenthal, 1985; Ruminek, Capasso, & Hendrick, 1977). There has also been more recent literature suggesting that such effects may not be trivial. For example, Fisher (2007) investigated self-reported sexual attitudes and behaviors in young male and female college students and found reliable differences in men's (but not women's) responses when the research assistant was female, as opposed to male. Given current concerns about the "reproducibility crisis" in social psychology and difficulties in replicating certain effects across laboratories, it may be worth looking more closely at the attributes of the research assistant(s) who ran and are running the studies. In many cases, the nature of these attributes will not matter at all. But in others, the sex, age, race, status, or even how the experimenter is dressed may be having an unintended but crucial impact on the findings.

With respect to what I would have done differently in relation to this study, the major lesson I relearned is the critical importance of doing one's homework when planning studies, including thoroughly reviewing relevant literature (old and new) on both the conceptual background to the research and relatedly, methodological constraints and possibilities. Only then can the research be planned, down to the smallest detail, including (crucially) who is going to run the studies and the inherent requirements of the job. This is not to suggest that we need to return to the days of wholesale discriminatory employment practices according to candidates' biosocial characteristics rather than (or as well as) their skills and experience. It does mean, however, that we need to take the power of the social situation seriously and to think much more carefully about potential experimenter effects given the type of study we plan to run with particular kinds of participants, both human and nonhuman (even, or especially, cats).

REFERENCES

Barnes, M., & Rosenthal, R. (1985). Interpersonal effects of experimenter attractiveness, attire, and gender. *Journal of Personality & Social Psychology, 48*, 435–446.

Fisher, T. (2007). Sex of experimenter and social norm effects on reports of sexual behavior in young men and women. *Archives of Sexual Behavior, 36*, 89–100. DOI 10.1007/s10508-006-9094-7

Ruminek, D., Capasso, D. R., & Hendrick, C. (1977). Experimenter sex effects in behavioral research. *Psychological Bulletin, 84*, 852–877.

CRITICAL THINKING QUESTIONS

1. Imagine that we are unsure whether experimenter sex is going to be a problem in a particular study. What steps might we take when planning the study to address this?

2. To what extent can we fully computerize the protocols for social psychological experiments? Could we ever do away with the need for human experimenters?

3. Is it ethical to recruit experimental assistants on the basis of a particular attribute such as race, sex, age, or physical attractiveness for running particular experiments?

44 THE CASE OF THE ENTERPRISING INSTRUCTOR

Regina F. Frey and Mark A. McDaniel
Washington University in St. Louis

In our work, we incorporate research from psychological science and discipline-based education research to develop classroom innovations, and we implement studies in authentic contexts to evaluate those innovations. From our experiences, we have realized the importance of continual communication with instructors (faculty practitioners) throughout the research project. Our example concerns an experimental intervention that we implemented in a general chemistry class. It was a true experiment, which is difficult to do in a classroom setting, with students randomly assigned to control and intervention groups. During the design of this project, we met numerous times with the instructors of the course discussing the experimental design, the details of the course logistics, and the instructor's course objectives. As with any effective collaboration, this led to clarification on both sides and slight changes in the project design. The first year of the project, the data collection and process went very smoothly, and the results gave evidence for our hypotheses. To ensure the results were robust, we (researchers and instructors) agreed to conduct a replication; that is, a second year in which the intervention was again examined. Because we had worked through the details for the first year, we did not meet again with the instructors to discuss the details. We all agreed to follow the same protocol from the first year. We were thrilled with how smoothly the project was proceeding.

At the end of the second year, we received a shocking surprise. As we were analyzing the data, we found out that the instructor had changed the course from the first year! Between the first and second year, the instructor had started learning about social psychological interventions (our project was evaluating one such intervention), and the instructor decided to add some social-psychological exercises to the recitations for underprepared students. This compromised our experiment at several levels. First, the exercises added by the instructor were similar to the intervention we were testing. Second, these underprepared students were precisely the students at whom our intervention was aimed. Therefore, of course, we had to remove that particular set of students from the analysis of the replication year. Our power for detecting significance was lowered, and most important without that segment of underprepared students, some of our findings from the first year changed.

Why would the instructor do such a thing? The instructor was very interested in helping her students and in continuing to improve her course. This is just the type of instructor with whom we want to work, but this interest also leads to the possibility that an instructor could make small changes to their course during the experiment without understanding the effect of these changes on the experiment. The instructor collaborating with us was very sorry. The mistake was a combination of her lack of training in social-science research protocols and our assumption that she understood what we meant when we requested that she keep her course the same from the first year to the second year. Perhaps we should have realized that she might make changes because this is her normal way of teaching. The upshot is that just before the second year, we should have reviewed with the instructor all of the details of her course and the protocol of our experiment.

WHAT DO YOU THINK LED YOU TO MAKE IT?

We had worked very closely with the instructor the first year and had worked through all of the details. The instructor asked very good questions about the experimental details and assisted by suggesting modifications to the procedure to better fit into her course. In addition, the experimental procedure went very smoothly during the first year. Therefore, for the replication of the experiment in the second year, we assumed the procedure would run exactly as in the first year. Consequently, we were not as vigilant for the second year. What we did not take into account was the instructor's lack of detailed understanding of the social-science research methods that our experiment followed. She did not fully appreciate the constraints that the procedure placed on her course. We also did not take into account (or realize) the instructor's passion for constantly making changes to her course in an effort to continually help her students succeed.

WHAT DID YOU LEARN FROM IT?

When working with instructors in evaluating teaching innovations in their courses, never assume that the instructors understand the full extent of the constraints that the study imposes on their course. Even if you have worked with the instructors before, the instructors' expertise is not in social-science research. It is not their responsibility to know the literature behind the implementation or the constraints of a research study. Therefore, when working with instructors, one needs to ask detailed questions about the course, such as the structure and logistics of the course, or if changes are being made from the previous year. In addition, after the discussion of the course and how the innovation is going to be implemented, the procedure needs to be written to ensure that all parties understand exactly how the innovation is going to be implemented and exactly the logistics of the course. This needs to occur every time the innovation is being implemented to ensure that the instructor is not making changes to the course that they did not think to tell you about. We also need to realize that the types of instructors that want to work with us on evaluating classroom innovations are ones who care deeply for their students and are constantly modifying their courses in order to improve them. This means that we need to realize how difficult it is for them to make changes in a controlled fashion. Robust evaluations of classroom innovations take multiple semesters, which could mean multiple years if the class is offered only once a year.

IF YOU WERE TODAY FACING THE SITUATION THAT LED UP TO THE MISTAKE, WHAT WOULD YOU DO DIFFERENTLY?

In the second (replication) year, we would meet with the instructor and review the details and constraints of the experiment. In addition, we would ask if she was thinking of making any changes in the course. We would again walk through, in detail, the structure and logistics of the course. This is to ensure that the instructor is not making any changes that she does not perceive as a modification but nevertheless may affect the validity of the study. If the instructor is planning modifications, then we and the instructor would together decide whether those changes could affect the integrity of the experiment and what the next steps would be. We suggest involving the instructor in these conversations as it is important to make the instructor a partner in the project. Respect the instructor and what they are is trying to do in the course.

WHAT MIGHT THE STUDENTS AND YOUNG PROFESSIONALS OF TODAY LEARN FROM IT?

When conducting classroom research, have high respect for your instructor colleague. Attempt to understand the project from their point of view. The most important criteria to the instructor are (1.) how this innovation is going to improve my students' experience or learning; (2.) how the students will view this innovation; and (3.) how the students will view the evaluation design (fair, number of surveys to fill out, amount of outside participation, etc.). In addition, we as researchers have to understand that the instructors do not think of this setting as a research laboratory; this is their class. There is emotion tied to their class and any changes to it that might occur as a consequence of a research study.

CRITICAL THINKING QUESTIONS

1. There are many challenges to conducting research in classrooms, some of which are illustrated in this essay. What are the advantages or reasons for expending the effort to conduct research in the classroom rather than in a psychology laboratory?

2. As discussed in this essay, when instructors participate in a study, they may have to postpone making other changes to the course that they might want to make immediately. What are the benefits (to society, to that particular course, to the instructor) of doing so relative to "depriving" that year's students of changes that now are postponed to the next year?

3. Thinking about how you or your friends might react if you were in a class in which an experiment was being conducted, would you (or friends) have objections to the class being involved in an experiment? If so, what kinds of things might the researchers and instructors do to mitigate any concerns you might have?

ERROR IN STATISTICAL ANALYSIS

45 SELF-HELP CAN BE NO HELP AT ALL
Some Unambiguous Advice[1]

Donald J. Foss
University of Houston

SELF-HELP CAN BE NO HELP AT ALL

Early in my psychology education I felt I had a pretty good grip on basic data analysis. After a series of dreary summer jobs during college, I received a National Science Foundation undergraduate summer fellowship prior to my senior year. Hooray! It was focused on statistics and also allowed me work in a psychology lab (low pay but highly rewarding). So I was ready for the stats classes in graduate school at Minnesota and did okay in them, even taking some that were not required. Then, after graduation, I got to do a post-doc at Harvard. It was an exciting time. Psychology was in the midst of a big change from thinking of itself as the study of behavior, to studying mental (cognitive) processes and products. Cambridge, Massachusetts, was at the epicenter of this change. It was possible to ask questions that were invigorating and new.

And I was ripe to make a foolish mistake. Part of it was due to ignorance and part to unwarranted pride. I thought my Minnesota-trained experimental and statistical skills matched up (at least) well with those of the other post-docs and grad students in the Harvard environment. At the same time, though, I was also anxious—and reluctant to ask for help because I did not want to appear ignorant.

Before I reveal my blunder, let me provide some additional context to give you an idea of the research question and the method used to test it. The following was a big goal (and still is): How do we understand spoken language? How do we characterize the mental products of comprehension, and how are those products constructed in our minds? One avenue for examining these issues in English is the (quite common) existence of ambiguous sentences. To take an extremely simple example, the last word in, *The man is holding a pipe,* can mean either a smoking device or a tube for conveying a fluid. Or, in a more complex example, the elephant in, *The elephant is ready to lift,* can be either the agent of the sentence—it is about to do some lifting; or the object—it has been prepared to be lifted.

[1]No kidding, I owe a debt of thanks to Arturo Hernandez, Barbara Kelsey, Benjamin Tamber-Rosenau, L. Allen Witt, and Chris Wong for helpful and constructive comments.

MacKay (1966) had proposed three possibilities for how we might deal with ambiguity. We might immediately (and unconsciously) somehow recover *both* interpretations and use other information to help choose between them. Or, we might momentarily *delay* getting either interpretation until we get enough information from the context to develop the correct interpretation. Or, we might develop just *one* interpretation and hold onto it unless further context tells us we have to change. MacKay had presented some evidence and arguments in favor of the delay theory. But in his experimental task the participants had taken a long time to respond. I wanted something more immediate, thinking that would be closer to natural comprehension.

Three of us (Foss, Bever, & Silver, 1968) constructed a set of ambiguous sentences and two unambiguous control sentences for each ambiguous one. Thus, for the ambiguous sentence, *The boy is looking up the street*, we had both, *The boy is gazing up the street*, and *The boy is looking up the address*. We also had a large set of normally unambiguous sentences. Each participant in our study heard a list of sentences and immediately after, each one was shown a picture that might or might not show what the sentence said. Their task was to say "right" as quickly as they could if the picture matched the sentence as they understood it or "wrong" if it did not. For the ambiguous sentences, the picture sometimes represented one of its meanings and sometimes the other one. We measured how long it took participants to start saying the response (the Reaction Time, RT) and whether they made a mistake.

If, as we suspected, the listener constructs just one interpretation, then the RT after an ambiguous sentence would be longer when the picture showed the other interpretation. That seems sensible. However, there is a possible problem: Maybe one of the two pictures is just harder to interpret than the other. We didn't want our time differences to be due to the pictures, so we designed and carried out a more complex experiment. I'll skip over the details, but I still believe that the logic of the design was nice, even elegant. However, the data got very messy.

Here's where the statistics come in. One reason things got messy is that the RTs were not normally distributed (i.e., they didn't yield a bell-shaped curve). Of course, that's the distribution they teach in beginning stats classes and the one assumed to be the case for many standard statistical tests of significance. So I transformed the data to more nearly normalize them by following another then-standard recommendation (i.e., taking the logarithm of each RT). Then, for reasons I'll also skim over—but due to the more complex experimental design I just mentioned—I did yet another transformation on the data. Finally, I conducted typical statistical analyses (e.g., *t*-tests) on the resulting numbers.

At the time, I felt confident that the analysis was correct and justified. Looking back, though, I get an image of the data set flopping around like a fish in the bottom of my experimental boat and me ruthlessly beating them into submission to get them to fit the required statistical assumptions. But the study (more-or-less) worked out, we had a good story to tell, it got published in a very respectable journal, and it's been cited over 100 times. So I didn't worry about it until I later gave it some more thought.

In retrospect, even though I think the basic idea holds (at least under certain circumstances), I'm not sure that our particular study would replicate, primarily because the tests and conclusions we drew from them may not have been appropriate for the transformed, possibly mangled, data. That's not equivalent to faking data or plagiarizing or other serious sins, but I didn't really know whether what I had done was right at the time I did it. And I could have.

In truth, while I knew enough about statistics to avoid some common problems, by the end of that project I really didn't know whether all the manipulations I had done would impress a real statistician or make him or her either faint or burst into laughter. Nor did I ask.

During that wonderful National Science Foundation (NSF) summer program, a very famous and path-breaking woman named Gertrude Cox (the "first lady of statistics") came to talk to us. She had collaborated with another outstanding statistician, William Cochran, and I learned about a now-classic book on experimental design by Cochran and Cox.

If I'd had the sense to think of it, in five minutes I could have walked to the office of William Cochran himself, who was then at Harvard. Or, even simpler, there were people just an elevator ride away—or even on the same floor as my office!—who knew much more about analyzing data than I did. Our study likely would have benefited enormously from consulting with one or more of them.

So (at least one of) my biggest research mistake(s) was due to foolish pride, what the Greeks called hubris. It had multiple sources, including a reluctance to acknowledge and admit what I didn't know. But now I know that there is always someone who knows more than I do, including things that can help me. That's true for you, too. I learned to ask for help—and to welcome others as collaborators. As should you. My experience may have a redeeming quality if it can help convey a simple yet very important lesson: **Embrace the fact that you are not an expert in everything. Seek help when you suspect that you might possibly benefit from it. Research partners are very valuable.**

When you hear an acceptance speech from someone who has received a major award (e.g., the Nobel Prize, an Academy Award), the supremely accomplished recipient almost always says that he or she couldn't have done it alone. They aren't kidding.

REFERENCES

Foss, D. J., Bever, T. G., & Silver, M. (1968). The comprehension and verification of ambiguous sentences. *Perception & Psychophysics*, *4*(5), 304–306. doi:10.3758/BF03210520

Mackay, D. G. (1966). To end ambiguous sentences. *Perception & Psychophysics*, *1*(12), 426–436. doi:10.3758/BF03215819

CRITICAL THINKING QUESTIONS

1. When is the last time you asked someone for help with a research problem? Was it easy for you to do it? Why, or why not?

2. Think about a current problem that interests you or that you are working on. Who could help you that you haven't thought to ask? Should you approach him or her?

3. If you ask someone for help, and you get it, should that person be a coauthor on your paper or simply get a footnote?

46

A THIRD-VARIABLE PROBLEM IN FACE RECOGNITION

Isabel Gauthier

Vanderbilt University

I study learning in visual-object recognition, in particular, how people change how they process objects as they gain expertise with a category. One interesting hallmark of expertise is how face processing differs from the way we recognize most objects, in a so-called holistic manner. If you ask someone to make a judgment about part of a face, let's say, whether the eyes are the ones of their friend Sally, and you tell them to ignore the mouth in the picture because you may have changed it, they cannot do this very well. People are unable to process Sally's eyes independently of the mouth they are shown with, and so we say they process the face "holistically." In contrast, most nonface objects are not processed in this way; we do not have trouble ignoring the rest of the object when paying attention to one of its parts.

Early in my career, I tested the theory that holistic processing is the result of expertise with faces. I predicted that if we trained people in the laboratory to become experts at recognizing novel objects (called "Greebles"), they would come to process them more holistically. The results supported this prediction, as the participants found it increasingly difficult to ignore Greeble parts as a result of training (Gauthier & Tarr, 2002).

Years later, I became interested in individual differences and considered a prediction that follows from the work I just discussed. People who are very good at face recognition should process faces more holistically than those who are poor at face recognition. In fact, we and others suspected that those who, through experience, had become very good at recognizing faces, were probably performing well *because* they were using a holistic strategy. Between 2010 and 2012, *Psychological Science* published three papers from three different labs on the relation between face-recognition ability and holistic processing of faces. The first paper (Konar, Bennett, & Sekuler, 2010) reported that there was no correlation between face-recognition ability and holistic processing. The second paper was from my lab (Richler, Cheung, & Gauthier, 2011), and in it, we argued that Konar and colleagues had failed to find a correlation because they were using a flawed measure of holistic processing (one that was confounded by response-bias issues; see Richler et al., 2011, supplemental information for a detailed explanation). With a different measure of holistic processing that did not have such issues, we found that holistic processing of faces was correlated with face-recognition ability. The third paper (Wang, Li, Fang, Tian, & Liu, 2012) also found such a correlation, and other papers were published soon after that also found face-recognition ability correlated with holistic processing.

As the dust appeared to settle on this issue, things got more complicated. At this point, my colleagues and I had noticed that all existing measures of holistic processing used in this work had low reliability. The tasks were quite sensitive at picking up evidence of holistic processing in a group of subjects, but they did not measure with much fidelity differences between people in holistic processing. The correlation between the magnitude of holistic processing on the first and second half of these tests was only about r = .2. Sadly, this is not rare for measures that are created for group studies and later repurposed to measure individual differences. Most critically, if a test does not even correlate with itself, it is difficult to expect it to correlate with anything else! And indeed, in the research I reviewed above, the correlations between holistic processing and face-recognition ability, while significant, were often fairly low.

Therefore, we set out to create a new test explicitly for the purpose of measuring, in a reliable way, individual differences in holistic processing. We published this more reliable test of holistic processing (Richler, Floyd, & Gauthier, 2014), proud to offer a tool that would be useful for many other researchers interested in individual differences. But there was one surprise: When we measured the correlation between holistic processing on this test and face-recognition ability, it was virtually zero! We replicated the study and found, again, no correlation. This made no sense to me: The new test was picking up larger holistic-processing effects than previous measures, with greater reliability, and yet the correlation we had previously observed had disappeared!

Much head scratching and speculation ensued, and it took a surprisingly long time to come up with the solution. The error we had made is clearly described in any introductory statistics textbook. It is the third-variable problem, whereby a third variable, one that researchers are often not even thinking about, accounts for the causal relation between two others.

In the present case, this variable is the repetition of faces on a given test. In the study of face recognition, it is very common for researchers to ask participants to complete a large number of trials (several hundred) that are created using a relatively small set of faces (the number varies, it could be 10, 20, but generally many fewer than 100). The measure of face-recognition ability that our research was using is called the Cambridge Face Memory Test (CFMT; Duchaine & Nakayama, 2006), and it has participants learn six specific faces that they have to recognize through a series of trials. The test essentially measures how well individuals can learn to recognize these faces in new images showing the faces in new viewpoints. Importantly, all the measures of holistic processing that had produced correlations had used a small number of faces that were repeated on many trials, measuring how well participants could attend to some parts and ignore other parts. These tests of holistic processing were not meant to be learning tests, but they *allowed* learning because of this repetition. In contrast, and for reasons that had nothing to do with avoiding learning, the new reliable test of holistic processing we had created used a completely new set of faces on each trial. In a new experiment, we were able to show that face-recognition ability as measured on the CFMT correlated with a test of holistic processing that repeated faces but not with an identical test that did not repeat faces (Richler, Floyd, Gauthier, 2015). In other words, we found that some people were better than others at using face repetition on tests of holistic processing, and that those were the same people who were better on the CFMT. To be clear, the CFMT measures face recognition ability, and our new test of holistic processing measured holistic processing, but in addition, each of them also measured how well people could learn from repeating faces throughout the test. Repetition of stimuli is just one of many aspects of a test that can contribute to its score: It is impossible to remove all such contributions to performance on a test, but when interpreting correlations between measures, it is always important to keep in mind there may be such a variable that could explain the relation.

This line of research left us with more puzzles to solve, because if expertise with nonface objects increased holistic processing, as I found in my dissertation, then we should expect this to be the case for faces, too. My colleagues and I are still working on this question, but what we learned in the process is that the third-variable problem lurks everywhere, and it is especially easy to miss when it comes from procedures that we barely think about, like repeating stimuli over trials to collect more data from each participant.

REFERENCES

Duchaine, B., & Nakayama, K. (2006). The Cambridge Face Memory Test: Results for 4 neurologically intact individuals and an investigation of its validity using inverted 5 face stimuli and prosopagnosic participants. *Neuropsychologia, 44,* 576–585.

Gauthier, I., & Tarr., M. J. (2002). Unraveling mechanisms for expert object recognition: Bridging brain activity and behavior. *JEP: HPP, 28*(2), 431–446.

Konar, Y., Bennett, P. J., & Sekuler, A. B. (2010). Holistic processing is not correlated with face-identification accuracy. *Psychological Science, 21,* 38–43.

Richler, J. J., Floyd, R. J., Gauthier, I. (2014). The Vanderbilt Holistic Face Processing Test: A short and reliable measure of holistic face processing. *Journal of Vision, 14*(11), 10.

Richler, J. J., Floyd, R. J., & Gauthier, I. (2015). About-face on face recognition ability and holistic processing, *Journal of Vision, 15*(9),15.

Richler, J. J., Cheung, O. S., & Gauthier, I. (2011). Holistic processing predicts face recognition. *Psychological Science, 22,* 464–471.

Wang, R., Li, J., Fang, H., Tian, M., & Liu, J. (2012). Individual differences in holistic processing predict face recognition ability. *Psychological Science, 23,* 169–177.

CRITICAL THINKING QUESTIONS

1. When we create a new test to measure a certain construct, what are other aspects of the test, beyond stimulus repetition, that could create spurious correlations with other tests?

2. Do you think any test ever only measures only one construct? If not, what do you think researchers can do to get a purer measure of a construct of interest?

3. Tradition in a field of research can provide us with rules of thumb that are helpful, but how might it contribute "blind spots" in our research?

PART VIII

GENERALIZABILITY OF FINDINGS

47

NOT ESTABLISHING THE CROSS-CULTURAL VALIDITY OF MEASURES OF KEY CONSTRUCTS IN A HIGH-STAKES FIELD EXPERIMENT

J. Lawrence Aber

New York University

One of the most important tasks in conducting psychological research is to establish that the measures one uses in research reliably and validly index the constructs one intends to measure. Examples of constructs and measures in my subfield of developmental psychology abound. For example, the security of young children's attachment to their primary caregivers (the construct) is best measured by the pattern of young children's behaviors before, during, and after a brief separation from their parents in the "strange situation" paradigm (the measure; Ainsworth, 1970). Similarly, preschool children's ability to delay gratification (the construct) is measured by minutes of time they wait for a preferred reward in the "Marshmallow Test" (the measure) (Mischel, Shoda, & Rodriquez, 1988). But how do we know if measures truly index the constructs we wish to investigate? The two key ways are by establishing the measures' reliability and validity. The reliability of a measure is an index of the consistency of responses to the measure. The validity of a measure is an index of the extent to which it is measuring what it is supposed to measure.

The biggest research mistake I've made recently was to rely on evidence demonstrating the reliability of several measures of school-aged children's "self-regulation" as adequate to support the validity of the measures. I made this mistake by using the measures in the new cultures of Lebanon and Niger where the measures have never been used before. Let me explain the research context, the mistake, and its scientific and real-world implications.

For the last several decades, I have been conducting field experiments of school-based interventions to improve both the social-emotional development and academic learning of children. I began this work with studies in low-income and/or conflict-affected communities in the United States (Aber, Brown, Jones, & Roderick, 2010; Aber, Brown, Jones, Berg, & Torrente, 2011; Jones, Brown, & Aber, 2011), but starting in 2010, I began similar work in low-income and/or conflict-affected countries (e.g., Democratic Republic of Congo, Niger, and Lebanon). My colleagues and I view such research as opportunities both to learn what interventions work best to promote children's learning and development and also to test basic theoretical propositions in the developmental and learning sciences.

For the last seven years, I have been collaborating with the International Rescue Committee (IRC) to rigorously evaluate one of their interventions called "Learning in a Healing Classroom" (LIHC; Aber et al., 2017a, 2017b). We developed a theory of change that describes how the intervention is supposed to change features of children's social-emotional processes and in turn their literacy and numeracy skills and their behavior problems. (See Figure 47.1.) As you see, we hypothesized that LIHC would improve four features of their social-emotional development: hostile attribution bias (HAB: the tendency to attribute hostile intent to an ambiguous behavior of a peer), anger dysregulation (AD: the tendency to become angry in a social situation), sadness dysregulation (SD: the tendency to become sad in a social situation), and aggressive reactions (AR; the tendency to behave aggressively in a social situation).

The measures used to index these constructs entail the use of stories (hypothetical vignettes) that ask children to imagine and report on how they would think, feel, and behave in challenging situations with peers at school. Such measures have been used successfully in intervention research for several decades in the United States (Dodge et al., 2015; Aber, Jones, Brown, Chaudry, & Samples, 1998). Because "self-regulation" is considered by many researchers and practitioners to be a cross-culturally important construct, recent studies have begun to test the reliability and validity of its measurement across quite different Western cultures (Dodge & Frame, 1982; Dodge et al., 2015; Di Giunta et al., 2017). The results of these efforts to establish the reliability and validity of these measures of HAB, AD, SD and AR were so promising that we decided to use modest adaptations to them in our impact evaluations of LIHC in the African and Middle Eastern cultures of Niger and Lebanon and to check the reliability and validity of the measures in these non-Western cultures using baseline (preintervention) data collection with the participating kids. This is where the mistake arose.

We used responses to six stories to measure each of the four constructs' "reliability." In this case, reliability meant that children's responses on each story were positively correlated with children's responses on the other five stories. The most common way to describe this type of reliability is with a summary statistic called "Cronbach's alpha." Alphas range from zero (there is no correlation among responses to the items in the scale) to 1 (there is perfect correlation among responses). Generally, researchers trust measures as reliable if alpha ≥ 0.70.

In our study in Lebanon, alpha ranged from 0.79 to 0.89 in our sample of 5- to 16-year-old kids. This meant that children's responses to different stories were highly correlated with each other, as they should be if they were measuring HAB, AD, SD, and AR. Also, all four measures were positively correlated with each of the other measures, as prior theory and research in Western countries would predict. I found these preliminary analyses so encouraging that I concluded that the measures of HAB, AD, SD, and AR were not only reliable but cross-culturally valid.

FIGURE 47.1   ■   Theory of Change: LIHC+Mindfulness

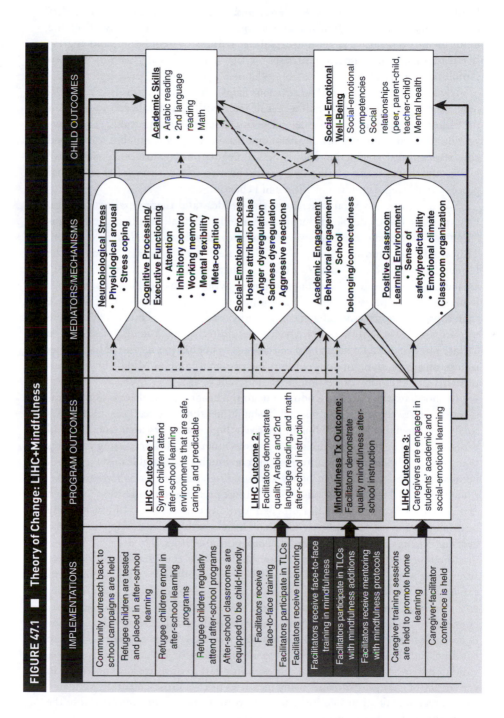

I failed to notice that there were severe "floor effects." What this means is that the vast majority of children responded "not at all likely" to nearly all of the items meant to measure anger dysregulation, sadness dysregulation, and aggressive reactions. This is a pattern of response that is not typically seen in Western samples of children.

It was only after testing the impact of LIHC on children's measures of self-regulation at "midline" (after half a year of intervention) that I began to question the cultural validity of the reliable and positively correlated measures. The intervention reduced children's hostile attribution bias (as we predicted), but it increased children's anger dysregulation and sadness dysregulation (against our predictions)! How could that be if these were reliable and valid measures of these social-emotional processes for refugee children in Niger and Lebanon?

We are left with several different ways to understand these puzzling findings. First, perhaps LIHC, despite its intention and design, actually made anger dysregulation and sadness dysregulation worse among Syrian refugee children in Lebanon. This would be a most serious problem, because it would be a violation of the Hippocratic oath: first do no harm! Second, perhaps the theory that low AD and SD are indices of positive adaptation doesn't apply to Syrian refugee children in Lebanon. It may be that expressing some anger and sadness dysregulation is more adaptive than expressing none, especially in conflict-affected countries. Third, perhaps these measures of AD and SD simply are not cross-culturally valid among Syrian refugee children in Lebanon. Perhaps anger and sadness dysregulation measured in this way is imposing Western definitions of these concepts on a complex Middle Eastern culture that views emotion expression in very different ways.

In short, are the puzzling findings due to the program, the theory, or the measures? In relatively low-stakes research, using a measure of uncertain validity is a small and reparable mistake. But in relatively high-stakes research, such as field experiments of interventions designed to serve vulnerable children, using measures of uncertain validity in a new culture is a big and much less reparable mistake. That's because practical actions (like policy and funding decisions on whether to continue to invest in interventions like LIHC) hinge precariously on results from such experiments. By using several measures of uncertain cross-cultural validity, I made a research mistake with serious potential implications both for the developmental and learning sciences and for the real world of programs for refugee children.

I believe I made this mistake because I judged that the reliability of the measures constituted adequate evidence of their cross-cultural validity. From this experience, I relearned how important it is to use measures of clear validity within new cultures. The best way to avoid this mistake is to use measures of key constructs that are already well validated within the culture in which the study is being conducted. But this option was not available to us at the time due to funding and time constraints. We faced a tough choice: We could use measures validated in other cultural contexts, or we could fail to measure key constructs in the theory of change. I consider using measures not yet cross-culturally validated to be a real mistake. But I consider not trying to measure concepts critical to the evaluation to be a bigger mistake.

REFERENCES

Aber. L., Brown, J., Jones, S., & Roderick, T. (2010). SEL: The history of a research–practice partnership. *Better: Evidence-based Education, 2*(2), 14–15.

Aber, L., Brown, J. L, & Jones, S. M., Berg, J., & Torrente, C. (2011). School-based strategies to prevent violence, trauma and psychopathology: The challenges of going to scale. *Development and Psychopathology, 23*(2011), 411–421.

Aber, J. L., Jones, S. M., Brown, J. L., Chaudry, N., & Samples, F., (1998). Resolving conflict creatively: Evaluating the developmental effects of a school-based violence prevention program in neighborhood and classroom context. *Development and Psychopathology, 10*(2), 187–213.

Aber, J. L., Torrente, C., Starkey, L., Johnston, B., Seidman, E., Halpin, P., . . . Wolf, S. (2017a). Impacts after one year of "Healing Classroom" on children's reading and math skills in DRC: Results from a cluster randomized trial. *Journal of Research on Educational Effectiveness,10*(3), 507–509.

Aber, J. L., Tubbs, C., Torrente, C., Halpin, P. F., Johnston, B., Starkey, L., . . . Wolf, S. (2017b). promoting children's learning and development in conflict-affected countries: Testing change process in the Democratic Republic of the Congo. *Development and Psychopathology, 29*, 53–67.

Ainsworth, M., & Bell, S. (1970). Attachment, exploration and separation: Illustrated by the behavior of one-year-olds in a strange situation. *Child Development, 41*(1), 49–67.

Di Giunta, L., Iselin, A. R., Eisenberg, N., Pastorelli, C., Gerbino, M., Lansford, J. E., . . . Thartori, E. (2017). Measurement invariance and convergent validity of anger and sadness self-regulation among youth from six cultural groups. *Assessment 24*(4), 484–502.

Dodge, K. A., & Frame, C. (1982). Social cognitive bias and deficits in aggressive boys. *Child Development, 53(3)*, 620–635.

Dodge, K. A., Malone, P. S., Lansford, J. E., Sorbring, E., Skinner, A. T., Tapanya, S., . . . Pastorelli, C. (2015). Hostile attributional bias and aggressive behavior in global context. *Proceedings of the National Academy of Sciences, 112*, 9310–9315. doi:10.1073/pnas.1418572112

Jones, S. M., Brown, J. L., & Aber, J. L. (2011). Two-year impacts of a universal school-based social-emotional and literacy intervention: An experiment in translational developmental research. *Child Development, 82*(2), 533–554.

Mischel, W., Shoda, Y., & Rodriquez, M. L. (1988). Delay of gratification in children. *Science, 244*(4909), 933–938.

CRITICAL THINKING QUESTIONS

1. Do you think that children's ability to regulate their angry and sad emotions are critical abilities in countries as different as the United States, Lebanon, and Niger? Why, or why not?

2. Do you think that researchers can reliably and validly measure anger and sadness dysregulation using the same methods in very different cross-cultural contexts? Why, or why not?

3. How serious a mistake do you think this researcher made?

4. Is there anything you could recommend to the researchers to help avoid making this mistake in the future?

48 ECOLOGICAL VALIDITY
Mistaking the Lab for Real Life

Karen E. Adolph

New York University

I have always prided myself on being "ecologically minded." I endorse the ecological approach of James Gibson (1979) and my graduate advisors, Eleanor Gibson (1988) and Ulric Neisser (1976), and I share their belief that the key to unlocking the mysteries of perception and action lies in the functional relations between animals and their natural environments. In *The Ecological Approach to Visual Perception*, James Gibson (1979, p. 3) wrote, "It is not true that the laboratory can never be like life. The laboratory must be like life!" Gibson didn't mean that researchers should only conduct naturalistic studies or try to simulate all the details of reality in the laboratory. He meant that controlled laboratory experiments must contain the critical characteristics—the "essential invariants"—of real-world perception and action (p. 305). Thus, ecological validity is central to ecological psychology: Experimental findings must generalize to the real-world phenomena we wish to explain.

In studies of infant locomotor development (my field), ecological validity is seldom a concern. Instead, for nearly a century, most researchers (including me) have encouraged barefoot, nearly naked infants to step on treadmills or take continuous, forward steps along straight paths over uniform ground (reviewed in Adolph & Robinson, 2013, 2015). Certainly no researcher believes that babies only generate alternating leg movements or only walk barefoot and naked along continuous, forward, straight paths. Rather, the practical limitations of recording technologies and researchers' desire to experimentally control biomechanical factors led to reliance on treadmill stepping and the "straight-path" test. Moreover, the long tradition of using these not-very-ecologically valid paradigms generated a wealth of robust, detailed data about developmental improvements in infants' gait (step length, timing between legs, joint angles, etc.). So what's the harm?

Eleanor Gibson's focus on the relations between perception and action led her to adopt a very different paradigm, in which infants navigate obstacles in their path. In Gibson's studies, and presumably in the real world, the ground is not uniform, and infants do not take continuous, forward, alternating steps. Babies stop. They detour. They engage in exploratory activities. They find alternative methods of locomotion or ask their caregivers for help. Infants detect "affordances" (or lack of them) for locomotion.

Gibson's most famous task is the "visual cliff"—a glass-covered, illusory drop-off. Gibson's followers expanded on her work with variations of the visual cliff and a wild assortment of other obstacles (reviewed in Adolph & Kretch, 2012). For example, I've tested infants at the edge of real drop-offs, gaps in the surface of support, uphill/ downhill and high/low friction slopes, narrow ledges and bridges, foam pits, and so on. In some cases, we altered infants' bodies with lead-weighted shoulder-packs, Teflon-soled shoes, or platform shoes. Sometimes caregivers told infants to go and sometimes to stop (reviewed in Adolph & Robinson, 2013, 2015).

Outside the laboratory, of course, no infant walks down steep slopes wearing Teflon-soled shoes, and no caregiver encourages infants to do so. Like Eleanor Gibson, I intentionally designed my tasks to be novel. In my view, locomotor development—indeed all of motor development—requires learning to perceive changing body-environment relations and to select and modify actions accordingly. Infants must learn to move while coping with novel changes in their bodies and the environment. Following James Gibson's mandate to make the lab like life, my tasks were designed to capture the novelty and variability of real-world locomotor development. So what's the problem?

My mistake was that I confused tests of infants' abilities (what they can do in structured lab tasks) with their real-world experiences (what they actually do outside the lab). I did not start by describing infants' real-world locomotor development. Instead, I simply assumed that the essential ingredients of natural locomotor experience are novelty and variability. After 20+ years of testing infants walking along straight paths, navigating novel obstacles, and coping with experimental changes to their bodies, I finally thought to ask: What are the real-life experiences that support learning to locomote? How, where, and why do mobile infants walk to places of their own choosing? We finally began to describe infants' spontaneous locomotion during free play at home and in laboratory playrooms.

Counter to common sense and a century of laboratory research, during real-world locomotion, infants do not primarily walk to destinations. Although infants walk to caregivers, toys, and snacks when tested in the straight-path test and on raised walkways with an obstacle blocking their path, such goals are not the typical impetus for real-world locomotion. Head-mounted eye tracking shows that destinations viewed while stationary rarely instigate locomotion, and bouts of locomotion rarely terminate at a destination (Cole, Robinson, & Adolph, 2016; Hoch, Rachwani, & Adolph, 2017; Karasik, Adolph, Tamis-LeMonda, & Zuckerman, 2012). Instead, infants stop walking in the middle of the floor or take steps in place. They walk twice as much with no one to play with than while playing with their caregivers, and they walk just as much in an empty room as in a toy-filled room (Hoch, O'Grady, & Adolph, in press). Apparently, movement is its own reward. Although my tasks with drop-offs, slopes, and so on provide a perfectly good test of infants' perception of affordances, they do not capture the essential characteristics of how infants learn to locomote during natural activity.

A second surprise was more fortuitous, given my many years of work in this field. Gait during free play validates the straight-path test. Using large instrumented floor, we replicated the developmental progression in infants' gait (speed, step length, etc.) during free play with all the starts and stops, omnidirectional steps, and curved paths that are eliminated in the straight-path test. This means that researchers needn't coerce infants to walk in unnatural ways. Moreover, discontinuous, omnidirectional, curved paths characterize infants' first steps and continue unabated over the next nine months (Lee, Cole, Golenia, & Adolph, 2018). But these essential characteristics of real-world walking are absent in the traditional straight-path task and correspondingly absent from theories of locomotor development.

A final surprise concerns the quantity and variety of natural locomotion. In a cluttered environment while playing with caregivers, toddlers average 2,400 steps and travel the distance of eight football fields per hour, traipsing en route over most available surfaces (Adolph et al., 2012). In short, infants acquire immense amounts of time-distributed, variable practice with locomotion—exactly the sort of training regimen that leads to functional, flexible behavior. Happily for me, the description of infants' natural locomotor development, however tardy, is consistent with my hypothesis that infants' real-world experiences support learning to perceive and exploit changing body-environment relations, and this hypothesis can now be tested in ecologically valid experiments.

What is the take-home message from my mistake? Researchers in any field must remind themselves that participants' abilities in structured lab tasks do not necessarily reflect participants' actual behaviors outside the lab. And the best way to ensure ecological validity in structured lab tasks is to start with a rich description of real-world behavior.

REFERENCES

Adolph, K. E., Cole, W. G., Komati, M., Garciaguirre, J. S., Badaly, D., Lingeman, J. M., . . . Sotsky, R. B. (2012). How do you learn to walk? Thousands of steps and dozens of falls per day. *Psychological Science, 23*, 1387–1394.

Adolph, K. E., & Kretch, K. S. (2012). Infants on the edge: Beyond the visual cliff. In A. Slater & P. Quinn (Eds.), *Developmental psychology: Revisiting the classic studies*. London, UK: Sage.

Adolph, K. E., & Robinson, S. R. (2013). The road to walking: What learning to walk tells us about development. In P. Zelazo (Ed.), *Oxford handbook of developmental psychology* (pp. 403–443). New York, NY: Oxford University Press.

Adolph, K. E., & Robinson, S. R. (2015). Motor development. In L. Liben & U. Muller (Eds.), *Handbook of child psychology and developmental science* (7th ed., Vol. 2 Cognitive Processes, pp. 114–157). New York, NY: Wiley.

Cole, W. G., Robinson, S. R., & Adolph, K. E. (2016). Bouts of steps: The organization of infant exploration. *Developmental Psychobiology, 58*, 341–354.

Gibson, E. J. (1988). Exploratory behavior in the development of perceiving, acting, and the acquiring of knowledge. *Annual Review of Psychology, 39*, 1–41.

Gibson, J. J. (1979). *The ecological approach to visual perception*. Boston, MA: Houghton Mifflin.

Hoch, J. E., O'Grady, S., & Adolph, K. E. (in press). It's the journey, not the destination: Locomotor exploration in infants. *Developmental Science.*

Hoch, J., Rachwani, J., & Adolph, K. E. (2017, April). *Why do infants move? Locomotor exploration is more random than destination directed.* Paper presented at the meeting of the Society for Research in Child Development, Austin, TX.

Karasik, L. B., Adolph, K. E., Tamis-LeMonda, C. S., & Zuckerman, A. (2012). Carry on: Spontaneous object carrying in 13-month-old crawling and walking infants. *Developmental Psychology, 48,* 389–397.

Lee, D. K., Cole, W. G., Golenia, L., & Adolph, K. E. (2018). The cost of simplifying complex developmental phenomena: A new perspective on learning to walk. *Developmental Science, 21,* e12615.

Neisser, U. (1976). *Cognition and reality: Principles and implications of cognitive psychology.* San Francisco, CA: W. H. Freeman.

CRITICAL THINKING QUESTIONS

1. How do tradition, practical constraints, and reductionist thinking contribute to laboratory studies that lack ecological validity?

2. How might the lack of ecological validity lead to erroneous theories?

3. What can you, as a researcher, do to ensure that the phenomena in your laboratory studies reflect the real-world phenomena you wish to explain?

Author Note: Work on this article was supported by National Institute of Health and Human Development Grants R37-HD33486 and R01-HD33486 to Karen E. Adolph.

49

A MAJOR ERROR IN THE EVALUATION OF PSYCHOLOGICAL TREATMENTS FOR ANXIETY

David H. Barlow
Boston University

A number of years ago, with the help of a large grant from the National Institute of Mental Health, my clinical research team and I were evaluating new treatments for generalized anxiety disorder (GAD), which consists of a debilitating and almost continuous experience of anxiety characterized by intense worry about any number of different situations and a state of very unpleasant arousal and muscle tension (Barlow, Rapee, & Brown, 1992). These individuals are always anticipating the next disaster that might be around the corner and so are in a continual state of anxious readiness that often results in substantial fatigue by the end of the day. The problem is, the worry and anxiety never really dissipate but switch from one topic to another. We treated one group with what at the time was a new application of cognitive therapy directed at their attributions and appraisals of the severity of the threat so that they could better cope with whatever stressful situations they encountered. In a second group, we evaluated the effects of deep muscle relaxation, which was focused more on the high levels of arousal and tension these individuals were feeling. Finally, we combined those two interventions, a combination we hypothesized would be the most effective since it addressed both facets of GAD. We randomly assigned 65 carefully diagnosed patients to one of these three treatment conditions and compared the outcomes to those from a waitlist control group who were assessed but did not receive treatment. Patients in the waitlist control group were all treated after the study was over. This type of experiment is called a "randomized clinical trial," which is the gold standard for evaluating the effects of drug or psychological treatments.

It is very important to establish in these clinical trials not only whether the treatment is better than no therapy at all but also whether is it better than an alternative therapy. These kinds of comparisons help us isolate the treatment's active ingredients or what is unique about the treatment as the important factor responsible for improvement, rather than alternative sources of explanation for any improvement, such as placebo effects, patient expectancies, or the natural healing process that occurs with the passage of time. In other words, is it valid to say that the treatment itself is effective? We call this type of validity "internal validity" because it refers to ruling out factors that may influence improvement other than the treatment itself.

But there is another kind of validity that is important in these types of trials, which we call "external validity." This refers to the extent to which an internally valid intervention is effective in different settings or under different circumstances from those where it was tested and how easily can it be disseminated and implemented in those settings. To take an extreme example, if doctors develop a treatment that is very expensive, and painful as well, many patients would be reluctant to undergo this treatment, particularly if an alternative treatment that was cheaper and less painful was nearly as good. There are other factors that determine if a treatment is externally valid in addition to acceptability and cost-effectiveness, including how generally effective the treatment is with different types of patients. So, if a treatment is not acceptable to patients, is too expensive, or works only with a few people, we would conclude it's not externally valid.

As you can probably guess, treating this many patients in a clinical trial over a period of three or four years in a research setting is expensive, since all patients receive free treatment, and also we must pay for the cost for research and personnel carrying out the roles as therapists and evaluators, and so on, so it's important to get it right. But it wasn't until the trial was over that we realized our mistake. Basically, the study was internally valid in that it was capable of ruling out many alternative sources of explanation for change, other than the treatment itself, but we had failed to recognize the substantial threats to external validity. This was because we thought it very important from the point of view of internal validity to make sure that all patients got exactly the same "dose" of treatment. So they each saw the therapist for same amount of time to make sure there weren't any differences in time spent with the therapist that could have introduced therapeutic healing factors not directly associated with the treatment procedures. For this reason, all patients received 15 sessions of treatment no matter how long the treatment actually was supposed to take. Thus, the treatment consisting of relaxing exercises alone might typically take five or six sessions, but we continued work with these patients on relaxation for 15 sessions. The combined treatment, on the other hand, covering both relaxation exercises and cognitive therapy, really should have taken a bit longer to be delivered in an intelligible and reasonable manner, but we insisted on fitting everything into 15 sessions.

What happened was that patients receiving relaxation exercises alone became bored with the treatment after five or six sessions and dropped out to a significantly greater extent than from the other treatments, somewhat confounding our ability to evaluate the results. In the condition where people received the combined treatment, on the other hand, only about half as many patients responded positively to treatment as in the other two conditions, and this was the group we expected to do the best! When we looked closely at what we had done, the problem seemed to be that we were attempting to cram so much information into each session that the patient never had a chance to really absorb the treatment sufficiently.

Since that time, the community of clinical scientists doing research on psychological and drug treatments has learned a great deal about the proper ways to conduct these clinical trials. We are always attempting to learn from each other's work and from each other's mistakes, so that the quality of the science we undertake improves, and we can make better determinations of which treatments are truly effective for patients or are "evidenced based." What we and others learned from this rather serious mistake is that, while it's extremely important to determine that the treatment is working because of the specific components of the treatment and not some unrecognized other factors (internal validity), it is just as important to evaluate treatments in the way they are likely to be delivered in frontline clinical settings such that they would feasible and acceptable to patients, as well as cost-effective (external validity.) Only by being sensitive to both types of validity can we conduct successful clinical trials.

REFERENCE

Barlow, D. H., Rapee, R. M., & Brown, T. A. (1992). Behavioral treatment of generalized anxiety disorders. *Behavior Therapy, 23, 551–570.*

CRITICAL THINKING QUESTIONS

1. Why could a clinical trial prove that a treatment is efficacious but still not have it adopted by clinicians and healthcare policymakers?

2. It has been established that deep relaxation exercises work for many anxiety disorders, but why didn't it work in this clinical trial?

3. Why is external validity as important as internal validity?

FAILURE TO UNDERSTAND THE "SYSTEM"

50 MISTAKES WERE MADE (BUT NOT BY ME)*

Stephen J. Ceci
Cornell University

I've made lots of mistakes, but the one that got me into hot water was when I was new to my career. I lacked the knowledge to mitigate the fallout before it caused enormous damage to my coauthor and myself. In fact, it led to my coauthor being denied tenure, which fortunately was retracted two years later in response to a lawsuit.

It was the fall of 1978, and I was a new assistant professor at the University of North Dakota. One day a senior colleague complained that his work was rejected by journal editors who accepted similar research by researchers at prestigious universities. I did not believe him, nor did my slightly more seasoned colleague, Doug Peters. We both suspected it was sour grapes, and before long, we were designing an experimental test of our colleague's allegation.

THE EXPERIMENT THAT GOT US INTO TROUBLE

Doug Peters and I gathered articles published in the top psychology journals in the previous 32 months. Each had been written by someone at a prestigious department of psychology (Stanford, Harvard, Yale, etc.). Our secretary retyped them, and we asked the original authors for permission to use these typescripts in an experimental test of journal fairness. We explained that we planned to send their typescript to the same journal that published it but with a fake name and institution on it; we would debrief editors and reviewers immediately after they sent us reviews/decisions, if they did not detect the ruse. Thirteen of these authors gave us permission. Simultaneously, we started collecting manuscripts written by colleagues at low-status institutions that had been rejected by these same journals. We planned to replace their low-status affiliations with prestigious ones (Harvard, Yale, and Stanford) and resubmit them to the same journals that rejected them.

Would editors fail to recognize already-published articles from their journals? If so, would these manuscripts be recognized by the reviewers as formerly published?

---

*With apologies to Carol Tavris's and Elliot Aronson's book by the same title.

If not, would they recommend rejection and, if so, on what grounds? On the other hand, would journals accept previously rejected manuscripts from low-status institutions when that affiliation was substituted for high-status ones? If both of these outcomes occurred, it would give some credence to our senior colleague's conspiracy theory.

The results from the thirteen resubmissions of accepted papers by authors at high-status institutions (one was excluded for technical reasons) were striking. Of the 38 reviewers and editors who handled them, only three (8%) detected the ruse, resulting in rejection by three editors. In these three cases we immediately debriefed the editors. The remaining nine manuscripts proceeded to be reviewed. Reviewers' failure to detect previously published work in major journals is interesting because they are touted by editors as experts on the topic. They should have been familiar with these papers because they had appeared in the same journals in the past 32 months—not so long as to be forgotten, yet not so recent as to still be on experts' to-read list. Of these nine undetected manuscripts, eight were rejected. Sixteen of the eighteen reviewers (89%) identified what they felt were fatal flaws in methodology and analyses, and they recommended against acceptance. The editors rejected the resubmissions and did not offer the option of revise and resubmit.

OBSTACLES IN CONDUCTING THE RESEARCH

From the beginning of this project, we encountered obstacles. An angry editor who detected the ruse notified our chairman. He threatened that because we were permitted to conduct such an unethical study it was fitting that our entire faculty be banned from publishing in his journal. In 1978, there was no established ethics review. We gave our chair a description of our plan, which stated we would obtain the approval of the original authors. We explained that we were not obtaining the approval of the journal editors/reviewers because doing so might compromise the study; the deception we proposed was mild compared to some experimental social psychology at the time.

Upon receipt of the editor's angry letter, the chair and senior faculty immediately reprimanded us; our secretary was ordered to stop typing manuscripts and letters (pre word-processors), and we received registered letters forbidding us to continue. Thus, we were forced to abandon an unfinished experimental condition (resubmitting the rejected manuscripts of authors at low-status institutions with high-status institutions on them). We were informed that until we signed an agreement to cease work on the study, all departmental resources would be withheld. This was not the most punitive action, however. Several months later, my coauthor Doug Peters, who was being considered for tenure, was criticized for exercising poor judgment in doing a study that could jeopardize the ability of colleagues to publish. He was denied tenure, which led to a lengthy appeals process and court case. Two years after being denied tenure, the university retracted its negative decision and awarded Peters retroactive tenure and promotion before the start of trial (Ceci & Peters, 1982).

The same angry editor also alerted other APA editors about our experiment, thus bringing our study to a screeching halt before it was completed. We published the results of the first part of the study, reporting the details of the editorial decisions to reject the papers that substituted low-status institutions for their original high-status ones (Peters & Ceci, 1980; 1982). By this time, the campaign to punish us had taken on national dimensions.

The journal that published our partial findings, *Behavioral and Brain Sciences*, published 56 commentaries, mostly from editors in various fields. Instantly, we were inundated with criticisms of two sorts. One concerned the ethics of deceiving editors and reviewers, and the other concerned publishing an incomplete design.

By today's standards, it is obvious that even though there were no institutional review boards (IRBs), we should have anticipated anger on the part of editors and reviewers. We were chided for "distressing and abusing" editors and reviewers. No fewer than seven commentators criticized us for being "ethically suspect" (Chubin, 1982), for example. "It is hard to see what benefits accrue to society . . . that outweigh the distress" (Beyer, 1982, p. 203). We had been too inexperienced to put ourselves in editors' and reviewers' shoes and "model-run" the procedures before launching them. We rationalized in the letter to our chair that what we were proposing was routine in experimental social psychology, which often employed deception more consequential than ours because, after all, we were not asking editors and reviewers to do anything different from what they routinely do—review manuscripts. In contrast, much research at the time deceived powerless subjects into thinking there was a crime in progress or to believe they were administering electric shocks to helpless victims. (Notably, none of these commentators had criticized deception studies that were common at that time.) The main difference between those studies and ours was that we deceived powerful people who controlled resources.

Fourteen commentators took us to task for publishing an incomplete experimental design. Of course, we planned a complete design, but we aborted it when the angry editor alerted other editors. We ceased all work when he did this, coincident with being forbidden to continue working on it. While commentators knew this, they still assailed us for going to press with an incomplete causal model. Others who heard about our study through the academic grapevine leveled accusations that our design was inadequate, and we should have withheld publication; we were depicted by some as incompetent miscreants.

So as mistakes go, ours nearly ended the career of Doug Peters, and even though he was granted retroactive tenure two years later under the shadow of a lawsuit, and he was promoted to full professor just a few years later, it haunted him until he retired two years ago.

REFERENCES

Beyer, J. M. (1902). Explaining an unsurprising demonstration: High rejection rates and scarcity of space. *Behavioral and Brain Sciences, 2*, 202–203.

Ceci, S. J., & Peters, D. (l982, September). Peer review: A study of reliability. *Change, 14*, 44–49.

Chubin, D. E. (1982). Reforming peer review: From recycling to reflexivity. *Behavioral and Brain Sciences, 2*, 204.

Peters, D., & Ceci, S. J. (l980). A manuscript masquerade: How well does the journal review process work? *The Sciences, 20*(7), 16–19.

Peters, D. P., & Ceci, S. J. (l982). A naturalistic study of psychology journals: The fate of published articles resubmitted. *Behavioral and Brain Sciences, 2*, 187–195.

CRITICAL THINKING QUESTIONS

1. Just because it is possible to publish controversial results in a prestigious journal does not necessarily mean that it is smart to publish them. If some day you have controversial findings, what are some of the relevant considerations in deciding whether you should publish them?

2. In the era of mandatory IRB review, do you think it is possible to replicate the Peters and Ceci study? What safeguards would you propose to gain IRB approval to replicate it?

3. The Peters and Ceci study resulted in both positive and negative outcomes for the authors. It nearly ended the career of one of the authors and prompted the other author to terminate his faculty appointment. But on the other hand, this study has been cited in excess of 1100 times (Google Scholar), making it one of the highest-impact publications by a psychologist at the University of North Dakota, and it led to important changes to the peer review process, notably changing from nonblind review to blind review in which the author(s)' identity and affiliation are unknown to reviewers. Given the mixed consequences, would you advise a new assistant professor today to launch an equally controversial study?

4. No mention was made about institutional culture, but at the time this study was launched (1978), the University of North Dakota's psychology department was intellectually conservative. It seemed to discourage risk taking by its faculty but also favored smaller pay differentials among the faculty and a greater sense of collective aims and effort. Other universities were different, and some actually embraced the Peters and Ceci study and recruited the authors, but they favored market-driven pay raises and perks and much greater differentials among faculty. Which type of institution do you think is the best fit for you?

A MISSED OPPORTUNITY TO IMPROVE ON CREDIBILITY ANALYSIS IN CRIMINAL LAW

51

Klaus Fiedler

University of Heidelberg

A cademic life is replete with errors and mistakes. So it should be easy to report one prominent example. But what is the biggest mistake one has committed as a behavioral scientist? My memorable mistake was in the field of applied psychology with severe and often existential consequences, related to my secondary professional identity as an expert witness in legal trials.

In criminal law, a decision on the guilt or innocence of a defendant has to be made in any case, even under high uncertainty, when no physical evidence is available and even in the absence of strong eyewitness testimony. In these most intricate cases of murder, rape, and serious assault, the judges' verdict still determines whether defendants go to jail for many years, lose their job, their family and, indeed, their existence. We all know these scenarios from the movies, but hardly anyone has ever experienced the reality of such court trials, in which scientists (typically psychologists) are assigned the role of expert witnesses whose judgment is to turn almost complete uncertainty into a verdict "beyond all reasonable doubt." What laypeople don't know is that the reality of many criminal court trials is even more scary and unbelievable than what the most dramatic movies depict.

The role I came to play for legal decisions in Germany started about two decades ago when I was invited to participate as an expert witness in several trials of the Federal High Court of Justice in Karlsruhe. This is the uppermost court in Germany. It is supposed to draw fundamental legal decisions, to which other, subordinate courts are then committed. A federal judge called me on the telephone and tackled my scientific superego, saying that it was my obligation to help them solve fundamental problems. In a first trial, I was part of a group of expert witnesses who helped the High Court to draw a decision against the use of a polygraph for lie detection. Despite some disagreement among experts, we arrived at a clear-cut decision, and the federal judges were obviously content with our work as scientific advisors.

So they soon came up with a new project, with a much wider bearing, namely, formulating scientifically sound rules for expert reviews of the credibility of witness reports. When no physical evidence (i.e., no finger prints, no DNA, no photo materials, and no computerized data) is available, then a single eyewitness's report often determines the verdict. That single witness is often the victim of rape or sexual assault, whose report typically provides aggravating evidence. The responsible job of a legal expert is to examine the witness's report and to arrive at a scientifically credible judgment about whether the witness has told the truth. In the absence of other evidence, the court will typically adopt the expert's opinion, deciding "guilty" when the expert classifies an aggravating witness report as veracious and "innocent" when the expert expresses doubts. The key role played by our professional peers in these existential decisions is enormous, and as I learned later from other criminal trials, expert mistakes and violations of scientific norms can be frightening. So, devising solid rules was very important.

A year later, we met again at the Federal High Court, and, in the context of an actual trial, several expert witnesses again presented their reviews as they might in a science symposium. This time, there was an impressive agreement among all experts, and we soon arrived at a set of guidelines for proper credibility analysis. These guidelines were distributed among all judges and criminal lawyers in Germany and—as I learned later from defense attorneys—had a profound impact on legal reality in Germany. The basic underlying principle was that credibility analysis must follow a distinct hypothesis-testing rule. Because of the Constitutional presumption that guilt has to be proven, an examination always has to start from the hypothesis that a defendant is innocent and, hence, that an incriminating witness report is invalid. The burden of proof in the diagnostic process is on establishing the alternative hypothesis that the witness report is true, and the defendant is therefore guilty.

We were all fascinated by the analogy to scientific hypothesis testing, and we congratulated each other for the big success. I was somehow reminded of the fruitful collaboration of American scientists and legal practitioners that is nicely documented in the article "From the Lab to the Police Station" (Wells et al., 2000). Our guidelines were indeed quite an accomplishment. Yet, in retrospect, I believe we missed an opportunity to make more strikes while the iron was hot, that is, as long as the judges in the High Court were so open to our advice. We failed to validate our guidelines at a more concrete level and to tackle specific deficits that would continue to undermine the quality of credibility analysis, as I would vividly experience in subsequent years. Indeed, I have to admit it should have been my role to chastise the expert panel for the failure to recognize these mistakes.

To illustrate, consider the most important method in credibility analysis (Rassin, 1999; Steller & Köhnken, 1989). It consists of a count of verbal symptoms that have been shown to be statistically related to the truth of a witness report (such as logical consistency, spatial-temporal links, spontaneous self-corrections). The starting hypothesis of innocence implies an initial zero count of truth symptoms. Only when a sufficient number of truth symptoms is found in the report will the alternative hypothesis be adopted that the defendant is guilty because the witness tells the truth. Whether the defendant is found guilty eventually depends on the overall number of truth symptoms detected in a witness's verbal report.

However, the overall number of obtained language features not only depends on whether the witness tells the truth but, first and foremost, on text length! A 10-page report is much more likely to contain many truth symptoms than a one-page report.

As an expert witness, I later had to struggle desperately with several cases in which this flagrant source of error was neglected. Experts simply ignored text length, thus confusing long reports with truthful reports. Conversely, it also happened that expert witnesses applied different ad hoc norms to short and long reports, considering one or two verbal symptoms in a very short report to be cogent evidence of truth (with disastrous consequences for the defendant). Or, to give another example, when a defendant's report overlapped 90% with an incriminating victim report, so that the critical text amounted to no more than 10% of the report, they would nevertheless count truth symptoms across the entire text. When I pointed out these obvious mistakes, experts would defend their practices, and judges would not listen to my methodological arguments. The iron was no longer hot. The small time window during which the legal system was open to psychological advice was closed. Our guidelines had been implemented, but only at an abstract level, too remote from the mundane problems that continue to cause tragic cases of injustice.

In retrospect, I'm afraid I missed the opportunity to contribute more to this serious legal issue. I don't know how much injustice could have been prevented, but I begin to understand that for scientists' life to be meaningful and fulfilling, scientists should not miss those stellar moments when they can apply their knowledge and skills to the solution of an important societal problem.

REFERENCES

Rassin, E. (1999). Criteria based content analysis: The less scientific road to truth. *Expert Evidence, 7,* 265–278.

Steller, M., & Köhnken, G. (1989). Criteria-based statement analysis. Credibility assessment of children's statements in sexual abuse cases. In D. C. Raskin (Ed.), *Psychological methods for investigation and evidence* (pp. 217–245). New York, NY: Springer.

Wells, G. L., Malpass, R. S., Lindsay, R. L., Fisher, R. P., Turtle, J. W., & Fulero, S. M. (2000). From the lab to the police station: A successful application of eyewitness research. *American Psychologist, 55*(6), 581–598.

CRITICAL THINKING QUESTIONS

1. What mistake did the expert panel make?

2. What could be done to take text length into account in credibility analysis?

3. What lesson is to be learned from this essay about scientists sharing their knowledge with the public?

52

THE IMPORTANCE OF PROFESSIONAL DISCOURSE

Jack M. Fletcher

University of Houston

The biggest mistake I have made in my professional career occurred when I strayed from a focus on concepts and methods to the author of the paper. I turned an argument about concepts and methods toward one that was personal and attacked the author for his writing style. In science, personal attacks, which are termed *ad hominem,* are always unfortunate because they address perceptions of people based on what they have written as opposed to the content of what they have written, thus shifting the focus away from scientific discourse. They also upset both the recipient of the attack and the attacker, sometimes when the response is also *ad hominem.*

My *ad hominem* mistake occurred early in my career. My mentor had a theory of reading disability that involved early difficulties with perceptual skills related to the processing of print. Another scientist published a series of studies questioning whether perceptual factors were involved in reading disability, identifying instead a problem with language skills. We wrote a paper criticizing the scientist over the methods used in his studies. He responded, and then we responded, again. Although the first paper was focused on methods, it had an edge that implied that anyone who thought the way this scientist thought was stupid. The second paper was overtly *ad hominem* and criticized the scientist for his writing style. I had never met the scientist, but my mentor was more than annoyed that the scientist had questioned his theory. Several years later, I met the scientist and found him engaging and interesting. I learned that it is much easier to criticize and attack a person one hasn't met, and that interest in personal attacks sometimes diminishes when the person is known beyond what they write. I regretted the *ad hominem* component of the article at the time, especially as research continued, and it became very clear that the scientist's hypotheses were correct. We became friends and eventually began to collaborate. One of my most highly cited papers is with this scientist.

From this experience, I learned to focus on ideas and methods and not make science personal. Although I frequently argue over ideas in the literature and on blog exchanges, I try to be careful not to make the arguments personal. I understand what it feels like to be subjected to personal attacks that include speculations about character and motive, having been the subject of *ad hominem* attacks. I remember especially being described as a "spin doctor of science" because of my subsequent research on beginning reading, which fed into a long-term debate about whether children need to be taught to read with phonics methods or simply allowed to discover reading through exposure. Our paper (Foorman, Francis, Fletcher, Schatschneider, & Mehta, 1998) was very controversial because it was interpreted as indicating that phonics worked best when, in fact, the paper showed that a comprehensive approach to reading instruction that included explicitly taught phonics was best for children struggling to learn to read. I believe that many individuals in the reading research and instruction community resort to personal attacks when they are not certain how to interpret scientific research and prefer to rely upon experience and observation.

In our current societal and political discourse, it is easy to observe *ad hominem* discourse where a person is attacked for motives, character, or other personal attributes instead of ideas or principles. This has been fueled by social media, such as Twitter and Facebook, but also bleeds into more conventional media, such as newspapers and blog exchanges within the professional community. In a recent study by Schroeder, Kardas, and Epley (2017), the investigators found that it was easy for people to attribute personal characteristics to printed material they read. In this situation, disagreements easily turn into perceptions of intellectual capacity and motive. However, when the same opinions are expressed by voice, attributions to personal characteristics were reduced, so that it was more difficult to personally denigrate the ideas even with disagreement.

I have learned to try and focus on the ideas and concepts involved in scientific discourse and to be wary when I begin to make personal attributions, even if I think they are correct or deserved. If I believe a piece I have written is too personal, I ask a colleague to read it and let it sit overnight before submitting or posting the material. I also think that this early experience, and others like it, have made me more relentlessly empirical, focusing on data and methods regardless of the idea of even my own hypothesis. I have become better, but hardly perfect, at appreciating and valuing diversity in viewpoints and the need for knowledge to accumulate. If I disagreed with the same scientist today, my first response would not be to write an article about the disagreement. I would engage the scientist first, make sure I understood my disagreement, and possibly even show him what I was writing before submitting it in the interest of fairly representing an alternative view.

Scientists, like politicians, are people. It is easy to think that someone is stupid, illiterate, or a jerk based on something he or she has written. But people are more complex, and we should always try and recognize that what a person writes or posts may lack a human context. By all means, argue and disagree, but do it without personal attacks, which don't really further scientific or societal discourse among people.

REFERENCES

Foorman, B. R., Francis, D. J., Fletcher, J. M., Schatschneider, C., & Mehta, P. (1998). The role of instruction in learning to read: Preventing reading failure in at-risk children. *Journal of Educational Psychology, 90,* 37–55.

Schroeder, J., Kardas, M., & Epley, N. (2017). The humanizing voice: Speech reveals, and text conceals, a more thoughtful mind in the midst of disagreement. *Psychological Science 28*(12), 1745–1762.

CRITICAL THINKING QUESTIONS

1. What does *ad hominem* mean?

2. Why are *ad hominem* approaches to discoursing about a problem? Do they facilitate or hinder the exchange of ideas?

3. Have you had experiences in which you engaged in *ad hominem* discourse or were the victim of this type of discourse? What did *you* feel when you in either situation?

"NEM DI GELT?" OR CAN ACCEPTING GRANT AWARDS BE A BAD THING?

Richard M. Lerner

Tufts University

Jun Wang

Texas A & M University

The famous comedian Henny Youngman summarized his philosophy of life with the Yiddish phrase, *"Nem di gelt,"* or "Take the money." Interestingly, academe seems to follow the comedian's philosophy.

Our developmental-science lab exists because of successful grantsmanship. We apply for money to fund our research, and we are happy when we learn that funders offer financial support for the research we propose to them. Perhaps especially among researchers working in universities wherein grant-funded research is especially prized (institutions termed Research 1 universities), our socialization as scholars has been to pursue external (outside-of-the-university) money to support our work. When we successfully obtain funds granted from government bodies or private foundations, we reap numerous benefits—reduced teaching loads, opportunities to recruit doctoral students and postdoctoral fellows to work with us, and rewards from our university: tenure, promotion, and merit raises. Simply, applying for and taking grant money from funders is an important building block of a productive research program and the essence of prestigious career advancement in academe.

So what could be amiss here? We design research to meet the highest standards of theoretical importance, methodological rigor, and ethical standards. What could be the downside of taking money offered by a funder to enact research we want to do? What could go wrong?

The answer may be "a lot." Taking money, even when a funder is highly enthusiastic about the research you proposed, may not always be wise. We have learned that if the enthusiasm of the researcher and the enthusiasm of the funder reinforce each other, decision making about the details of the research may be problematic. The *nem di gelt* philosophy led to our biggest mistake.

Our lab studies the role of character education in positive youth development, and one of our projects assessed whether the coaches of youth sport programs could be taught to promote good character among the adolescents on their teams. Did coaches, who were trained to prioritize teaching youth that sport should be associated with respect for one's opponents, fair competition, and good sportsmanship, actually work with their athletes differently than coaches not receiving such training? We had a funder who was as eager as we were to answer these questions. In fact, the funder wanted us to get started on our research right away. The funder wanted to use the results of our research to frame future funding decisions about character education programs, and of course, we wanted to give them the best evidence we could provide.

However, the *timing* of the funding was not optimal. The funder said we could receive the funding immediately and that we should give an answer to the questions we posed within six months—a time frame that was not optimal for a pre-post intervention study developed from scratch, especially considering that the funding was offered at a time when we would need to launch the research during the youth baseball season. We knew that the challenges associated with studying this outdoor sport would be considerably greater than would be the case for an indoor sport, such as youth basketball season. Youth basketball games in New England are 40 minutes long on average, occur on a court of standard dimensions located within an enclosed gymnasium, involve only four or five players and, as well, involve coaches located in a constrained location (on or by the bench). We had a good videotaping method to use to record and then code the coaches' behaviors in the constrained setting of basketball courts. However, youth baseball games occur on fields of different sizes in outside areas (where rain could cancel or delay games), with nine players on a team, with coaches in different locations on the field, and with games lasting between six innings to two hours. We were uncertain how our videotaping method would transfer from the basketball to the baseball setting, but the funder said that its money needed to be allocated immediately, and immediately meant studying youth baseball coaches.

We asked the funder to allow us to delay the timing of the grant so that we could study the basketball setting. However, the funder—and the leaders of the character education program we were partnering with to address our questions—urged us to adapt our videotaping procedures so we could get started and to give them evidence-based advice, as soon as possible. *Our mistake was that we agreed to take the money when it was offered* and, therefore, study baseball coaches and not basketball coaches. In New England, the baseball season is relatively short, there are often weather cancellations, and fields vary in their configurations. We launched the project relying on a series of best bets that ended up being wrong. For example, we bet that the efficacy of the technical changes needed to adapt our basketball methods to collect valid baseball data would work sufficiently well; for instance, we thought that audio recordings would be as sensitive in open fields with multiple coaches moving in multiple and often unpredictable directions as they would be inside of gymnasiums with one or two coaches located in relatively fixed locations. In turn, we bet that the number of games that would be cancelled due to weather would be akin to the past few seasons, and thus, that we would have a large enough sample of games by the end of the season to provide a sufficiently statistically powerful data set. We were wrong on both these bets and on several others.

As a consequence, at the end of the study, the data we had were not of the quality that either we or the funder desired. We had too many methodological limitations to make any useful inferences from the data we collected. Both we and the funder were disappointed and, even more, frustrated. However, by the end of the baseball season, the youth basketball season was soon to begin. We requested from the funder a no-cost extension of the grant period and said we would use our own money (which came from our lab's small discretionary fund account) to do the study correctly—and as we had initially envisioned! Perhaps not surprisingly, the funder also had the philosophy of "Nem di gelt," and our offer was accepted. We conducted the study with basketball coaches and generated the high-quality data and interesting and useful findings we had initially envisioned.

Our lesson then is that there may be a high price to pay—in regard to actually costing money and the quality of one's reputation—by taking money just because it is available. Sometimes enthusiasm gets in the way of prudence, and when a researcher faces such a situation, perhaps his or her philosophy should be, "*Du zalst nisht nemen di gelt*," that is, "Don't take the money."

CRITICAL THINKING QUESTIONS

1. What would happen to universities if the strong commitment to pursuing external funding was lessened? Would tuition increases be required?

2. Should the careers of faculty hinge on obtaining external research funds? Should excellence in teaching be regarded as highly as excellence in research?

3. Do you think that the best researchers make the best teachers?

KEEP YOUR FRIENDS CLOSE BUT KEEP YOUR ENEMIES CLOSER

With Whom Should You Share Your Creative Ideas?

David B. Pisoni
Indiana University

When I began working in the field of speech perception in the late 1960s, there were no personal computers available for research. The lack of computers made it extremely difficult, if not impossible, to carry out novel experimental research using synthesized speech signals unless you were able to work at Haskins Laboratories or MIT where there were computer-controlled speech synthesizers. To do research on speech perception, it was necessary to make reel-to-reel audiotapes of your test stimuli and play them back to listeners. This was the way we did research back in the day.

When I arrived at Indiana University in August of 1971, I had several boxes of audiotapes with me that I had used in my dissertation research along with copies of a set of consonant-vowel (CV) syllables that I had created at Haskins Laboratories in the summer of 1969. At some point during my early years at Indiana, I was invited to give my first invited talk at another university. This was a very exciting event because I had never given an invited talk before, except for my job interview at Indiana, and I was very eager to tell people about the novel findings from my dissertation. My visit was very intense, and I had numerous conversations with people, including several conversations with my host, who would eventually turn out to be a lifelong research competitor. I was very naïve, and I did not realize that my host was actually pumping me for information about what I was planning to do in the future and what kinds of studies I had under way. My host had recently published several papers describing an experimental methodology that provided a way to trace out the time course of auditory perceptual recognition, but he had used simple tones in his earlier research and was eager to use more complex speech signals like the ones I had created. I had read all of his published papers very carefully, and I had some pretty good ideas about what I wanted to do next in my own research using his experimental methodology with speech stimuli. During the course of my visit, I shared my ideas about these new experiments quite freely and even described several studies that were actually under way using the set of synthetic CV syllables I had created in 1969.

One thing led to another, and my host asked if I would mind sharing my set of synthetic speech stimuli with him. Again, I have to emphasize here that I was very young and naïve at the time. In fact, my host and several of his close colleagues often referred to me as "Young Dave Pisoni" during my visit. I had no idea that my host would take my speech stimuli and carry out the same experiments that I already had under way in my lab. In fact, I never knew anything about his studies using my synthetic speech stimuli until I read the published paper in a journal and saw a footnote thanking me for providing him with the experimental materials.

This publication came as a big surprise to me at the time because I had never really thought much about the consequences of giving someone my stimulus materials or sharing my ideas for future research. I probably should have been much more suspicious and considered this in greater depth before sending him the stimuli, but I was honored that someone was interested in my research ideas. At the time this event happened, I did not have my own computer yet, and I was still using reel-to-reel audiotapes to carry out research. By the time I got my own minicomputer and had it up and running, my host's paper had been published, and my ideas were scooped by another person who was thinking of the very same studies that I was thinking about, but he got there first. He beat me to the punch, so to speak.

What have I learned from this early experience, and what advice and suggestions would I give young people working in the field of psychology today? First, if you think you have a good idea for a research study, you need to be very careful whom you share your ideas with. As Francis Ford Coppola wrote in *The Godfather*, "Keep your friends close, but keep your enemies closer." You need to know whom you are talking to, and you need to know if you can trust this person with your ideas and not to use them for his or her own gain. Other than reading my host's published papers and spending time talking to him on my visit, I really did not know very much about him or his operating strategy. It turned out that in later years he was an extremely competitive and ambitious person who always wanted to be on top. My experiences as a graduate student at Michigan and my interactions with more experienced researchers at Haskins and MIT never involved any sort of competitive environment and never fully prepared me for a situation like this one. If anything, the people I had firsthand experience in dealing with were all very senior people in the field who were nurturing and supportive and always had my best interests in mind. They were not competitors, and they served as valuable mentors helping me to develop my own research program and professional career. My host, on the other hand, was much younger than the people I worked with at Michigan, Haskins, and MIT, and he was out to make a name for himself even at the expense of a younger and naïve person like me who had just completed graduate school and taken on my first academic position. If you have a good idea for a research study, make sure you know something about the person you are sharing it with. Don't always assume that people will be straightforward and honest with your ideas. Doing research, any kind of research, is a highly competitive enterprise, and there are a lot of people in the field who would take advantage of a young, inexperienced person without thinking of the consequences. In my field, speech perception, as in most areas of basic and clinical research, everyone is thinking about the same fundamental research issues. Academically speaking, what matters in the end is who publishes the results of a research study first and who gets the credit for the discovery. I got scooped at an early age because I was naïve and unaware that there are some untrustworthy people out there in the academic world, and I needed to become educated about competition at an early stage of my career. This one early experience served to enlighten me about what ideas I should share with people and what ideas I should keep to myself. Be sure you know whom you are sharing your ideas with, and don't always assume that everyone is a warm, nurturing, and supportive person. There are sharks out there in the waters looking for new ideas. Creative ideas are at the core of the research enterprise in any scientific field, and the sooner you realize how important this is, the sooner you will be able to protect your own intellectual property and make sure you get the full credit you deserve for your insights and discoveries. Fortunately, this experience only happened to me once in my career, but it had a lasting effect on my thinking and how I go about doing research and sharing ideas with other colleagues and students.

CRITICAL THINKING QUESTIONS

1. Why is competition a good thing in research? Why is it bad?

2. Why is collaboration a good approach for carrying out basic and translational research today? Is collaboration always a good approach to research?

3. How do you retain your individuality in a collaborative setting/relationship?

4. What should you know about someone before you collaborate with him or her?

5. What should you know about someone before you describe your research ideas and plans for the future?

6. When can you trust someone, and when should you exercise caution in talking about your own research ideas?

7. When can you share your not-yet-published results/manuscript? When are new research findings publicly available for anyone to examine?

55 WALKING ETHICAL TIGHTROPES IN RESEARCH COLLABORATIONS

Jonathan A. Plucker
Johns Hopkins University

The biggest research lesson I have learned in a quarter century as a psychologist is that ethics matter, and ethical issues are complicated, never easy, and omnipresent. Indeed, if you are doing lots of research and don't ever come across an ethical concern, you probably need to step back and make sure you are paying enough attention! Ethics become even more complicated when collaboration is involved. Working with others is often a research necessity. When handled well, working with other people and organizations can be a huge benefit to one's research: better quality ideas, more sophisticated designs, fewer errors, quicker turnaround, more visibility, bigger impact. At the same time, especially when money is involved, collaborations can get tricky in a hurry. I had one such collaboration relatively early in my career, and I regret my mishandling of it to this day.

My team had a subcontract with a for-profit contract research firm, in which the firm took a big chunk of money off the top and then had us conduct the actual research. This is a fairly standard setup, often referred to as a "pass-through" arrangement, in which government entities give research and evaluation contracts to large, for-profit or not-for-profit firms; then those companies subcontract with researchers who actually do the work. These relationships are more common than many researchers realize, and they have the potential to benefit everyone: The for-profit gets a slice of the contract and maintains market share in the contract research world without adding payroll, the client gets the work done, and the researchers get funding to do interesting work. Everyone pays a small price to get a bigger benefit that would be hard to obtain without the partnership. It doesn't always work out this way, but that's the general mechanism.

In this particular collaboration, my team found our for-profit contact to be slow with feedback, and moreover, his comments were vague and unhelpful. To complicate things further, the client paying for the research (a senior program coordinator at a state department of education) kept complaining that the for-profit was costing his state tons of money but producing little benefit. In every call over a two-year period (including with the for-profit on the line), the client asked if we would do the research without the for-profit, freeing up money he could use on direct services for children in his program.

We declined (usually by changing the subject), until one day when, in a moment of frustration with the pass-through arrangement, I said sure, we could do it without the for-profit. The client was pleased, and my team was happy that I was willing to get them out of the relationship. But I had a bad feeling in the pit of my stomach, as what was meant as a breezy comment felt a little underhanded, as I was working behind the back of the people at the for-profit firm.

I later learned that the client immediately called our contact at the for-profit firm and reported that I'd said we did not need them anymore. Within a week, our contact at the for-profit stopped returning our calls, and I realized I had handled the situation poorly (to put it mildly). When we finally got them on the phone, they eviscerated us, accusing us of being underhanded and biting the hand that fed us, among other unpleasant things.

All of that was fair—we never looked at it from their point of view, only ours and the client's (which was confirmation bias on our part, as the client was telling us what we wanted to hear). The eventual outcome was ironic: The client kept the project with the for-profit but dropped *us*! And the for-profit, not surprisingly, never approached us again about collaborating, refused to pay us for completed work on an unrelated project, and on at least one occasion deliberately undercut us when they found out we were in pursuit of a specific contract. We made an enemy for life, and a powerful enemy at that! The fact that it was an unforced ethical error made it feel all the worse.

I could write a book about all the issues at play here, but there were definitely some key take-aways from my mistake. Regarding collaborations, always put yourself in the other person's shoes, especially during tense moments (which are unavoidable). By ignoring the perspective of the for-profit, I endangered not only that research but also several other projects, and people's livelihoods depended on those contracts. The for-profit's response was disproportionate, bordering on frothy revenge, but I had poked Karma[1] in the eye when I should have known better, and I—along with people important to me—paid for it. The fact that three wrongs (the for-profit not pulling its weight, the client being mischievous, and my underhandedness) didn't make a right was not lost on me.

When you enter a collaboration, do so with your eyes wide open. What is the collaborator's reputation regarding communication, following through on commitments, and long-term relationships? If your collaborator, whether an organization or an individual, is well-established but has few long-term partners, you should tread carefully. When the collaboration is up and running, transparency and clear communication are critically important. We should have never been on the phone with the client without also having our contact at the for-profit on the line. Doing so helps ensure transparency but also guards against one partner playing you against the other. As my mother

---

[1] Karma is a concept from Hinduism and Buddhism representing the idea that your intent and actions have direct consequences. In other words, you reap what you sow! It is generally represented in popular culture as a person ensuring you feel the consequences of your positive and negative actions.

used to say, if a person is bad-mouthing someone else to you, they are almost certainly bad-mouthing you to someone else. Keeping things transparent, especially when communicating, has little downside and keeps everyone accountable.

If a collaboration turns out to be less than ideal, I learned that one should finish the work as best as one can and just not work with that partner again in the future (i.e., don't throw a live hand grenade into the collaboration). Of course, a truly horrible collaboration may need to be ended on the spot, but since this incident, I have been able to end most of my weaker collaborations by getting them to the end products as quickly as possible and then politely walking away. The fact that those partners rarely approach me afterward about future collaborations suggests they are just as relieved to be finished with me!

Regarding personal ethics, immediately after this incident, I briefly wondered if I should work to be better at what I euphemistically thought of as "politicking," when what I really meant was "underhandedness." When I caught myself thinking this, I felt even *worse*, which hadn't seemed possible. Did I, or do you, really want to be more highly skilled at underhandedness and backstabbing? I like to think that Karma tapped me on the shoulder at that moment and whispered, "Easy there, big guy. That's not a good path forward for you."

My mistake is not meant to say collaborations are ethical minefields that are always difficult. Like any relationship, a research partnership is hard work, but the payoff for a successful collaboration can be tremendous. I have had dozens, if not hundreds, of successful collaborations, and my work and career have benefited in countless ways. But entering into these experiences with a personal code of ethics fortified by due diligence, perspective, transparency, and patience will ensure positive experiences for you and your colleagues.

CRITICAL THINKING QUESTIONS

1. My unsuccessful collaborations have almost always resulted from my not preparing for negative developments at the outset, assuming that everything would go perfectly. In order to avoid a rose-colored-glasses phenomenon, what are some steps you can take at the start of a research collaboration to better anticipate and solve problems that may emerge?

2. When you run into ethical dilemmas, having an "ethics mentor" to serve as a resource and sounding board can be invaluable. What are important characteristics of an ethics mentor? Who can serve in this role for you?

3. Some ethical research mistakes have legal ramifications, but many (such as the situation described in this essay) do not. Should that influence how you handle an ethical problem?

SOCIETAL COSTS OUTWEIGH SOCIETAL BENEFITS

56 THE DANGER OF SUPERFICIAL SUCCESS

James C. Kaufman
University of Connecticut

When I was asked to write about my biggest research mistake, my first thought was to consider some type of methods or statistical error. Indeed, I have many to draw from—but what I ultimately settled on was something entirely different. My biggest research mistake was pursuing a line of inquiry early in my career because it was superficially rewarding and easy, regardless of its purpose.

In graduate school, I became intrigued with the historiometric technique pioneered by Simonton (2009), in which you comb through biographies or other existing data as a way of studying eminent creators. As an aspiring creative writer, I began entering all sorts of information about eminent writers from a large encyclopedia-like volume (pre-Wikipedia). When I completed this behemoth dataset, I began analyzing and playing with the data and uncovered a curious hiccup that stood out: Female poets were more likely to show signs of mental illness than any other kind of writer (from male poets to female fiction writers or journalists). I did a second study on eminent women and found a similar pattern. I called it the Sylvia Plath Effect (Kaufman, 2001), after the famous suicidal poet, and published. I followed up this paper with a few similar studies (Kaufman, 2003, 2005).

Through a variety of circumstances (my university hired a public relations firm to hype faculty research, and this type of finding was both easily digestible and the type of study that appealed to general interest in celebrity suffering), the Sylvia Plath Effect made a bit of a news splash. It was covered by many newspapers, magazines, and blogs. There were even five or six independent rock songs with the same name. It helped establish my name in the field of creativity. At this point, you may understandably be wondering why I would consider this line of work to be my biggest research mistake.

I grew to regret this work as I saw the real-world impact. Poets worried about their mental health. Some people saw it as a reason to mock poets. It helped reinforce the mental illness-creativity connection, as it was frequently misinterpreted to mean that if you wanted to be a well-known poet, you needed to be mentally ill. As a creativity researcher, I wanted to promote being creative as a good thing. I wanted to encourage people to tap into their creativity and nurture it in others. Yet my own past work was shooting down my goals.

I developed the WGASA [Who Gives A S**t Anyway] rule, named for the former monorail at the Wild Animal Park in Southern California. Many decades ago, they held a contest to name the monorail. As the board members examined the many suggestions, one wrote on a chalkboard "WGASA" (contrary to popular legend, everyone was well aware of what it meant). In other words, why were they spending so much time on a trivial matter (Kaufman, 2016)? I have called this acronym the WGASA rule, which essentially means that any academic research should have a real-life purpose. It does not need to have an immediate application—a great deal of outstanding scholarship has been done to explore key topics or ask important questions. Similarly, there is an argument to be made for basic science being studied for the sake of scientific growth. What I consider to qualify for the WGASA rule are studies or lines of work that are esoteric to the point of being irrelevant—research conducted in a vacuum with no impact on anything but the scientist's vita.

The corollary to the WGASA rule, which I see as being even more important, is that psychological research should ideally lead to more positive outcomes than negative outcomes. There are so many contentious topics out there (intelligence and race/culture is one that immediately comes to mind), and scholars often argue that the ultimate goal of science is truth. Taking unpopular stances is necessary, and the existence of tenure helps protect such free speech. But at the end of the day, there is also a certain amount of responsibility that comes with conducting psychological research.

I do not question in any way scientists' right to study whatever they want to study. If they want to spend a lifetime pursuing research that will increase stigma against any group or give credence to people who seek an excuse to hate, then that is their prerogative. Less dramatically, if people want to study topics that make for easy publications but do absolutely nothing to improve the world in the slightest way, then that is also their choice.

But drawing from my own experience, I would urge young scholars to think carefully about their choice of topics to investigate. More than 15 years after the Sylvia Plath Effect, and despite so many other studies and theories aimed at helping people, it remains the work for which I am best known. At the very least, I believe I have learned from my mistakes. As I tell my own students, life is too short to invest time and energy on work that has no life beyond publication. More importantly, life is too precious to use one's gifts to exploit or demean others. If the natural extension or application of your work will end up doing absolutely nothing or—even worse—make any group of people's life a little worse, then it is time to reconsider your career choices.

REFERENCES

Kaufman, J. C. (2001). The Sylvia Plath effect: Mental illness in eminent creative writers. *Journal of Creative Behavior, 35*, 37–50.

Kaufman, J. C. (2003). The cost of the muse: Poets die young. *Death Studies, 27,* 813–822.

Kaufman, J. C. (2005). The door that leads into madness: Eastern European poets and mental illness. *Creativity Research Journal, 17,* 99–103.

Kaufman, J. C. (2016). *Creativity 101* (2nd ed). New York, NY: Springer.

Simonton, D. K. (2009). *Genius 101.* New York, NY: Springer.

CRITICAL THINKING QUESTIONS

1. In class, do you prefer to challenge yourself or take the easiest path?

2. Is it important to you for your eventual career to impact people in a positive way? How would you compare the importance of helping others to, for example, your happiness or salary?

3. The impact of science and technology is easier to see in our day-to-day lives. Can you think of a way that social science research has impacted your own life?

KINDS OF RESEARCH MISTAKES

Robert J. Sternberg
Cornell University

In this book, you have read about the kinds of research mistakes even eminent researchers have made in their research. What are some take-away lessons that you can learn from all this? A temptation in reading a book like this one is seeing these errors and thinking that whereas the authors of the chapters may have done these things, the reader himself or herself, of course, would never make such a mistake. I was intrigued, therefore, to discover that I have made every single one of these kinds of mistakes—at least once and usually multiple times—in my own career. I would like to review the kinds of mistakes, therefore, and mention my own instances just as a warning that these kinds of mistake are not limited to authors of particular chapters, and they are not once-in-a-career blunders. They happen to us all, and can happen at any time.

I. FAILURE IN CONCEPTUALIZING RESEARCH

Failure in conceptualizing research comprises the largest category simply in terms of the number of essays devoted to it. Failures of this kind can take many forms: underpowering a study, intending to answer one question but then designing a study that actually answers a different question, thinking one sees all alternative outcomes for a study only to find out that the actual outcome does not fit any of the preconceived potential outcomes, choosing data analyses that do not meet the assumptions of one's data, and so forth.

My dissertation data analysis was a good example of a failure to conceptualize my research correctly. I analyzed the data for my dissertation, looking at alternative mathematical models that might fit the data (Sternberg, 1977). The first were not terrible, but disappointingly, none of the models fit particularly well. This outcome is not one that anyone ever hopes for, but especially not in a dissertation upon which one's PhD hinges.

I decided to examine the residuals in my modeling equations. Sure enough, I had made a systematic error in conceptualizing the data. I had assumed that all of my stimulus material would be processed analytically, but that was not the case. Some of the stimuli were processed holistically, in particular, stimuli for which analytical comparisons simply were not necessary. When I recast the mathematical models to allow for dual holistic and analytical processing, the fits jumped up, and one model was the clear favorite.

When I wrote up the data, I presented my original model but also explained how my original expectations were wrong and how the data showed that subjects were using a strategy different from what I had anticipated. I realized that people are not mindless data processors: They fit their data processing to the types of stimuli with which they are presented.

II. PREMATURELY JUMPING TO CONCLUSIONS

Prematurely jumping to conclusions occurs when one looks at data (or anything else) and then quickly sees what one wants to see instead of what is there. We all, to some extent, see what we want to see. The question is whether we are willing to make the effort and take the time to ensure that what we are seeing is what is there.

My colleagues and I published a confirmatory factor analysis of a test I had designed to measure a set of abilities, in particular, analytical, creative, and practical abilities (Sternberg, Castejón, Prieto, Hautamäki, & Grigorenko 2001). Conventional theories of intelligence would argue that there should be only a single general factor, perhaps with other second- and third-order factors embedded within (Sternberg & Grigorenko, 2002). I initially saw three factors emerge from the data, in particular, the analytical, creative, and practical factors. But fact be told, the factors, although existent, were weak. Those data scarcely provided a strong argument for my theory of three separate aspects of intelligence. It would not be until some years later (Sternberg, 2010) that I would realize that if one uses only multiple-choice items, one cannot adequately separate creative and practical abilities from analytical ones. Multiple-choice items are just not good measures of creative and practical skills, a finding that should not be particularly astonishing. I probably should have seen this clearly in 2002, but I didn't. I was not quite ready to see what was staring me in the face in my data.

III. FOLLOWING A GARDEN PATH

When one follows a garden path, one follows a lead that leads to a dead end. What once may have seemed like a promising path for research, for data analysis, or whatever, proves to be a path to nowhere.

Some years ago, I became interested in conflict resolution. In particular, I had some ideas about styles of conflict resolution—consistent individual differences in how people resolve conflicts. For example, some people may consistently behave in physically aggressive ways, others in verbally aggressive ways, still others in trying to tamp down the conflict, and so on. I even pulled off two articles in a prestigious social-psychology journal on the topic (Sternberg & Dobson, 1987; Sternberg & Soriano, 1984). The problem was that the research was leading me nowhere. I had no doubt that I could continue to do research in the area. But I had strong doubts that the research would lead anywhere I was interested in going. I had dead-ended with it. Even though I had two published articles in a prestigious journal, I dropped the research area. It just wasn't leading me anywhere.

IV. USING MEASURES OF DUBIOUS RELIABILITY/VALIDITY

Other people may use dubious measures; of course, none of us would! Measures of dubious reliability are ones that do not produce consistent levels of performance, over time or across items within the measures. Measures of dubious validity simply do not measure what they are supposed to measure.

I would like to say that, by my level of advancement, I am immune to such a foolish mistake. Apparently not. I recently did a study with an undergraduate on a topic of mutual interest—ethical reasoning. We devised our own measure of ethical reasoning. But in order to show that the measure was valid, we needed to validate it against another measure that had been generally accepted as measuring the same construct or at least a similar one. We chose a measure that is available in the literature and that we believed to be well-reputed. Once we collected the data, we tried to score and analyze the results comparing our new measure to the old measure. We found, to our dismay, that the well-reputed measure was of seriously inferior quality. It possessed no psychometric quality that one would want in a measure against which one validates one's new scale. As a result, we were unable to assess whether our measure did indeed assess ethical reasoning. We had assumed that, because the measure was widely used, it was good. We could not have been more wrong! I should have known that reputation of a test is very different from the quality of a test (Sternberg, 1981b, 1985, 1986, 1997a, 1997b). But in this instance, I just failed to recognize it.

V. CARELESSNESS

All researchers know that they should never ever be careless—in designing studies, in analyzing data, in writing up data, or whatever. But almost all of us are careless, one time or another. Perhaps we take a shortcut, or we just do not think carefully about what we are doing.

A set of colleagues and I once submitted a paper to a journal. I actually cannot remember which paper it was. What I do remember is that I waited until after the submission to check carefully the tables in the paper, which were prepared by the colleague who did the data analysis. I could not believe what I was seeing. I don't know how it happened, but the tables were riddled with small errors. None of the errors amounted to much, but the data just weren't right. I could say, well, what a loser colleague that person was, except that it was certainly my responsibility, as a coauthor, to check the data before the paper was submitted, not after. The errors did not change any conclusions, but they were errors nevertheless. I wrote to the journal editor, described what had happened, and blamed myself (appropriately). The journal editor permitted us to resubmit with changed tables, and the paper was eventually published—with the correct data.

VI. OVERRELYING ON OTHERS

I suspect that anyone who has been in the field of psychological science for any amount of time has made the mistake of overrelying on others.

I just recently had an instance in which I got badly burned by overrelying on someone. The someone was a well-regarded professional, and I felt confident in relying on him. I was organizing a symposium, and his job was to write the final discussion paper for the symposium. There was a firm due date, and, as the due date got closer, I reminded him several times that I would need the discussion. He assured me multiple times that although he was slightly delayed in starting the task of writing the discussion, all was on track for his getting it done on time. I was glad about this, because it reached the point where it would be too late to get anyone else to do it, given the due date. A couple of days before the discussion was due, he wrote me to say that he would not be doing the discussion after all—and that he did not think the task was worth doing in the first place. I couldn't believe what I was reading. If he felt that way, I sure wish he had told me months ago, not in the final days before the discussion was due. The upshot was that I spent two very long days of my life—the last two before the discussion was due—writing the discussion. I got it done and submitted the entire symposium on the day it was due.

In retrospect, I probably should have realized that the signs were bad, but I trusted the individual. And the individual has a good reputation in the field. The lesson I learned, and one I always tell students, is that one always needs a Plan B in case Plan A fails. In this case, I was informed so late by the intended discussant that I had to become Plan B. But I would say it again: Never rely on a colleague to the point where you have no backup if the colleague does not come through for you.

VII. ERROR IN STATISTICAL ANALYSIS

My colleagues and I once made the most obvious statistical error there is. Fortunately, we corrected it before the study in which it was made was submitted for publication (Sternberg, Nokes et al., 2001). We were assessing the academic (analytical) and practical intelligence of Luo children in rural Kenya. We devised tests of both academic and practical intelligence and administered them to the children in our study. We were interested simply in whether the correlation between academic and practical intelligence would be statistically significant. Standard theories of intelligence would predict that they correlation would be significant (see Sternberg & Grigorenko, 2002), whereas our theory, as it existed at the time, did not predict a significant correlation (Sternberg, 1997a, 1997b). So the null hypothesis of no correlation would be refuted by the alternative hypothesis of a positive correlation. It seemed, therefore, perfectly appropriate, indeed, statistically conservative, to use a one-tailed test for the statistical significance of the correlation: My own hypothesis would be refuted by significance, and it is easier to get significance with a one-tailed test.

The correlation proved to be statistically significant, but there was a problem: The correlation was significantly negative! The better one did on the test of academic intelligence, the worse one did on the test of practical intelligence, and vice versa. We came to realize that, in the society we were studying, the "smart" kids left school early because they had the opportunity to acquire an apprenticeship and eventually earn money, whereas the "not so smart" kids stayed in school because they were not offered apprenticeships. Hence, higher academic scores were associated with lower practical scores, and vice versa. We just never predicted this finding, and no theory at the time, at least that we were aware of, did. Of course, we had to change to a two-tailed statistical test, but we did so after the fact. So, first we made an error in conceptualization, and as a result of it, we did the wrong statistical analysis. We were able to correct our error—but after the fact. We learned that one should be extremely cautious about using one-tailed tests. Sometimes, one obtains findings in a direction one just might never expect *a priori*.

VIII. GENERALIZABILITY OF FINDINGS

Failures of generalization almost always involve our generalizing results beyond where we reasonably can generalize them. Anyone who claims never to have made this error is simply lying or deluded. In my early work in the 1980s, I did countless experiments on Yale college students, and flagrantly generalized the results to "people in general" (e.g., Sternberg, 1981a, 1981b; Sternberg & Davidson, 1982). This does not mean that the results were not generalizable: It just means that I had no real basis for saying they were generalizable. It was not until I started doing cultural research later in my career (e.g., Sternberg, 2004, 2014) that I realized just how limited research is that does not seek to test out subjects across various cultural milieus. And it was not until I became an academic administrator at diverse institutions that I could see, with my own eyes, that Yale students were anything but typical even of college students (Sternberg, 2016b). At one level, I always had known this. But at another level, I had to see it to believe it. For example, I went from one institution in which almost all my students were political liberal to another institution in which the large majority were politically conservative—and all were equally persuaded of their beliefs.

IX. FAILURE TO UNDERSTAND THE "SYSTEM"

I have written several books on negotiating the "system" of psychological science (e.g., Sternberg, 2016a, 2017); so one would think that by this time, and after my having been president of the American Psychological Association and an administrator at various universities, I would understand the "system." But I keep learning new things, even today. One reason is that what constitutes the "system" changes.

Not all that long ago, I was pushing for a job candidate to be hired. But there was another candidate whom others were more interested in. I could not figure out exactly why. There may have been a lot of reasons, but one, I learned, is that the other candidate published in "higher-impact" journals. Impact factors are determined by the number of times articles in particular journals are cited. When I started my career, we psychological scientists all knew that different journals were of different qualities, but there were no "impact factors" available. So, for some of my colleagues, the impact factors mattered, and they saw my preferred candidate as inferior. There are many scientists who believe that "impact factors" are of dubious validity (see Ceci & Williams, in press). But the system had changed, and a new measure, even one of dubious validity, was swaying the opinions of many of my colleagues. They had their view, I had mine; I lost. I just did not realize how important this dubious statistic had become in the system of hiring.

X. SOCIETAL COSTS OUTWEIGH SOCIETAL BENEFITS

Many psychological scientists do not think much or even care much about the societal costs and benefits of what they do. But then, others do, such as James Kaufman, who wrote the sole chapter in this section. For me, this was always an important issue. I always wanted my research to benefit not just science, but also, society. I have never purposely done, and would never purposely do, any research in which I thought the societal costs would outweigh the societal benefits. And yet, in my distant past, I once inadvertently did such research.

As an undergraduate, I worked part-time in the Yale University Undergraduate Admissions Office. Upon graduation, I briefly took a job working as a special assistant to the dean of undergraduate admissions. One of my main responsibilities was doing research on the admissions process.

One study I did was a cost-benefit analysis of the Yale Admissions Office interview as it existed at the time (Sternberg, 1973). The question I addressed in the study was whether the admissions-office interview was worth the time and effort that went into it. My analysis revealed that the interview was largely invalid as a measure for admissions, but nevertheless, students liked the interview. I therefore concluded, in the publication based on the study, that the interview should be retained because, although it was invalid, students on average liked it, and therefore it was a good marketing device for the university.

Now, 45 years after the publication of the article, I find it hard to believe that a younger Bob Sternberg would ever publish such an article. I was basically arguing that what at the time was a useless waste of time for students should be retained because students liked it. Ironically, they liked it almost certainly in part because their estimate of how well they did in the interview was substantially higher than the rating of the interviewer. That is, they were falsely confident about their self-presentation. So I was recommending retaining an assessment because students liked it in large part because they thought they did much better than they did. I recommended continuation of a practice that was time consuming and potentially costly to the students, and at the same time, useless for the admissions office. Of course, that was back in 1973, and I certainly would not want to generalize to any interviews that may be done today, more than 40 years later!

So there you have it. I've made all 10 of the kinds of mistakes noted in this book. I hope you can learn from the book and thereby avoid making some, perhaps many, of these mistakes. I wish I'd had this book—before I made these mistakes. Best of luck to you in your future research!

REFERENCES

Ceci, S. J., & Williams, M. W. (2019). Journal publishing starts with an attitude. In R. J. Sternberg (Ed.), *Guide to publishing in psychology journals* (2nd ed, pp. 192–203). Thousand Oaks, CA: Sage.

Sternberg, R. J. (1973). Cost–benefit analysis of the Yale admissions office interview. *College and University, 48,* 154–164.

Sternberg, R. J. (1977). *Intelligence, information processing, and analogical reasoning: The componential analysis of human abilities.* Hillsdale, NJ: Lawrence Erlbaum Associates.

Sternberg, R. J. (1981a). A componential theory of intellectual giftedness. *Gifted Child Quarterly, 25,* 86–93.

Sternberg, R. J. (1981b). Testing and cognitive psychology. *American Psychologist, 36,* 1181–1189.

Sternberg, R. J. (2004). Culture and intelligence. *American Psychologist, 59*(5), 325–338.

Sternberg, R. J. (1985). Human intelligence: The model is the message. *Science, 230,* 1111–1118.

Sternberg, R. J. (1986). Inside intelligence. *American Scientist, 74,* 137–143.

Sternberg, R. J. (1997a). *Successful intelligence.* New York, NY: Plume.

Sternberg, R. J. (1997b). What does it mean to be smart? *Educational Leadership, 54*(6), 20–24.

Sternberg, R. J. (2010). *College admissions for the 21st century.* Cambridge, MA: Harvard University Press.

Sternberg, R. J. (2014). The development of adaptive competence. *Developmental Review, 34,* 208–224.

Sternberg, R. J. (2016a). *Psychology 101½: The unspoken rules for success in academia* (2nd ed.). Washington, DC: American Psychological Association.

Sternberg, R. J. (2016b). *What universities can be: A new model for preparing students for active concerned citizenship and ethical leadership.* Ithaca, NY: Cornell University Press.

Sternberg, R. J. (2017). *Starting your career in academic psychology.* Washington, DC: APA Books.

Sternberg, R. J., Castejón, J. L., Prieto, M. D., Hautamäki, J., & Grigorenko, E. L. (2001). Confirmatory factor analysis of the Sternberg triarchic abilities test in three international samples: An empirical test of the triarchic theory of intelligence. *European Journal of Psychological Assessment, 17*(1), 1–16.

Sternberg, R. J., & Davidson, J. E. (1982, June). The mind of the puzzler. *Psychology Today, 16,* 37–44.

Sternberg, R. J., & Dobson, D. M. (1987). Resolving interpersonal conflicts: An analysis of stylistic consistency. *Journal of Personality and Social Psychology, 52,* 794–812.

Sternberg, R. J., & Grigorenko E. L. (Eds.). (2002). *The general factor of intelligence: How general is it?* Mahwah, NJ: Lawrence Erlbaum Associates.

Sternberg, R. J., Nokes, K., Geissler, P. W., Prince, R., Okatcha, F., Bundy, D. A., & Grigorenko, E. L. (2001). The relationship between academic and practical intelligence: A case study in Kenya. *Intelligence, 29,* 401–418.

Sternberg, R. J., & Soriano, L. J. (1984). Styles of conflict resolution. *Journal of Personality and Social Psychology, 47,* 115–126.

INDEX